THE
RESOLUTION
OF AFRICAN CONFLICTS

Edited by
ALFRED NHEMA & PAUL TIYAMBE ZELEZA

The Roots of African Conflicts

The Resolution of African Conflicts

THE
RESOLUTION
OF AFRICAN CONFLICTS

The Management of Conflict Resolution & Post-Conflict Reconstruction

Edited by

ALFRED NHEMA
Executive Secretary, The Organization for Social Science Research in Eastern & Southern Africa (OSSREA) Addis Ababa

&

PAUL TIYAMBE ZELEZA
University of Illinois at Chicago

Published
in association with
OSSREA
Addis Ababa

JAMES CURREY
Oxford

OHIO UNIVERSITY PRESS
Athens, OH

UNISA PRESS
Pretoria

OSSREA in association with

James Currey Ltd
73 Botley Road
Oxford OX2 0BS
www.jamescurrey.co.uk

Ohio University Press
19 Circle Drive
The Ridges
Athens, Ohio 45701
www.ohioedu/oupress
www.ohioswallow.com

Unisa Press
PO Box 392
Unisa
Muckleneuk 0003
www.unisa.ac.za/press

© James Currey Ltd, 2008
First published 2008

1 2 3 4 5 12 11 10 09 08

ISBN 978-1-84701-302-6 (James Currey paper)
ISBN 10: 0-8214-1808-4 (Ohio University Press paper)
ISBN 13: 978-0-8214-1808-6 (Ohio University Press paper)
ISBN 978-1-86888-493-3 (Unisa Press paper)

British Library Cataloguing in Publication Data
The resolution of African conflicts : the management of
conflict resolution & post-conflict reconstruction
1. Conflict management - Africa 2. Postwar reconstruction -
Africa
I. Nhema, Alfred G. II. Zeleza, Paul Tiyambe, 1955-
303.6'9'096

Library of Congress Cataloging-in-Publication Data
available on request

Typeset in 10/11 pt Photina with Castellar display
by Long House, Cumbria
Printed and bound in Malaysia

Contents

10
Peace & War
in Post-Conflict Mozambique

11
Post-1990 Constitutional Reforms in Africa
A Preliminary Assessment of the Prospects
for Constitutional Governance & Constitutionalism

List of Tables & Figures

Tables

Figures

Acknowledgements

This book is the outcome of the OSSREA's Research Programme on *African Conflicts* which sponsored an international conference titled 'African Conflicts: Management, Resolution, Post-conflict Recovery and Development', held at the United Nations Conference Centre (UNCC) in Addis Ababa, Ethiopia, from 29 November to 1 December 2004. The conference's major objective was to provide a platform by means of which various stakeholders could present their findings on various themes focusing on conflict management and resolution as well as post-conflict recovery and development. The conference also provided a forum through which participants could share experiences learnt in the area of conflict management and recovery.

Over 180 participants attended the Conference which was officially opened by His Excellency Ato Girma Woldegiorgis, the President of the Federal Democratic Republic of Ethiopia. International participants included academics, researchers, members of the diplomatic corps, members of Parliament, representatives of regional and international organizations, non-governmental organizations' operatives, policy-makers and donors.

A total of sixty-two papers were presented at the Conference under the following nine themes:

• Conflict Prevention, Management and Resolution
• Economic Policies and Poverty Reduction
• Elections, Political Parties and Sustainable Development
• Elections, Political Parties and Democratic Consolidation
• Ethnic Conflict, Policies and Development
• Democracy Consolidation and Development
• Peace-building, Post-conflict Rehabilitation and Development
• Religion, Health and Society
• Human Rights, Gender and Human Security

The papers in this volume and its companion volume, Zeleza & Nhema (eds), *The Roots of African Conflicts: The Causes & Costs*, review several strategies meant to ensure conflict resolution and post-conflict recovery in Africa. The ranges of interventions which are examined in the various chapters include, *inter alia*, negotiation frameworks within the extant economic, social, political and cultural configurations; the role of international actors and regional organizations like the African Union, the International Criminal Court and sub-regional organizations; the utilization of continental early warning systems; and finally a discussion of the role of democratic constitutional governance as a panacea for conflict resolution in Africa.

OSSREA acknowledges the support of the Swedish International Development Cooperation Agency (Sida/Sarec), the Norwegian Agency for Development Cooperation (NORAD), and the Netherlands Ministry of Foreign Affairs for their financial support for this initiative and other OSSREA research activities.

We also appreciate the input of the OSSREA Secretariat who in many ways have contributed to the success of this project.

Alfred Gwarega Nhema
Executive Secretary
The Organization for Social Science Research
in Eastern and Southern Africa (OSSREA)
Addis Ababa

Paul Tiyambe Zeleza
Professor and Head
Department of African American Studies
University of Illinois at Chicago

Notes on Contributors

Victor A.O. Adetula is an Associate Professor of Political Science at the University of Jos, Nigeria. He previously served as the Director of the Centre for Development Studies, University of Jos, and as Senior Program Manager in the Democracy and Governance Office of USAID in Abuja, Nigeria. His most recent publications include a co-edited book, *Border Crime and Community Insecurity in Nigeria* (2002), and the following book chapters: 'Ethnicity and the Dynamics of City Politics: The Case of Jos' in Abdulmaliq Simone and Abdelghani Abouhani (eds), *Urban and Africa: Changing Contours of Survival in the City* (2005) and 'African Development, Peace and Conflict' in Shadrack Best (ed.), *Introduction to Peace and Conflict Studies in West Africa* (2005).

Aisha Ahmad completed her Master's degree in International Relations at the University of Toronto, Canada, and is currently a doctoral candidate at the University of Cambridge, UK. Her research focuses on disarmament of warlords in Afghanistan and the security dynamics of the post-Taliban period. Her works can be found at http://www.cbc.ca/news/viewpoint/vp_ahmad/20050721.html

Kasaija Phillip Apuuli is a Lecturer in Public International Law and Diplomacy at Makerere University, Kampala, Uganda. His recent publications include 'International Law and Uganda's Involvement in the Democratic Republic of Congo', in *University of Miami International and Comparative Law Review* 10, 1 (2002), 'The Inter-governmental Authority on Development's (IGAD) Conflict Early Warning and Response Mechanism (CEWARN): A Ray of Hope in Conflict Prevention?' in Alfred G. Nhema (ed.), *The Quest for Peace in Africa: Transformations, Democracy and Public Policy* (2004) and 'The Politics of Conflict Resolution in the Democratic Republic of Congo (DRC): The Inter-Congolese Dialogue Process', *African Journal on Conflict Resolution* 4 (1) (2004).

Jacobus Kamfer (Jakkie) Cilliers is Executive Director, Institute for Security Studies/Institut d'Études de Sécurité (ISS), a regional research think-tank with offices in Addis Ababa, Nairobi, Pretoria and Cape Town, working on peace and security issues in Africa. His most recent publications include *Human Security in Africa: A Conceptual Framework for Review* (2004), the following ISS research papers, 'Progress with the African Standby Force' (2005) and 'Towards a Continental Early Warning System for Africa', and 'UN Reform and Funding Peacekeeping in Africa,' *African Security Review* 14 (2) (2005).

Charles Manga Fombad is Professor of Law, Department of Law, Univer-

sity of Botswana. He is also Professor *Honorarius* of the Department of Jurisprudence, School of Law, University of South Africa. His main publications
include: *Botswana Law of Delict* (2001), *Cameroon Constitutional Law* (2003)
and *The Botswana Legal System* (with E.K. Quansah) (2006) and over 45
articles in journals and more than 10 book chapters.

Christof Hartmann is Professor of International and Development Politics,
Duisburg-Essen University, Germany. He has published on democratization,
elections, conflict management, and the role of political institutions in sub-
Saharan Africa and Asia. He is editor of *Elections in Asia and the Pacific* (2
vols.) (with Dieter Nohlen and Florian Grotz) (2001) and author of several
books about African politics including, *Externe Faktoren im Demokratisie-
rungsprozeß* (1999) and *Ethnizität, Präsidentschaftswahlen und Demokratie*
(1999). Recent publications in English include 'Paths of Electoral Reform in
Africa,' in Andreas Mehler (ed.), *Elections and Political Parties in Contemporary
Sub-Saharan Africa* (2005) and 'Local Elections in the SADC Countries: A
Comparative Analysis of Local Electoral Institutions', *Journal of African
Elections* (2004).

Idris Salim El Hassan is Associate Professor in Social Anthropology and
Dean of the Community Development Unit, University of Khartoum, Sudan.
He is the author of several books, including *Religion in Society: Nimerie and
the Turuq* (1993) and *Sudanese Visions in Science Knowledge and Culture* (2001)
(in Arabic) and has published numerous articles on gender, education,
culture and religion in various journals and edited collections.

Khabele Matlosa is the Director, Research, Publications and Information
Department at the Electoral Institute of Southern Africa, in Johannesburg,
South Africa. He has been an election observer and adviser in various SADC
countries, and is co-editor-in-chief of the *Journal of African Elections*, and
guest editor of the *African Journal of Conflict Resolution*, 4 (2) (2004). His
latest publications include 'Caught between Transition and Democratic
Consolidation: Dilemmas of Political Change in Southern Africa' in *Southern
Africa Post-apartheid? The Search for Democratic Governance* (2004), 'SADC's
Electoral Guidelines: What is new?', in *Global Dialogue* 10 (1) (2005) and
*HIV/AIDS and Democratic Governance in South Africa: Illustrating the impact on
electoral processes* (co-authored with P. Strand, A Strode and K. Chirambo)
(2005).

Brazao Mazula was Vice Chancellor of Eduardo Mondlane University in
Mozambique from 1995 to early 2007. He has a Ph.D. from the University
of São Paulo in Brazil, and is the author of numerous works including
Cultural and Ideological Education in Moçambique 1975–1985 (1995), and the
edited collection, *Elections, Democracy and Development* (1996). He has served
in various capacities in Mozambique including as chair of the National
Electoral Commission.

Alfred Nhema is Executive Secretary of the Organization for Social Science
Research in Eastern and Southern Africa (OSSREA) in Addis Ababa,

Ethiopia. He has published on development issues in developing countries and is author of *Democracy in Zimbabwe: From Liberation to Liberalization* (2002), and editor of *The Quest for Peace in Africa: Transformations, Democracy and Public Policy* (2004).

Pontian Godfrey Okoth is Professor of History at Maseno University and an adjunct professor at the Centre for Disaster Management and Humanitarian Assistance, Western University of Science and Technology, Kakamega, Kenya. His publications include: *United States Foreign Policy Toward Kenya* (1992), *Africa at the Beginning of the Twenty First Century* (2000) and *Conflict in Contemporary Africa* (2000). He is also author of numerous articles and book chapters.

Ursula Scheidegger is a doctoral student in the Department of Political Studies at the University of the Witwatersrand in Johannesburg, South Africa. Her Ph.D. is on 'Transformations From Below, Social Capital, and the South African Transition'.

Edwin C. Rutto is a Programme Officer at the Africa Peace Forum in Nairobi. He works on the IGAD-CEWARN programme and is engaged in research. He holds a Master of Arts degree in International Studies from the Institute of Diplomacy and International Studies, University of Nairobi.

Kizito Sabala is a conflict analyst and senior researcher at the Africa Peace Forum based in Nairobi, and a doctoral candidate at the Institute of Diplomacy and International Studies, University of Nairobi. His publications include *African Commitments to Controlling Small Arms and Light Weapons: A review of NEPAD Countries,* (2004) and several APFO reports, including *State Forces and Major Armed Opposition Groups in the Great Lakes Region* (2000), *Peace Initiatives in the Democratic Republic of Congo* (2000), and *Situation Analysis of the Great Lakes Region of Africa* (2000).

List of Acronyms

AC	Amnesty Commission
ACCORD	African Centre for the Cooperative Resolution of Disputes
ADF	Allied Defence Forces
AHSI	African Human Security Initiative
ANAD	L'Accord de Non-aggression et d'Assistance en matière de Défence (Francophone Non-aggression and Defence Agreement
ANC	African National Congress
ARLPI	Acholi Religious Leaders' Peace Initiative
ARP	Alexandra Renewal Project
AU	African Union
BCP	Basutoland Congress Party
BNP	Basotho National Party
CAAU	Constitutive Act of the African Union
CEAO	Communanté Economique de l'Afrique de l' Ouest
CEO	Chief Executive Officer
CEWS	Continental Early Warning System
CHOGM	Commonwealth Heads of Government Meeting
CODESA	Convention for a Democratic South Africa
CODESRIA	Council for the Development of Social Science Research in Africa
COMESA	Common Market for East-ern and Southern Africa
CPA	Comprehensive Peace Agreement
CPF	Community Policing Forum
CPMR	Conflict Prevention, Management and Resolution
CPP	Commission for the Consolidation of Peace
DA	Democratic Alliance
DDDR	Demilitarization, Disarmament, Demobilization and Rehabilitation
DDR	Disarmament, Demobilization and Reintegration
DMA	District Management Area
DRC	Democratic Republic of Congo
EAC	East Africa Community
ECCAS	Economic Community of Central African States
ECF	Electoral Commissions Forum
ECOMOG	ECOWAS Cease-Fire Operation Monitoring Operation Group
ECOWAS	Economic Community of West African States
EISA	Electoral Institute of Southern Africa
EMB	Electoral Management Body
EU	European Union
FEDEMO	Federal Democratic Movement
FRELIMO	Front for the Liberation of Mozambique
GDP	Gross domestic product
GoS	Government of Sudan
GOSS	Government of Southern Sudan
HIPC	Heavily Indebted Poor Countries
HSM	Holy Spirit Movement (I&II)
ICC	International Criminal Court
ICTR	International Criminal Tribunal for Rwanda
ICTY	International Criminal Tribunal for the Former Yugoslavia
IDPs	Internally Displaced Persons
IEC	Independent Electoral Commission

IGAD	Intergovernmental Authority on Development
IGADD	Intergovernmental Authority on Drought and Development
ILO	International Labour Organization
LRA	Lord's Resistance Army
MAP	Millennium Partnership for the African Recovery Programme
MDC	Movement for Democratic Change
MMC	Multi-Member Constituency
MMP	Mixed-Member Proportional System
MP	Member of Parliament
MPLA	Popular Movement for the Liberation of Angola
MRA	Mano River Area
MRU	Mano River Union
NAI	New African Initiative
NCSC	National Civil Service Commission
NDRC	National Disarmament and Rehabilitation Commission
NEPAD	New Economic Partnership for African Development
NGO	Non-Governmental Organization
NRA	National Resistance Army
NRM	National Resistance Movement/Army
OAU	Organization of African Unity
OSSREA	Organization of Social Science Research in Eastern and Southern Africa
PC	Presidential Council
PR	Proportional Representation
PR	Proportional Representative (Councillor)
PSC	Peace and Security Council (of the African Union)
PTA	Parent-Teacher Association
RDP	Reconstruction and Development Program
RECs	Regional Economic Communities
RENAMO	Mozambican National Resistance
SADC	Southern African Development Community
SADCC	Southern African Development Coordination Conference
SADC-PF	Southern African Development Community Parliamentary Forum
SALW	Small Arms and Light Weapons
SAPES	Southern African Political Economy Series
SMC	Single-Member Constituency
SNRC	Somali National Reconciliation Conference
SPLA	Sudan People's Liberation Army
SPLM	Sudan's People's Liberation Movement
SWAPO	South West Africa People's Organization
TFG	Transitional Federal Government
UMA	Arab-Maghrib Union
UN	United Nations
UNDAF	United Nations Development Framework
UNDP	United Nations Development Program
UNITA	Union for the Total Liberation of Angola
UNLA	Uganda National Liberation Army
UNOSOM	United Nations Operations in Somalia
UPA	Uganda People's Army
UPDA	Uganda People's Defence Army
UPDF	Uganda People's Defence Forces
UPDM	Uganda People's Defence Movement
WB	World Bank
WLR	Weekly Law Reports
WNBF	West Nile Bank Front
ZANU-Ndonga	Zimbabwe African National Union-Ndonga
ZANU-PF	Zimbabwe African National Union Patriotic Front
ZEC	Zimbabwe Electoral Commission
ZESN	Zimbabwe Electoral Support Network

Introduction
The Resolution of African Conflicts
ALFRED NHEMA

The almost universal approval given to peace and security as prerequisites for democracy and economic development makes the task of critically examining the conditions as to why some societies and countries go to war and others not highly challenging. Despite the increasing acceptance that poverty is still one of the major root causes of conflicts in Africa, the jury is still out on what conditions can free the continent from the yoke of conflicts and what materials and procedures at the levels of theory and praxis analysts should use in seeking durable answers. Given this lack of clarity, there is a tendency to explain or to define peace, security and democratization, by describing their realization or institutionalization as panaceas for durable peace and security in Africa.

Although peace and security are prerequisites for democracy and economic development, in a continent like Africa, where poverty and conflicts have been a backdrop for decades, an analysis of the major causes of conflicts that are critical to the resolution of African conflicts is critical.

Conflicts in Africa: An Overview

Any attempt to resolve conflicts in Africa has to take into account the root causes of some of the current problems in Africa, as examined in Zeleza and Nhema, *The Roots of African Conflics: The Causes & Costs*. These are often traced back to the colonial era when Europeans scrambled for territories with scant regard for ethnic boundaries, with the result that today's independent states are polyglot mixtures of cultural and linguistic groups.

A nation can be described as an entity of people who have developed solidarity on the basis of shared values, customs and institutions. A state, on the other hand, is:

> An organization within the society (that) coexists and interacts with other formal and informal organizations from families to economic enterprises or religious organizations. It is, however, distinguished from the myriad of other organizations in seeking predominance over them and in aiming to institute binding rules regarding the other organization's activities. (Azarya 1989: 408)

1

In an ideal situation, *national* loyalty is expected to blend with state loyalty, giving rise to an environment in which the state acquires legitimacy and political authority across all national or ethnic groups. Cultural, linguistic and political barriers that accentuate differences are supposed to have been resolved at that stage. However, history shows that the multi-ethnic states of Africa can hardly be defined as cohesive nation states in which the inhabitants have developed solidarity on the basis of shared customs and values. This situation tends to create an environment in some countries where some disaffected citizens owe a greater allegiance to their ethnic group than to their state.

Although the founding members of the Organization of African Unity were aware of the 'artificiality' of some of the inherited states in the immediate postcolonial period, they chose to recognize the inherited colonial borders in the hope that, with time, the leaders of the newly independent state elites would create conditions necessary for the creation of a consolidated state first, and build a cohesive nation-state later on in the future. By all accounts, it is evident that the tension between nation and state still accounts for some of the major conflicts in Africa. Unless political accommodative arrangements can be crafted in those countries where ethnic conflict is still rife, such states will remain fragile indeed.

Lack of democratization can be cited as one of the root causes of conflicts. Conflicts in Africa can be minimized in an environment that encourages substantive participation in the economic, political and social realms. Any attempt to exclude the ordinary citizen from such participation creates a rift between the rulers and the governed. Open political systems that safeguard basic civil liberties, basic needs and freedom of expression are less likely to be confronted by debilitating conflicts. In those countries where democratic freedoms are denied, very often citizens have had to take up arms, thereby generating conflict the effects of which have retarded socio-economic development and progress (Nhema 2004).

Yet another issue that continues to plague the African political dispensation is the lack of legal safeguards commonly referred to as the rule of law. African countries have still to create individual legal safeguards that subordinate politics to law. As long as the political systems and the elites operating under them are not subjected to the rule of law, such a system will give rise to those in political power paying scant attention to the development of a constitutional state that can protect human rights and civil liberties.

It has also become quite apparent that some forms of Western-style democratic systems are struggling to take root in most of Africa. While most of the countries have adopted constitutions that purport to serve the needs of the people through periodic elections, most of them are struggling to put in place the concrete electoral frameworks necessary and essential for a viable democratic order (Bujra and Adejumobi 2003).

Following the collapse of the Berlin Wall, most countries in Africa have accepted the 'first past the post' electoral system of governance undergirded by its concept of simple majority rule orientation. However, while such a system thrives in mature polities that have resolved the state-nation dichotomy in a satisfactory manner, in some African countries the simple majority electoral system, if not well managed, can create more divisions in society along ethnic lines. In an environment in which voters still owe their loyalty to the nation rather than the state, electoral systems based on simple majorities may create exclusionary rather than inclusionary political systems based on ethnic loyalties. Political realities in some countries may dictate that some form of unity government accommodation of the winners and losers be effected in the post-electoral dispensation, as such political arrangements will take into account diverse interests of society and avoid a 'winners take all' approach.

The role of external powers has also been cited as one of the causes of African conflicts. For much of the Cold War period, the rivalry between the superpowers fueled much of the conflict in Africa, where, in such countries as Mozambique, Angola and Ethiopia, African proxies fought for either the USSR or the United States. But since the demise of the Soviet Union, the nature of warfare in Africa has shifted to mostly intra- and inter-state conflict. Concomitantly with this change has been a lowering of the geo-strategic importance given to Africa by the Western powers. Hence, in the presence of conflict and failing states, the West has either failed to respond, or responded with some reluctance, as exemplified in the situations prevailing in such countries as Somalia, Rwanda, Burundi and the Democratic Republic of Congo (DRC).

One disconcerting development in post-Cold War Africa is the manner in which conflicts are being financed. While before the Cold War rivals provided funds for weapons, mineral resources such as petroleum and diamonds have become alternate sources of revenues for combatants. For example, it was access to diamonds that enabled the fighting to go on for years in Angola, Liberia and Sierra Leone. In these arrangements, gun traffickers have been active conspirators in channeling weapons to the continent as long as they had access to the precious metals and petroleum products that are the largest export products of Africa.

Debates have raged over the role of local, national and international actors in conflict resolution and post-conflict strategies in Africa. It is indisputable that, for any conflict resolution strategy to work, the various opposing forces must have confidence in the various mediation strategies and particularly those individuals and institutions that are involved in the process. There is a new realization in Africa that, while the role of external actors is indeed laudable, Africa will have to rely increasingly on its own to provide the long-term solutions to its own problems within the framework of its sub-regional groupings and the African Union and the United Nations. It can be noted that what are lacking very often in the initiatives that are currently being implemented by the African Union are the financial resources and logistical support so essential in making sure that the peacekeepers fulfill their mandate in an efficient and compre-hensive manner. More resources would therefore have to be devoted by African leaders to their peace-making operations in the continent.

According to recent studies, there have been more than thirty wars recorded in Africa since 1970. These wars, involving Algeria, Angola, Chad, Democratic Republic of the Congo, Ethiopia, Liberia, Namibia, Mozambique, Rwanda, Sierra Leone, Somalia, South Africa, Sudan, Uganda and Western Sahara, had both inter-state and intra-state characteristics. These wars have been responsible for the death and displacement of millions (Laremont 2002).

What is heartening is that Africa is now experiencing a dwindling number of countries that are still entangled in brutal and violent conflicts during the last decade. The twenty-year-old war unleashed by the Lord's Resistance Army (LRA) that has ravaged northern Uganda looked as if it might come to an end with the tentative cease-fire agreement of August 2006. While a final peace agreement has not been reached between the Ugandan government and the LRA, the fact that such a positive development has taken place should be appreciated. In Dar Fur, Sudan, the African Union's peacekeeping force has extended its mandate that was supposed to end in September 2006 by a further three months. Operatives of the Somalia transitional government and its opponents, the Council of Islamic Courts, which has taken over most of Somalia, met for peace talks in Khartoum in 2006. In the DRC, the various warring factions subjected themselves to a recent election in 2006 that initially failed to provide an outright winner. The West African country of Côte d'Ivoire continues to inspire observers with its incessant efforts aimed at finding a lasting solution to its political impasse. All these developments signify that Africans now realize that, without enduring peace, meaningful development will continue to elude the continent.

The developments highlighted in the preceding discussion are indications that efforts to resolve African conflicts are bearing fruit. These imperatives towards peace need to be supported by policies at the local, national, regional and international levels which ensure that the incentives motivating people to engage in war are blighted by real alternatives and the creation of conditions in which the majority of African people can enjoy economic, political and social progress.

Outline of the Volume

The papers in this volume review several strategies meant to ensure conflict resolution and post-conflict recovery in Africa. The ranges of interventions which are examined in the various chapters include, *inter alia*: negotiation frameworks within the extant economic, social, political and cultural configurations; the role of international actors and regional organizations like the African Union, the International Criminal Court and sub-regional organizations; the utilization of continental early warning systems; and finally a discussion on the role of democratic constitutional governance as a panacea for conflict resolution in Africa.

Following this introductory chapter, Victor Adetula's contribution provides a framework for a working peace system by examining the role of sub-regional integration attempts in Africa. He utilizes interesting empirical examples of the roles played by the various sub-regional organizations in the prevention and management of conflicts in Africa. These include interventions by the Economic Community of West African States (ECOWAS) in Liberia, Sierra Leone, Guinea Bissau, the South African Development

Community (SADC) in Lesotho and Mozambique, the Inter-Governmental Authority on Development (IGAD) in Sudan and Somalia, and the Arab-Maghrib Union (UMA) in Western Sahara. His in-depth analysis examines the various challenges faced in African sub-regional 'peacekeeping and conflict management initiatives and efforts'. He wraps up his chapter by delving into future scenarios that focus on the role of African sub-regional organizations within the context of regional initiatives by the African Union and the New Partnership for Africa's Development (NEPAD).

The second chapter by Godfrey Okoth focuses on the role the Organization of African Unity (OAU) and its successor, the African Union (AU), are playing in maintaining peace in Africa. He maintains that the OAU did not provide strong leadership to help resolve conflicts on the continent. He argues that explanations for this weak performance by the OAU fall into three categories. The first explanation involves institutional weaknesses that stemmed from the Organization's Charter. The second explanation is based on structural weaknesses related to organizational hierarchy and leadership motivations. The final explanation is historical, relating to past lessons learned through experience. The chapter ends by assessing the performance of the challenges facing the AU and some of its recent attempts at conflict resolution. Okoth's general conclusion is that, unlike its predecessor, the AU is a more professional, and less of a political, outfit and thereby well suited to fulfill its stated objectives.

The third chapter by Jakkie Cilliers focuses on the Continental Early Warning System (CEWS) of the African Union. It maintains that there should be a shared 'commitment between African leaders and African civil society organizations engaged in peace and security issues, research institutions in particular, for a joint responsibility for democracy, human rights and development'. The chapter further challenges both civil society organizations and the African leaders to help each other adhere to both actual and 'rhetorical commitments' made by the AU on various decisions and 'declarations as well as in legal documents such as the African Charter on Human and Peoples' Rights on the basis that the nature of African governance is a key determinant of insecurity and instability'. The chapter's insightful conclusions focus on the role external agencies, research institutions and civil society groups can play in complementing the work of the CEWS by supporting the activities of the AU's Peace and Security Council in its quest to attain stability which is a prerequisite to sustainable development in Africa.

Apuuli's chapter is an exposé of the conflict raging between the Lord's Resistance Army (LRA) led by Joseph Kony and the Ugandan government. It maintains that the agreement which officially paves the way for the International Criminal Court (ICC) to launch an official investigation into the activities of the LRA presents intriguing issues, since there are numerous crimes in the conflict that have been committed by both sides – the LRA and the government forces thereby offending 'the jurisdiction *rationae materiae* of the ICC Statute and other international legal instruments'.

Ursula Scheidegger's discourse on local government and the beneficial and destructive potential of social capital in post-apartheid South Africa makes interesting reading with its case study focusing on 'three local government wards [in Johannesburg's metropolitan area] that cut across former segregation boundaries ... where local government is not only an important agent of development and redistribution but also a structure providing for popular participation'. She contends that, while the negotiated transition process resulted in a new social, economic and political order based on a democratic constitution and represented by a democratically elected government, not much has changed in terms of the economic and social structures, perceptions, values and beliefs that were entrenched during the apartheid era. Such a socio-economic context shapes the way and manner in which social assets are 'distributed and managed' in post-apartheid South Africa. The challenge, then, is that social capital emanating from these social relations create an environment in which 'the adoption of cooperative values and the generation of trust cutting across social divisions are a challenge'.

Christof Hartmann shares a similar focus with regard to the theme of local government and its role in the management of conflicts in fragmented societies. Hartmann puts forward a model that looks at institutional dimensions and variables in local government systems and how those variables impact on the mitigation of potential conflicts in South Africa, Namibia and Mauritius.

Sudan's conflict resolution process with the Sudan Liberation Movement (SPLM) is examined in detail by Idris Salim El Hassan. His thesis is that, while the agreements are expressions of 'conflict settlement arrangements' aimed at achieving the 'socio-economic development of a united Sudan based on equality, justice, non-discrimination and non-marginalization', the legal and political forms of the agreements do not adequately address the 'technicalities and socio-economic contexts that will condition the implementation' of the peace agreement signed on 26 May 2004. The chapter offers a detailed account of the Sudanese economy and the role of the civil service and the key challenges facing the creation of a 'new Sudan'. His interesting conclusions are that, to avert the resurgence of war, there is a need not only to examine critically issues of meeting the aspirations of the various parties and addressing the realities on the ground but also to accelerate efforts aimed at building mutual trust and tolerance between the formerly contending parties.

Khabele Matlosa's intriguing contribution on elections and conflict in Southern Africa presents an increasingly acceptable view in Africa that elections 'if well managed ... are crucial instruments for conflict management in war-torn societies. Conversely, elections can also accentuate existing conflicts among belligerent parties.' He precedes his analysis of elections in Southern Africa by conceptualizing governance and then delves into empirical examples of how elections have evolved in selected SADC countries that include Angola, Lesotho, Mozambique and Zimbabwe, to mention but a few.

Chapter 9 by Kizito Sabala, Aisha Ahmad and Edwin Rutto examines the peace-building process in Somalia and the challenges faced by postwar Somalia led by the Transitional Federal Government. These range from the general insecurity in the country to the breakdown of physical infrastructure and the lack of cohesion among the various clans and sub-clans.

The chapter also analyzes the role that IGAD can play in assisting the reconstruction of the country after decades of civil war and concludes by noting that any attempts to reconstruct Somalia must take into account 'the need to consolidate social cohesion' which the authors contend can curb the 'influence of warlords and the problems of clanism, and foster a sense of Somali nationalism'.

The insightful study by Brazão Mazula, Eduardo Sitoe, Obede Baloi and Guilherme Mbilana on the post-conflict scenario in Mozambique adopts a case-study approach that focuses on the conflicts that occurred in the districts of Changara, Tete province (Central region) and Montepuez, in the Northern Province of Cabo Delgado. These are then used as empirical examples illuminating the complexities involved in peace-building, reconstruction and peace consolidation in the country.

The volume ends with an assessment of the prospects for constitutional governance and constitutionalism in Africa by Charles Fombad. The author argues that, while constitutional reforms and governance in Africa have become the norm rather than the exception, 'the mere existence of these new or revised constitutions and their effective enforcement may not necessarily be the panacea that would cure the multifaceted ... problems ... beset(ting) the continent nor (will they) even guarantee constitutionalism'. Fombad further posits that, while there has been progress made in commitments to constitutionalism by some states in Africa like Botswana, Ghana and South Africa, it is still not clear whether the majority of African leaders have the political will to adhere to constitutionalism.

All in all, it is apparent from these papers that there is little doubt that the challenges African countries and institutions face in the conflict resolution and reconstruction of post-conflict societies are truly daunting. The main concern and major goal for Africa should be to create conditions conducive to peace and opportunities for development and a decent life for the majority of the African people. In fact, it is a vicious cycle: Africa needs peace for development but it also needs development to enhance peace. Any strategies therefore to create peace must consider this reciprocal relationship between peace and development. To be sure, there is no magic formula and no singular strategy or set of tactics that can guarantee success. What also comes out lucidly from the chapters in this book is that the range of mechanisms to resolve conflicts are as varied as are the types of conflicts, and that strenuous efforts continue to be made by national, regional and international players to end such conflicts. The papers in this volume are therefore an effort to equip such efforts conceptually and practically.

References

Azarya,Victor. 1989. 'Reordering State-society Relations: Incorporation and disengagement'. Cited in M. Bratton, 'Beyond the State: Civil society and associational life in Africa'. *World Politics*. XLI (3): 407–30, p. 187.

Bujra, Abdalla and Adejumobi, Said, eds. 2003. *Breaking Barriers, Creating New Hopes: Democracy, civil society and good governance in Africa*. Addis Ababa: DPMF Book Series.

Laremont, Ricardo René, ed. 2002. *The Causes of War and the Consequences of Peacekeeping in Africa*. Portsmouth, NH: Heinemann.

Nhema, Alfred G., ed. 2002. *Democracy in Zimbabwe: From liberation to liberalization.* Harare: University of Zimbabwe Press.

Nhema, Alfred G., ed. 2004. *The Quest for Peace in Africa: Transformations, democracy and public policy.* Addis Ababa: International Books with OSSREA.

OSSREA. 2005. *Proceedings of the International conference on African conflicts: Management, resolution, post-conflict recovery and development.* Addis Ababa: OSSREA Publications.

1

The Role of Sub-Regional Integration Schemes in Conflict Prevention & Management in Africa
A Framework for a Working Peace System

VICTOR A. O. ADETULA

Many African conflicts have their roots in domestic politics. However, all the conflicts have a regional context. One feature of African conflicts is their domino effect, which most leaders in Africa dread since a conflict starting in one specific area may soon engulf the entire region because most African conflicts spill over easily. This makes a regional approach to the resolution of African conflicts imperative. The above considerations, and also the growing awareness in Africa that the pursuit of economic development by regional integration schemes is only possible under a peaceful atmosphere, have been at the base of the increased attention given to issues of peace and security by African regional and sub-regional organizations, especially since the end of the Cold War. These apply to the role played by the Economic Community of West African States (ECOWAS) in Liberia, Sierra Leone and Guinea Bissau, the South African Development Community (SADC) in Lesotho and Mozambique, the Inter-Governmental Authority on Development (IGAD) in Sudan and Somalia, and the Arab-Maghrib Union (UMA) in Western Sahara.

This chapter interrogates our conceptual and theoretical understanding of the role of sub-regional integrative and cooperative schemes in the prevention and management of African conflicts. It is suggested that a new awareness is growing in Africa about the role of sub-regional organizations in the prevention and management of conflicts. The success of the ECOWAS Cease-Fire Operation Monitoring Operation Group (ECOMOG) is well known, and so are criticisms of it. The chapter analyzes the socio-political context of the intervention operations of some African sub-regional organizations, the specific historical motivation, and the prospects for peace and security. The new trend and some of the issues in the emergent sub-regional collective security systems in Africa are related to the growing link between democratic governance and regional peace and security. As President Mandela once said: 'We [African leaders] must accept that we cannot abuse the concept of national sovereignty to deny the rest of the continent the right and duty to intervene, when, behind those boundaries, people are being slaughtered to protect tyranny' (1998:2). Eboe Hutchful (1998: 1) lends credence to Mandela's notion of 'sovereignty as responsibility', noting that the 'defence of democracy and proper governance' is indeed 'appropriate grounds' for intervention in the 'internal affairs of other states'. The thinking among the new African democrats therefore seeks to promote good governance over and above a state-centric notion of sovereignty. The newly established African Union (AU) and to some extent the New Economic Partnership for African Development (NEPAD) share in this new thinking. A systematic study of the new political response to issues of regional security and its links with democratic governance will enrich our understanding not only of the relationship between regionalism and collective security, which redefines regional integration, but also the traditional purpose of regional integration, to include collective concerns for issues of good governance, security, peace and order.

The chapter is divided into five sections. The first section introduces the main issues in the study, while the second section presents an overview of the conceptual and theoretical issues and also looks at the interpretations and influences of the 'idealists' and 'realists' on the roles of regional and sub-regional organizations in conflict prevention and management since the end of the Cold War. The third section analyzes the practical engagement of African sub-regional organizations with conflict management. The fourth section examines the limitations and shortfalls in African sub-regional peacekeeping and conflict management initiatives and efforts. A discussion of the future role of African sub-regional organizations, in particular the continent-wide regional initiatives of NEPAD and the AU, concludes the chapter.

Overview of Conceptual & Theoretical Issues

The conceptual point of departure in this chapter revolves around the concept of 'democratic security', which eschews the restricted traditional notion of security that has dominated international relations, security studies and strategic studies. The notion of 'democratic security' pointedly avoids the error of concentrating exclusively on the state to the exclusion of the people. The concept of 'security' is frequently misused. The 'realist' school whose prominence in the development of contemporary theory and practice of international relations remains uncontested promotes the focus on state power in inter-state relationships. In spite of the increasingly inter-dependent character of inter-state relations in the modern state system, the statist notion of security significantly influenced the evolution, goals and directions of international organizations. Concepts such as collective, regional as well as global security emerged out of concern for the security of states and in defence of states rather than the security of people. The study by Inis Claude (1971:216) on the development of international organizations in the twentieth century shows the evident preoccupation with the concept of collective security as well as the 'antiwar orientations' that informed the efforts to construct international organizations.

The League of Nations was established in 1919 with the expectation that it would transcend 'politics' in its operations, and that its establishment would mark the birth of a new world order! The League, however, failed to prevent the outbreak of the Second World War. But that in itself could not end the obsession of many statesmen with collective security. In 1945 the United Nations was formed, still around the concept of collective security, with deference to the position of the 'realist' on 'power politics', which won the day. As Mark Zacher (1979: 2) put it, 'statesmen now recognised that without the inclusion of the Great Powers – whose partial exclusion had, of course, contributed to the League's demise – the new organization would likely share the fate of its predecessor.'

It is instructive to note that, in the talks and discussions preceding the formation of the United Nations Organization, there was a clear consensus on the hegemony and unity of the Great Powers as a condition for the new security system. Another issue of note is the question of whether the new security system should be oriented toward regionalism, as advocated by Moscow and London, or toward universalism, as Washington favoured. The Great Powers put forward proposals for the San Francisco Conference in June 1945 for the universalist orientation, to create an international collective security organization. However, changes were made that allowed and expected regional organizations to manage conflicts among their members. This was prompted by three considerations: (i) a regional approach to inter-state conflicts held more promise of eliciting collaboration; (ii) global rivalries and divisions might inhibit the United Nations from dealing with some types of conflicts; and (iii) some countries were just too enthusiastic about the interventions of the Great Powers in their regions (Zacher, 1979: 2). Whatever the strength of these concerns, they provided, in some sense, the justification for the provisions in Articles 51–54 of the UN Charter. It was against this background that the Organization of African Unity (OAU) was set up in 1963 as the collective regional security apparatus for Africa.

However, despite the creation of the United Nations and regional organizations, the record is replete with unsuccessful attempts at collective security; wanton breaches of global peace and security litter the annals of world politics since 1945. And contrary to general expectation that the end of the Cold War would drastically reduce the incidence of political conflicts in Africa, violent conflicts have continued and become even more salient and prevalent across the continent.

Nevertheless, the end of the Cold War brought some changes in the concept and practice of international relations. There was a resurgence of the 'idealist' school on how to manage the way states relate to one another in a 'new world order'. This new thinking sought to redefine international relations, not in terms of the old 'power politics' or the use of force; rather it presented a new system of collective security that 'would require the great powers to renounce both the use of force in disputes among themselves and unilateral action in regional conflicts. It would also require Security Council agreement that regional conflicts endangering territorial integrity will be dealt with through economic sanctions – and, if necessary, military action – imposed by collective decision and with the used of multinational forces' (McNamara 1991: 100). Robert McNamara, a leading protagonist of the new school of international relations, warned that: 'a system of collective security implies collective decision making.

Correspondingly, all partners must share the financial costs, the political risks, and the dangers of casualties and bloodshed.'

The idealists' scenario of the international system is one of a 'multipolar world' that would need and impose new relationships, responsibilities and obligations on states and international organizations alike, based on the rule of law. It would be a 'new world order' that would 'establish the military neutrality of the developing countries vis-à-vis the great powers; commit the great powers to end military support of conflicts in the developing countries; support a system of collective security to guarantee territorial integrity, with a mechanism for resolving regional conflicts; and increase technical and financial assistance to the developing countries' (McNamara 1991: 99). The management of international violence since the end of East-West ideological rivalries clearly belies the idealist expectations presented above. The Gulf War, the crises in Somalia, Haiti, Yugoslavia, Bosnia, and most recently in Afghanistan and Iraq, are just a few examples of the failures of the 'new thinking'.

The influence of the new idealism on Africa with respect to conflict management is worth examining. At the continental level, the Organization of African Unity (OAU) dominated the scene with a mandate to resolve conflicts. The 'regionalist' approach of the OAU found easy accommodation within the new idealism. However, besides lacking the political courage, the institutional capacity of the OAU for managing conflicts was largely inadequate. Although the OAU Charter provided for the organization to settle African disputes and conflicts, its performance in this area was hardly impressive. Indeed, its role was appropriated by sub-regional organizations like the Economic Community of West African States (ECOWAS). Clearly, by the end of the Cold War the OAU had still not emerged as a regional organization with sufficient clout to manage African conflicts.

In postcolonial Africa motives for regional cooperation have been broadened to include economic, social and political interests in addition to the need for greater international bargaining power. It is very rare today to find an African country that has not shown overt interest in at least one of the several existing regional cooperation schemes on the continent. Also, lately in many African circles the regional approach to conflict prevention and management is gaining ground. The broadening of the role and functions of African regional integration schemes to include responsibility for peace-building and conflict management efforts generally adds credence to the conceptualization of regional integration as a dialectical unity of social, economic and political processes. This conceptualization is at the core of the link between regionalism and collective security.

Engagements of Sub-regional Groupings

The Economic Community of West African States is large. Its 15 (16 until 2000 when Mauritania withdrew its membership) member countries include seven countries which belonged to the Communanté Economique de l'Afrique de l' Ouest (CEAO), and three countries that are in the Mano River Union (MRU). It was set up in 1975 with the stated objectives:

[T]o promote cooperation and development in all fields of economic activity, particularly in the fields of industry, transport, telecommunications, energy, agriculture, natural resources, commerce, monetary and financial questions and in social and cultural matters for the purpose of raising the standard of living of its peoples, of increasing and maintaining economic stability, of fostering closer relations among its members and of contributing to the progress and development of the African continent. (*Treaty of the Economic Community of West African States, 1975*, Article 2 (1))

Modeled as a customs union, the ECOWAS Treaty and Protocol provide a plethora of integrative instruments in the form of several monetary, fiscal, administrative, institutional and legal measures. With its intervention in Liberia and Sierra Leone, ECOWAS has come to be more associated with regional security.

Although the ECOWAS Treaty (1975) was silent on conflict management and prevention, it was appreciated quite early that no meaningful cooperation could take place within the sub-region without peace and security. The Protocol on Non-Aggression, and the Protocol Relating to Mutual Assistance on Defence were incorporated into the ECOWAS Treaty in 1978 and 1981, respectively, to address this concern. Unfortunately, this did not prevent internal dissension, conflict, and large-scale violence in the sub-region. The Liberian civil war broke out in December 1989. In August 1990 ECOWAS sent a peace enforcement force – the ECOWAS Cease-Fire Monitoring Group (ECOMOG) – to Liberia. When the Liberian civil war broke out it was reckoned to be an internal problem by the international community, in which other states or the United Nations did not need to intervene. Thus at the time the ECOMOG force moved into Liberia it was almost certain that neither the United Nations nor the United States was going to intervene to bring about peace. When the UN did eventually come in, its involvement was limited to sending some observers and providing some cash to fund the operations of ECOMOG. Sesay (2002) notes that ECOWAS 'rose creditably to the challenges of conflict management and peace keeping in West Africa at a time when the great powers had literally abandoned West Africa, and indeed the continent as a whole, and focused their attention on Bosnia in Europe'. While most sections of the international community delayed and appeared to be confused, Liberia's neighbours and other countries in West Africa were grappling with the inflow of refugees. This development no doubt affected the perceptions of the ECOWAS member states that identified the Liberian crisis as a threat to the peace and economic well-being of the sub-region.

At the May 1990 ECOWAS Summit in Banjul, the Heads of State took serious note of the prevailing disputes in the sub-region, with special reference to the Liberian crisis. Subsequently, an ECOWAS Standing Mediation Committee of five members was set up to look into conflicts which had disruptive effects on normal life within the member states and on the smooth running of the Community, with a mandate to act for and on behalf of the Heads of State. In August 1990, a Summit Meeting of the Committee was convened in Banjul, with invitations extended to the neighbours of Liberia (Côte d'Ivoire, Guinea and Sierra Leone) This summit produced a Peace Plan for Liberia, which included an immediate cease-fire to be observed by the warring parties; the setting up of the ECOWAS Cease-Fire Monitoring Group (ECOMOG) to keep the peace and restore law and order and ensure respect for the cease-fire; the institution by Liberians of a broad-based interim government by means of a national conference of political parties, warring parties, and other interest groups; the withdrawal of President Doe from Liberia; the holding of free and fair elections within twelve months to establish a democratically elected government; the presence of the ECOWAS to observe the elections; and the setting up of a special emergency fund for ECOWAS operations in Liberia. In official circles in some West African countries, especially Nigeria, the intervention was seen in terms of the defence of peace and security in the sub-region as well as in the spirit of good neighbourliness. But support for the initial operations of ECOMOG in Liberia was not total, as some member states of ECOWAS only approved of ECOMOG operations very reluctantly.[1] All the same, the Peace Plan was endorsed by the Assembly of the Heads of State and Government at its meeting on 27–8 November 1990.

The ECOWAS Cease-Fire Monitoring Group that intervened in Liberia was an *ad hoc* sub-regional response to the challenges of peacekeeping and conflict management. It therefore expected to be confronted with challenges. President Olusegun Obasanjo (2001: vii) was later to point out that 'ECOMOG fell badly short of its ideals in many ways'; for instance, there were the realities on the ground in Liberia, such as hostility towards ECOMOG troops on the part of belligerent NPFL forces which launched several attacks on ECOMOG positions, and also the population, paving the way for the amendment of the ECOMOG mandate. This came in the form of an authorization for ECOMOG to engage in Peace Enforcement Action in Liberia. With this, ECOMOG was able to defend itself decisively, restore safe haven status to Monrovia so that it could continue to provide sanctuary for refugees and displaced persons, and also to impress on the warring parties in particular the NPFL, that a military option to the resolution of the Liberian crisis was unacceptable and that the only acceptable procedure was by way of free and fair elections.

The operations of ECOMOG within the framework of Peace Enforcement Action allowed it to defend itself against aggression and to execute counter-offensive actions such as retaliatory expeditions against the National Patriotic Front of Liberia (NPFL). Although ECOMOG responded to the persistent insurgencies of the rebels with the use of force, which pushed the rebel forces back, these operations were clearly beyond the traditional conception of peacekeeping operations. However, the results were received with excitement in many circles: ECOMOG was able to establish buffer zones between the warring parties, facilitate the movement of relief supplies, repair and reactivate essential services, as well as evacuate hundreds of thousands of Liberians and other nationals trapped in Monrovia and other parts of the country during the war. It was also able to repatriate Liberians after the cease-fire, chair meetings between the warring parties during the negotiation of cease-fire agreements, and monitor implementation of the agreements. Moreover, in conjunction with the United Nations and other international non-governmental organizations like President Jimmy Carter's International Negotiation Network, ECOMOG conducted and monitored elections in Liberia after the cessation of hostilities.

It is interesting to note that, between May 1990 when ECOWAS first met on the Liberian crisis and August 1995 when the Abuja Peace Accord was signed, there were over thirty meetings and summits which resulted in more than fifteen agreements. The Abuja Accord signed on 19 August 1995 and the Accra Accord signed in July 1996 paved the way for the transition programme that led to an elected government in July 1997. The engagement of ECOWAS with conflict prevention and management enterprises in Guinea Bissau and Sierra Leone brought new lessons, all of which eventually led to the adoption in December 1999 of an ECOWAS' Mechanism for Conflict Prevention, Management, Resolution, Peace Keeping and Security. Together with the 1978 Protocol on Non-Aggression and the 1981 Protocol Relating to Mutual Assistance on Defence, the Mechanism provides the foundation for ECOWAS's collective security system.

Liberia, Sierra Leone and Guinea have a great deal in common. All three are members of the Mano River Union (MRU),[2] which was established on 3 October 1973 to accelerate development by means of integration within the Mano River Area (MRA). The MRU instituted a common external tariff in April 1977. It also introduced intra-union free trade in May 1981. In 1986, a Non-aggression Treaty was signed by the member states. Such was the level of cooperation among the three Mano River Basin countries before 1989 when Charles Taylor launched his rebellion near the Guinea/Liberia/Sierra Leone border. Not surprisingly, the Liberia civil war had serious consequences for Sierra Leone and Guinea. Guinea, for instance, had to bear the burden of an influx of refugees, and it was not long before the conflict in Liberia spilled over into Sierra Leone. The intractability of these conflicts can be explained, in part, in terms of their complex and multiple linkages. It is significant that the presence of Sierra Leonean rebel forces along the border of the other two countries helped the spill-over of violence into Guinea and Liberia, and the growth of region-wide conflict: Taylor's Liberia supported Sierra-Leonean and Guinean rebels while Guinea also supported Liberian rebels.

The armed attack launched in Sierra Leone in 1991 by the Revolutionary United Front (RUF) from the Liberia/Sierra Leone border was followed in 1996 by a military coup against the government of President Tejan Kabbah by the Armed Forces Revolutionary Council (AFRC) which later joined the RUF to form a military government. The international community condemned these developments. On 8 October 1997 the UN Security Council imposed an oil and arms embargo on Sierra Leone and also authorized ECOWAS to ensure its implementation by the use of ECOMOG. The pressure recorded significant success as the AFRC/RUF government was able to hold on to power for only about nine months. ECOWAS/ECOMOG reinstated Tejan Kabbah as President of Sierra Leone on 10 March 1998.

Three major peace negotiations on the conflict in Sierra Leone took place, which resulted in the following agreements: the Abidjan Peace Agreement of 30 November 1996; the Conakry (ECOWAS) Peace Plan of 23 October 1997; and the Lomé Peace Agreement of 7 July 1999. The progress made with respect to the implementation of the Lomé Peace

Agreement is commendable. The government of Sierra Leone has established all the mechanisms and institutions for peace negotiated in the Agreement, which include the establishment of the Commission for the Consolidation of Peace (CCP) that is working on a programme of transformation of ex-combatants. The internal peace process is also progressing with the involvement of civil society organizations. Nevertheless, six years after the reinstatement of President Kabbah the political situation in Sierra Leone was still very far from stable.

In the meantime, in June 1998 the former Chief of Staff of the Armed Forces of Guinea Bissau, Brigadier-General Ousumane Mane initiated an armed attack against the government of President Joao Vieira. The government, with military aid from Senegal and the Republic of Guinea, was able to maintain its hold on the power, and in July 1998 the warring parties agreed to a cease-fire. Relentless efforts by the international community to negotiate peace culminated in the Abuja Peace Agreement of November 1998, which ushered in other processes leading to elections held in January 2000. The development of sub-regional mechanisms for conflict management and peace-keeping has progressed much further in West Africa than in any other parts of Africa. The achievements of ECOWAS in Liberia and Sierra Leone have earned the regional organization a measure of international recognition.

The Southern African Development Community (SADC), has a model of regional collective security that is almost identical to that of ECOWAS/ECOMOG. It should be noted that SADC had a security function that dated back to the apartheid era in South Africa. At the time SADC was founded in July 1979, South Africa was involved in a number of regional conflicts, and the aim of the Southern African Development Coordination Conference, as it was then called, was to provide collective security, and also to reduce economic dependence on South Africa. Since the end of the apartheid era, SADC has undergone a radical realignment, with South Africa becoming its *de facto* leader rather than its primary target. SADC's 1992 Treaty states clearly that the consolidation, defence, and maintenance of democracy, peace, security and stability are among the main objectives of the organization.

As with Nigeria in ECOWAS/ECOMOG, having South Africa on board has contributed to the effectiveness of SADC's security and economic functions. In 1996 SADC established the SADC Organ of Politics, Defence and Security, which arose out of the need for a common security regime in Southern Africa. It was envisaged that the SADC Organ would become the institutional framework within which SADC countries would coordinate their policies and activities in the areas of politics, defence and security. The objectives of the body at the time of its formation included: to safeguard the people and development in the region against instability arising from civil disorder, inter-state conflict and external aggression; to undertake conflict prevention, management and resolution activities by mediating in inter-state and intra-state disputes and conflicts, pre-empting conflicts through an early warning system and using diplomacy and peacekeeping to achieve sustainable peace; to promote the development of a common foreign policy in areas of mutual interest; to develop close cooperation between the police and security services of the region and to encourage the observance of human rights. The Organ's principles state that disputes will be settled by negotiation, mediation and arbitration, and that military intervention will be entertained only after all possible alternatives have been pursued in accordance with the Charter of the OAU and the United Nations (SADC 1996). Although the organization recorded some success in mediating conflicts in the Comoros and the Democratic Republic of Congo (DRC), the dream of a regional security community is still far from being realized. Disagreement among members over different interpretations of certain sections of the Charter has resulted in the Organ being suspended.

The Inter-governmental Authority on Development (IGAD) has begun to assert a role for itself in the resolution of sub-regional conflict in the Horn of Africa. IGAD is a sub-regional organization that has the primary task of coordinating certain regional resource issues. It was established in 1986 and was initially known as the Inter-governmental Authority on Drought and Development (IGADD). Its membership now consists of six countries: Djibouti, Eritrea, Ethiopia, Kenya, Sudan and Uganda. It was in March 1996 that the Heads of IGAD amended the organization's charter to cover political and economic issues, including conflict resolution. With respect to conflict management, the periodic summits of IGAD have provided the necessary forum for heads of state to meet and discuss conflict issues, among other things. For example, at the 1986 IGAD summit the leaders of Ethiopia and Somalia had the opportunity to initiate talks that eventually led to détente and the demilitarization of their borders (Deng 1996: 137). Because of perceived threats from conflicts in Somalia and Sudan, security issues received prompt attention in IGAD's agenda, especially in the early 1990s. Although its efforts were not completely successful, IGAD mediated in the civil war in Sudan in September 1993, and made some headway in 1994. It resumed its role in 1997 but not very much has been accomplished beyond keeping the process going.

The Horn of Africa is bedeviled by serious inter- and intra-state conflicts. All the countries in IGAD have had significant internal security problems. For example, Sudan has been in conflict for more than two decades. Neither Sudan nor Ethiopia has demonstrated the actual or potential attributes of a 'core state' to assume leadership responsibility within IGAD. In addition, IGAD is confronted with the problem of lack of funds. None of the member states is rich enough to provide support, in the sense that Nigeria supported ECOMOG operations in both Liberia and Sierra Leone. Hence, the accomplishments of IGAD have remained quite marginal compared with those of either ECOWAS or even SADC.

Apart from ECOWAS, SADC and IGAD, there are a handful of less-known sub-regional initiatives on conflict prevention and management operating in Africa. These include the ECCAS, the Arab-Maghrib Union and the little-known community of Sahelian-Saharan states[3] that once mooted the idea of creating an intervention force to help settle the border dispute between Eritrea and Ethiopia. It is interesting to note that the recently revived East African Community (EAC) has bounced back to life giving due consideration to matters of regional security and peace. In June 1998, the three EAC member states – Kenya, Tanzania and Uganda – together with the US undertook their first joint peacekeeping exercise.

In West Africa the Accord de Non-Aggression et d'Assistance en Matière de Défence (ANAD) was signed in June 1977 by Burkina Faso, Mali, Mauritania, Niger, Senegal, Côte d'Ivoire and Togo. Benin and Guinea Conakry were granted observer status at its meetings. ANAD's main objective at its creation was to promote security and stability in order to enhance economic development. It was not a supranational body, and neither did it develop any military policy. It stated quite clearly that it was a defensive alliance, and that any attack on any member would be interpreted as an attack on the entire alliance (Alao 2004). Its mode of operation includes dialogue and negotiation to resolve conflict among its members, and the use of a peace intervention force should the former fail. Also, it is stipulated that an external attack against a member state would entail the following course of action: first, a search for a diplomatic solution, to be followed by the imposition of sanctions short of the use of force, and finally, as a last resort, the use of armed force to counter and reverse the aggression. Although it was originally conceived as a non-aggression and mutual defence pact ANAD has today transcended the initial status of sub-regional security to include areas of high-level integration such as common policy formulation and cooperation on broader issues of human security.

Noticeably where sub-regional mechanisms for conflict management have recorded appreciable success, as in the case of ECOWAS/ECOMOG in West Africa, it is arguably the result of paying regard to issues of good governance and democratization. Sesay (2002) argues that the sub-regional groupings that have enjoyed relative success stress the central role of democratization and good governance in their programmes of conflict management and resolution. Some of the principles espoused in the Revised Treaty of the Economic Community of West African States (ECOWAS n.d) and other major declarations on the various conflicts in West Africa under-line the notion that democratization coupled with responsive and responsible governance is the most effective conflict management tool. In contrast, where it has been difficult to get members of sub-regional schemes to agree to operate conflict management mechanisms with due considera-tion to issues of good governance and democracy, the returns on invest-ment in collective security have been rather low.

Limitations & Shortfalls

Despite some success stories, conflict management mechanisms of sub-regional organizations in Africa, including the larger ones such as ECOWAS and SADC, are still largely underdeveloped, and generally lacking in established institutional frameworks and structures. Because of the absence of institutionalized structures for conflict management, conflict resolution initiatives have mostly taken *ad hoc* forms. In the Liberian conflict, for example, the ECOWAS Heads of State and Government established a Community Standing Mediation Committee, which in turn created the ECOMOG at its inaugural session. In Sierra Leone, the ECOWAS Heads of

State and Government did not formally approve of the ECOMOG force until some three months after its intervention. And in Guinea Bissau, the ministerial-level ECOWAS Defence Council voted to extend ECOMOG's mandate to Guinea Bissau even before the ECOWAS Heads of State and Government had time to address the issue. Abiodun Alao (2001) noted, for instance, that of all the existing sub-regional organizations in Africa, 'only ANAD was specifically created for defence and security purposes. Others were forced by developments in their respective regions to incorporate defence and security calculations into their agenda'. The establishment of the ECOWAS Mechanism for Conflict Prevention, Management Resolution, Peacekeeping and Security in December 1999 is commendable as a commitment by ECOWAS to create a permanent machinery for ensuring lasting peace and stability. However, the Mechanism does not address the critical issue of who will determine when and how the military force under the Mechanism will be deployed.

The SADC also shares similar deficiencies. In fact, unlike ECOWAS, SADC lacks integrated systems, processes, and methods to deal with issues such as human rights and the advancement of democracy and good governance. The lack of consensus among SADC member states on 'how the Organ should relate to the SADC Summit', coupled with the lack of 'the requisite political will and institutional capacity', has not helped SADC to evolve a regional security community (Dieter et al. 2001: 65). Also, the ideological division among member states has continued to hamper the work of the Organ. For example, while the group comprising Angola, Zimbabwe and Namibia is disposed towards military solutions to conflict, another group made up of South Africa, Mozambique and to some extent Zambia supports the principles and objectives of the SADC Organ.

The ECOWAS, SADC, and IGAD lack early warning systems and risk assessment capacities and are therefore pretty weak in conflict prevention. Both ECOWAS and IGAD lack reconnaissance and logistical capacities. Here South Africa has the edge by reason of its capabilities and other military assets of Southern Africa including Zimbabwe.

Despite their obvious shortcomings, sub-regional organizations still largely represent primary units of security and conflict management for the African continent. Both the United Nations and other major actors in the international community have given explicit approval to the increased engagement of sub-regional organizations in conflict management. This is so especially in the light of a catalogue of failed efforts on the part of continent-wide organizations like the OAU to manage African conflicts effectively.

Conclusion

Since the end of the Cold War it has become abundantly clear that Africa must rely less on the generosity of the North to manage its conflicts. Since Operation Restore Hope in Somalia in 1992, the Western countries have become less enthusiastic about getting involved in Africa's 'intractable conflicts'. It is significant that Africa has accepted this reality on its own and has adjusted accordingly, beginning from the establishment of the OAU

Mechanism for Conflict Prevention, Management and Resolution in 1993. The New Partnership for African Development (NEPAD) and the African Union (AU) are two related regional initiatives committed to the philosophy of self-reliance.

The African Union (AU) is the latest of Africa's broad regional cooperation schemes. Its objectives, which include strengthening the founding principles of the OAU Charter, are more comprehensive than those of the OAU in acknowledging the multi-faceted challenges confronting the continent, especially in the area of peace and security. The Constitutive Act of the AU (CAAU), in its objective, places a premium on the promotion of peace, security and stability in Africa (Article 3 (f)). Also, enshrined in its principles are the peaceful resolution of conflicts, the prohibition of the use of force or threats to use force, and rights of intervention in the affairs of member states in the case of 'grave circumstances' related to war crimes, genocide, and crimes against humanity (Articles 4 (c) , (f), and (h) respectively). At the inaugural AU summit in 2002, it was agreed that a Peace and Security Council (PSC) be established with the responsibility of preventing, managing and resolving conflicts in Africa. The PSC has been set up and efforts are being made by African leaders to ensure that it is structured in a way that guarantees its effectiveness. Unlike the OAU mechanism, the AU has the 'right to intervene in a member state pursuant to a decision of the PSC in respect of grave circumstances, namely war crimes, genocide, and crimes against humanity'. Also, the most recent African plan for economic development is the New Partnership for African Development that is based on the New African Initiative (NAI), a merger of the Millennium Partnership for the African Recovery Programme (MAP) and the Omega Plan. NEPAD emphasizes the importance of collective peace and security as a prerequisite for development in the realm of conflict management.

The future of the relationships between the AU and the sub-regional organizations will depend, however, in no small measure, upon the development of both the AU and the various sub-regional organizations themselves. This, of course, has several political ramifications, demanding complex institutions and structures, and extensive political will, as well as unity of objectives and commitments at national, sub-regional and continental levels. Suffice it to say here that the successful development of both the AU and the various sub-regional organizations in Africa depends first and foremost on the commitment of African states to redefine regional and sub-regional integration in a way that moves the process beyond state-centered approaches to include, among other things, the increased participation of civil society – the people and their representatives in associations, professional societies, farmers' groups, women's groups and so on, as well as political parties – in regional integration processes. Without sufficient participation of these groups either in the political process where decisions relating to regional cooperation and integration programmes, including conflict issues, are taken or in adequate consultation, efforts and initiatives stand the risk of becoming easy prey for sabotage. Although there is some new thinking in this direction, as already expressed in NEPAD and the AU, these new initiatives need to be translated into concrete agendas and programmes for civil society engagement with the state and other structures and processes of regional integration.

References

Alao, A. 2001.'The Role of African Regional and Sub-regional Organizations in Conflict Prevention and Resolution', *Journal of Humanitarian Assistance: New Issues in Refugee Research*, Working Paper No. 23 http://www.jha.ac/articles/u023.htm.

Claude,I. L. 1971. *Swords into Plowshares: The Problems of Progress of International Organization.* 4th edn. New York: Random House.

Deng, F.M. 1996. *Sovereignty As Responsibility: Conflict Management in Africa.* Washington, DC: The Brookings Institution.

Dieter H., G. Lamb and H. Melber. 2001. 'Prospect for Regional Co-operation in Southern Africa'. Discussion Paper No. 11, in *Regionalism and Regional Integration in Africa: A Debate of Current Aspects and Issues.* Uppsala: Nordiska Afrikaintitutet, 54–74.

Economic Community of West African States (ECOWAS) 1975. *Treaty of the Economic Community of West African States (ECOWAS)*, Lagos: ECOWAS Executive Secretariat.

Economic Community of West African States (ECOWAS). n.d. *Revised Treaty of the Economic Community of West African States (ECOWAS)*, Abuja: ECOWAS Executive Secretariat.

Hutchful, E. 1998. 'Demilitarization in Africa: An Update.' Discussion paper prepared for Conference on Leadership Challenges of Demilitarization in Africa, organized by Center for Peace and Reconciliation, in conjunction with the Africa Leadership Forum and the United Nations Development Program (UNDP)-Tanzania, Arusha, Tanzania, 22–24 July.

Mandela, N. 1998. Address of the President of the Republic of South Africa, Nelson Mandela, to the Summit Meeting of the Organization of African Unity (OAU) Heads of State and Government, Ouagadougou, Burkina Faso, 8 June.

McNamara, S. R. 1992. 'The Post-Cold War World: Implications for Military Expenditure in the Developing Countries', in Lawrence H. Summers and Shekhar Shar, eds, *Proceedings of the World Bank Annual Conference on Development Economics, 1991*, Washington, DC: World Bank, 95–126.

Obasanjo, O. 2001. 'Integration Vision for the 21st Century', in Anatole Ayissi. ed., *Cooperation in West Africa: An Agenda for the 21st Century*, Geneva: United Nations Institute for Disarmament Research (UNIDIR) vii–xi, available at http://www.unidir.org/pdf/ouvrages/pdf-2-92-9045-140-8-en.pdf

Sesay, A. 2002 'The Role of ECOWAS in Promoting Peace and Security in West Africa', *DPMN Bulletin*, IX (3) June http://www.dpmf.org/role-ecowas-peace-amadu.html

Southern African Development Community. 1996. *Communiqué: Summit of Heads of State or Government of the SADC, June.*

Zacher, W. M. 1979. *International Conflicts and Collective Security, 1946-77.* New York: Praeger.

Notes

1 Some prominent members of ECOWAS, notably Côte d'Ivoire and Burkina Faso, were later to challenge the legitimacy of ECOMOG.

2 Liberia and Sierra Leone are foundation members of MRU. Guinea joined later on 25 October 1980.

3 Member countries include Burkina Faso, Chad, Libya, Mali, Niger and Sudan.

2

Conflict Resolution in Africa
The Role of the OAU & the AU

P. GODFREY OKOTH

This chapter starts from the premise that the post-Cold War era presents international organizations with increasingly complex problems concerning conflict resolution. The United States and the former Soviet Union have increasingly withdrawn from active involvement in preventing and resolving conflicts in Africa. This is despite the fact that Africa's struggles that are increasingly associated with ethnic conflicts are exacerbated by the continued availability of arms dating back to Cold War rivalries. In many instances, the United Nations has responded to international calls to intervene in these crises, including its mission to Somalia, Rwanda and Burundi, among others. Such interventions have been particularly difficult, however, in view of the scope of the destruction and violence resulting from these civil wars. Faced with a growing number of demands for conflict resolution, the UN has become over-burdened and is calling for more regional intervention efforts to be made. Thus, it is important to determine what role regional organizations are able to play in resolving these conflicts.

The chapter comprises an examination of the role the Organization of African Unity (OAU) played and the role the successor of the OAU, namely, the African Union (AU), is now playing in keeping the peace in Africa. We argue that the OAU did not provide strong leadership to help resolve conflicts on the continent; nor did it take many significant actions to address the increasing number of conflicts that broke out.

We maintain that explanations for this weak performance by the OAU fall into three categories. The first explanation involves institutional weaknesses stemming from the Organization's Charter. The second explanation is based on structural weaknesses related to organizational hierarchy and leadership motivations. The final explanation is historical, relating to past lessons learned through experience.

Because the OAU failed to carry out radical reforms, it ceased to exist, and from its ashes the AU emerged. The AU is expected to enhance continental unity and significantly improve Africa's ability to participate in the new era of globalization.

Institutional Weaknesses of the OAU Charter

One aspect of the OAU that had a direct impact on its ability and willingness to intervene in regional conflicts was its Charter, which in several ways curtailed the number of options the organization had for dealing with conflicts. Although conditions existed in which an action taken without regard for principles might produce a better outcome than strict compliance, adherence to the Charter provided order for an already chaotic continent. An examination of the principles enshrined in the OAU Charter helps explain the limitations that the OAU faced in handling conflict resolution and provides insight into the normative preferences of its members. Although the priorities of the OAU had shifted over time to reflect numerous changes on the continent, the Organization's founding principles had not been altered and imposed limitations on the degree of involvement the OAU could take to intervene in conflict situations (El-Ayouty 1994). Furthermore, some of these principles were contradictory, presenting member states with the difficult task of determining those that took precedence in a given situation and thus often resulting in the maintenance of the *status quo* rather than in organizational action.

During its inception in May 1963, the OAU's highest priority was to help all African countries achieve independence (Foltz 1991). As many African countries became independent over the following decade, the OAU focused particularly on ending apartheid and on promoting a separate African identity in the world arena. By promoting the non-aligned movement in the third world and calling for 'African solutions of African problems,' it sought further independence from its colonial heritage. In the post-Cold War era, debates about pursuing globalization or regionalism still persisted but new goals and debates also emerged. The OAU's priorities then included such diverse goals as the promotion of economic integration, development, and human rights (El-Ayouty 1994:1). The principles on which the OAU was founded, however, remained largely unchanged despite the changes in its priorities. The founding principles still reflected the organization's initial concern with independence and severely limited the types of actions the OAU was allowed to take to resolve regional conflicts and to facilitate the achievement of its new priorities.

Two of the most binding principles to which member states of the organization were committed are those of sovereignty and non-intervention (Foltz 1991). Neither the OAU nor any member state was permitted to interfere in the sovereign, internal affairs of the other member states. In order to safeguard their hard-won independence, African states sought to prevent any unwanted interference by neighbouring states in their domestic affairs. These principles, although intended to promote state security, did not necessarily promote peace in the region. Maintenance of the non-intervention principle regardless of internal conditions severely restricted the OAU's ability to engage in many conflict resolution activities, particularly in the case of civil wars. The OAU was only allowed to intervene at the infrequent request of the member state concerned, or in case of an inter-state conflict. Historically, even when floods of refugees and the emergence of rebel groups in other states threatened regional stability, the OAU did not use these mitigating factors to justify uninvited intervention. For example, the conflict in the Sudan displaced thousands of refugees and resulted in instability within the region and hostile relations with neighboring states. The OAU, however, chose not to get actively involved (Jonah 1994:1). The only way that it was able to get round the sovereignty principle was when all order had broken down within the state and there was no longer any 'government' from which to ask permission to intervene (as in the case of Somalia in 1992). Even this justification, however, was not often invoked. In most cases the OAU simply offered its good offices and mediation services to help resolve conflicts. These services were utilized by the combatants, but usually not until the warring parties had worn themselves out and caused a great deal of destruction that might have been prevented by earlier intervention.

According to experiences in Somalia (UNOSOM I, II, UNITF) and Chad (OAU peacekeeping force 1981), peacekeeping forces were not always a recommended solution to civil war. In the case of Somalia, despite the fact that the large military presence was able temporarily to end military engagement, negotiated settlements were not forthcoming. The presence of foreign troops aroused such hostility that the negotiators were unable to secure any kind of agreement from the combatants, resulting in the eventual withdrawal of the forces. The OAU forces in Chad were even less effective because of smaller numbers, fewer resources, and a very disorganized chain of command. The peacekeepers' ineffectiveness resulted in the eventual military victory of Habre's forces and the peacekeepers' withdrawal after only six months of operation (Okoth 1983:148-164). There were other methods of intervention, however, such as arms and economic embargoes or even preventive diplomacy, which would be viable options for the OAU to pursue if it were not limited by the principle of non-intervention. As the priorities of the OAU shifted over time, the limitation on intervention due to unaltered Charter principles became increasingly problematic, preventing or limiting intervention even when human rights were being violated, and thus bringing the new priorities into conflict with the founding principles.

Another principle that limited the conflict resolution options of the OAU was that of territorial integrity, to uphold the boundaries of all member states as they were established at each state's independence. This was particularly true in cases in which internal factions were seeking secession from a member state. The OAU was bound by its Charter to uphold the *status quo* of territorial divisions regardless of the validity or persuasiveness of the secessionists. It was thus restricted in the types of negotiated settlements it could propose and support (new boundary lines are not an option). This automatic support for current boundaries (and thus by implication the member state's government) often resulted in distrust of the OAU by rebel groups preventing serious dialogue from occurring at all. Thus, even mediation efforts, which did not threaten state sovereignty, were limited in their effectiveness *(Weekly Review* 1998: 26).

Just as sovereignty often prevented intervention and commitment to upholding territorial integrity limited the scope of peaceful settlement options, contradictions between principles also tended to result in inaction by the OAU (Asante 1987). One such contradiction was the OAU's declared support for the principle of self-determination (used to support anti-colonial movements in the 1960s and 1970s) and the organization's maintenance of territorial boundaries. The arbitrary borders established by the colonial powers split up numerous nationalities, while in other cases quite diverse groups are combined as in the Sudan and Chad. Rather than supporting their various claims for secession from or annexation of territories, however, the OAU chose to uphold the current borders to prevent the total breakdown of order. Although the policy of preventing the fracturing of member states was a sound one, it was left without a mechanism to deal with claims for secession. Thus, the contradiction between territorial maintenance and self-determination remained.

A second contradiction stemmed from the OAU's desire to promote 'peaceful settlement of disputes' between its members, and its aversion to intervening in the sovereign affairs of its members. The Organization occasionally used the few peaceful settlement mechanisms at its disposal to resolve territorial disputes between neighboring states, but it rarely made even token efforts to resolve violent civil conflicts. Even if the OAU were more willing to actively intervene, it had no mechanism for such ventures. The creation of the Central Mechanism for Prevention and Management of Conciliation and Arbitration suggests, however, that the OAU was attempting to pursue 'peaceful settlements of disputes' more seriously in the future (Da Costa 1995). The new mechanism placed greater emphasis on cost-effective preventive diplomacy and on breaking Africa's dependence on outside mediators other than the Commission. The mechanism also sought to create an empowered African High Command that would be more effective than the decision-making body of the Commission, which was largely overshadowed by the Assembly.

This examination of the principles of the OAU Charter suggests that they posed significant though not insurmountable restrictions on the organization's options to resolve conflict in the region. These principles (sovereignty, non-interference, territorial integrity, self-determination) and organizational priorities (independence, economic growth, the protection of human rights) shaped and guided the decisions and actions of the OAU as it considered whether to intervene in a conflict and what manner of intervention would be appropriate and effective. The next section examines further how the structural limitations of the organization affected its intervention decisions.

Structural Weaknesses of the OAU

When explaining the weak performance of the OAU on the issue of conflict intervention, the organization and decision-making structures of the OAU had as much if not more significance than the Charter principles did. Organizational structures indicated whether the OAU had some degree of autonomy or whether it was completely dependent on its member states when it took action.

An examination of the OAU's organizational structure indicates that it suffered several structural weaknesses that limited its autonomy and its ability to conduct conflict resolution activities. The supreme decision-making body of the organization was the Assembly of Heads of State and Government, which met at least once a year. The Council of Ministers was responsible to the Assembly and implemented its decisions. The Secretariat, headed by the Secretary General, merely supervised the implementation of Assembly and Council decisions. In this hierarchical structure, the Secretary General of the OAU was far weaker than the UN Secretary General. He had very little authority and a relatively small staff to work with and was thus constrained to handle mainly those issues that the Assembly passed on to him. Without any power to act on his initiative, the OAU Secretary General was reduced to being a bureaucrat rather than an influential actor in many situations (Saxena 1993:2). He occasionally assumed the key role in negotiations to resolve conflicts, but this role was most frequently taken by state leaders on an *ad hoc* basis, thereby further weakening the Secretary General's influence (Jonah 1994:5). When these *ad hoc* negotiations were conducted and the Commission for Mediation and Conciliation specifically designed for mediating in disputes between member states was ignored, the OAU essentially became a rubber stamp rather than a crucial actor with regard to the agreements that were reached (Sesay 1982).

The hierarchical structure that placed all power in the hands of state leaders and removed much of the authority of the Secretary General tended to support the *status quo* rather than give the OAU an active role to resolve conflicts on the continent. Leaders who chose to guard their own power cautiously found intervention problematic unless the stability of their own regime was directly threatened by a regional crisis (Jonah 1994:5). Each Head of State was potentially threatened when intervention precedents were established, and few decisions were therefore made to actively intervene. Furthermore, the Assembly was a cumbersome decision-making body with over fifty members, where cohesion and consensus were difficult to achieve. Member states appeared to be unable to transcend national interests to promote regional interests, thus further reinforcing the inertia of the OAU (Layachi 1994:1).

Institutional structure was not only indicative of the limitations of the OAU for deciding whether or not to intervene to resolve a conflict; it could also indicate the degree of expertise and management that the Organization was capable of commanding. A highly bureaucratized OAU might have been slow moving and inefficient, but it was also able to draw on a wide variety of resources that were not directly linked to its member states. Many of these bureaucracies had certain procedures and jurisdictions that allowed them a fairly wide range of activities in situations in which they had previously been given authority. This scope and authority allowed them to act more immediately in crises than the formal decision-making body that met only once a year except for extraordinary sessions.

The institutional structure of the OAU was quite simple compared with that of other international organizations. The OAU had few commissions or committees to conduct missions of their own. As noted above, such committees could potentially have a great deal of power to act within their designated jurisdictions without direct orders from the formal decision-making body, and this could remove power from the hands of the Assembly. Such committees in the OAU, however, were usually established only temporarily by the Assembly to perform specific functions such as fact-finding investigations, and were subsequently disbanded. This lack of permanent and semi-autonomous organizational committees made the OAU particularly dependent on its member states not only for decision-making concerning intervention, but also for resource contributions (military, economic and diplomatic).

The weakness of the OAU stemming from its dependence on the member states was further compounded by the internal weaknesses of the member states themselves. When member-states were struggling economically, they had insufficient funds to contribute to the OAU. Furthermore, when member states faced domestic political challenges, they had little time or effort to devote to broader regional issues. The OAU's structural limitations combined with the lack of resources further weakened its ability to act to resolve regional conflicts.

Historical Weaknesses

The argument that any options and actions undertaken by the OAU had to be based on previous experiences, successes, and failures might partly account for the organization's weak leadership in resolving regional conflicts. In the thirty-seven years of its existence, the OAU was more active in intervening in border disputes between member states than in responding to civil wars, but had little success in either type of intervention (Andemichael 1994: 1). The preference for handling border disputes rather than internal conflicts stemmed from the organization's Charter principle of upholding territorial integrity and its respect for member states' sovereignty. The largest intervention action the OAU took with regard to a civil war resulted in complete failure. The 3,265 peacekeeping troops sent into Chad in 1981 did very little to achieve a peaceful solution to the war, making almost no effort to prevent Habre's forces from gaining military victory over those of President Oueddei (Okoth 1983).

Despite the principle of upholding territorial integrity and its commitment to the peaceful resolution of disputes between member states, the OAU was not particularly active or successful in resolving border disputes between Kenya and Somalia in 1977, limiting its action to appealing to the two states to respect the provisions of its Charter concerning territorial integrity. Even when a conflict was directly linked to a liberation struggle, one of the Organization's early priorities, as in the case of Mozambique/ Rhodesia (1975–80), there was not much action taken. The OAU gave limited diplomatic condemnation to Rhodesia and moral support to Mozambique against border incursions by Rhodesian soldiers in pursuit of freedom fighters. One of its few successes occurred in 1978 when a mediation committee was able to successfully propose a peace formula for the border dispute between Ethiopia and the Sudan (Sesay 1982: 11). But success eluded the organization in the 1978/79 Uganda-Tanzania War (Okoth 1987).

This poor record of intervention revealing the OAU's limitations led the organization to be even more cautious when considering intervention in its final years of existence. Such caution was warranted in view of the post-Cold War conditions in Africa. The end of the Cold War removed many of the forces that manipulated nationality tensions to prevent violent conflict, making current conditions much more difficult to handle than previous conflicts. Authoritarian governments were no longer aided by the super-powers in putting down domestic strife in order to maintain stability on the continent. As a result, there were now a growing number of conflicts where there was less international interest in helping to resolve them. Not only was there less international aid available, but the very nature of these conflicts presented problems for the OAU at several levels. Many of these conflicts were increasingly civil wars in which the organization was prohibited by its Charter principles from intervening. Intervention decisions were made even more difficult by the fact that human suffering due to violence was becoming an acceptable justification for international inter-vention, regardless of sovereignty principles. Thus, the OAU faced a contra-diction each time that violence broke out threatening human rights and demanding its attention. The organization was not only confronted with the difficulty of dealing with violence in civil wars, but had also to determine what stand to take concerning the increasing pressures for boundary changes which the OAU could not condone (Okoth 1987). The final factor that made conflict conditions particularly problematic for the OAU was that the conditions leading to many of the disputes stemmed from political and economic demands. This suggests that, if the OAU wanted to achieve long-term peace, it had also to promote economic growth to achieve political stability (Asante 1987: 7). But this would be an immense additional task for the organization to handle.

Some Strengths & Goals of the OAU

Thus far this examination of the OAU has focused on the limitations the organization faced in conflict resolution that stemmed from its Charter principles, organizational structure, and historical experiences. It is clear that the OAU had limited desire, resources and capabilities to resolve conflicts peacefully in Africa. But it was not without some potential. Even when conflicts presented problematic conditions for the OAU, it was able to set goals to address these problems in order to avoid becoming totally irrelevant on the continent. Indeed, it did possess some assets that could be drawn upon in conflict situations. By focusing on these assets one can determine what goals were reasonable and possible for the OAU to pursue.

Despite its unremarkable record of resolving conflicts and the difficult conditions that it faced, the organization did have some strengths that should be taken into account when proposing goals for conflict resolution in the region. One of the strengths that the organization could draw upon more readily than the UN was its familiarity with the circumstances surrounding conflicts and its understanding of the political culture and the motivations of the various faction leaders. This allowed the diplomats to get at the underlying causes of the conflict and conduct more productive negotiations during both the early and late stages of intervention. Without this expertise, diplomats could put negotiations at risk by failing to include key actors (such as the UN's exclusion of many of the clan leaders in its talks in Somalia in 1993) or by proposing unacceptable alternatives to the parties involved. The OAU appeared to have a psychological effect on the combatants that allowed it to be effective in encouraging them to settle their conflict through negotiations (Sesay 1982:11).

Another strength of the OAU was that it was the only pan-African organization that included all the African states. The organization provided a unique forum for its members to voice their concerns, complaints, and disputes. The principle of equality among all members allowed smaller states to have more of a voice than they might otherwise have had on the continent (although some more powerful states still carried more influence than the weaker ones). Not all disputes could be settled in such a forum, but its existence did provide member states with an opportunity to resolve disputes before they became violent (and destabilizing). Furthermore, the fact that the OAU was composed entirely of members that were part of the region meant that the members had a direct interest in any conflict in the region. This gave the OAU more motivation to act than other international organizations which had less at stake. The OAU took the initial steps to resolve regional conflicts, particularly since the UN frequently maintained that it usually could not act in a conflict unless regional options had already been attempted (Andemichael 1994:14).

The fact that the OAU placed a strong emphasis on unity and consensus was also an asset. Consensus, although difficult to achieve and maintain, strengthened the organization, allowing it to command greater international attention and to exercise greater international influence. There were also more resources to draw upon from member states and no contrary forces stemming from members opposed to a particular action. This was especially important for the OAU since it did not have extensive resources and conflict resolution endeavours were frequently resource-intensive.

Based on conflict conditions in Africa and the strengths and weaknesses of the OAU, three limited goals appeared to be reasonable for the OAU to pursue with regard to conflict resolution. Since the organization was not equipped to handle large operations for long periods of time, it was reasonable to assume that the necessity for extensive operations could be reduced if greater priority was given to promoting preventive diplomacy rather than taking a 'hands off' approach to internal struggles in member states. The OAU could actively engage members (and/or factions) in dispute in dialogue to prevent them from resorting to military means to resolve their problems. This did not guarantee the prevention of conflicts, but it was a cost-efficient, timely goal that the OAU was capable of pursuing. The organization also had strong diplomatic resources to draw on to facilitate endeavours that were less costly than military operations.

Since the consequences of regional violence were destabilizing to the member states and a new organizational priority was to protect human rights, a second goal should have been to promote actions that could reduce the destabilizing effects of refugee flows and extensive human suffering due to regional violence. Pursuit of this goal did not need to interfere with the sovereignty of a member state. It could be achieved by focusing on providing humanitarian aid and alleviating immediate suffering. Short-term solutions could include efforts to negotiate a cease-fire to protect civilians, even if further settlements that could be viewed as threats to sovereignty were not attempted at that time.

A third and more difficult goal for the OAU would be to mount some response in a crisis to prevent the eruption of greater violence. Such an option could include military and/or diplomatic intervention to temporarily stop hostilities and seek a negotiated peace, though the extent of the operation might be limited not only by member concerns but also by lack of resources. The consequences, if the OAU chose not to pursue such a goal, could include a great escalation in violence before the international community decided to take action to alleviate the violence. If the OAU chose not to act when regional violence broke out, the situation could become much worse before it was better. If the OAU decided to try to respond to a crisis early, it could prevent more dire outcomes later even if such action was difficult for the organization to take. Such a response would go beyond merely providing relief to civilians who were suffering from the conflict. It would also require reforms within the organization to accomplish this. Necessary changes to the OAU would include a timely response mechanism, a general consensus that there should be a response, and the commitment of member states to contribute the necessary resources. Since the OAU had only limited resources, such a response to a crisis could not involve a long-term operation or mission to achieve a final solution to the conflict. Utilizing response mechanisms such as monitoring, embargoes, and international condemnation of violence could still make an important impact.

Nevertheless, it is clear that the OAU was largely incapable of meeting the challenges facing the continent. This is not surprising. The fundamental weakness of the organization was reflected in its inability effectively to contain, manage or terminate conflicts on the continent, to fashion a workable development paradigm, or to prevail upon member states to meet their financial and other commitments. Nearly four decades after its formation, new issues emerged which challenged the efficacy of the OAU's institutions even further: the forces of globalization, the dominance of neo-liberal doctrines, the phenomenon of rebel movements, national and international terrorism, and the threat of general human insecurity. These were among the numerous issues that could not be effectively addressed by the largely anachronistic institutions of the OAU. Its Cold War institutions were incompatible with post-Cold War realities. It is against this backdrop that the AU was formed in July 2002 – to perform the tasks that the OAU was unable to handle. However, before we assess the performance of the AU let us examine the main features of the constitutive act of the union.

The Main Features of the Constitutive Act of the AU

The Constitutive Act of the AU (Saxena 2004:182), like the OAU Charter, in our view does not contain a blueprint for the formation of a United States of Africa. Article 2 (b) of the Constitutive Act, *inter alia*, provides that the Union shall 'defend the sovereignty, territorial integrity and independence of its member states'. There is no mention of dismantling the territorial boundaries of African states as a preliminary step necessary for the formation of the United States of Africa. Not only that, Articles 4 (a) and (h) also talk of the 'sovereign equality' of member states, and insist on paying respect to the 'borders existing on the achievement of independence', almost as the OAU Charter did in its Article III. There are other provisions in the Constitutive Act, such as 'non-interference by any Member State in the internal affairs of another' (Article 4 [g]) and 'co-existence of Member States' (Article 4 [I]), all of which go to show that the new document also supports the maintenance of the *status quo* in Africa insofar as the question of giving institutional shape to the ideal of African unity is concerned. Of course, this does not mean that future generations cannot amend the agreement and proceed with integration when they feel that the time is right for such a move.

The Constitutive Act of the AU, however, is somewhat more elaborate than the OAU Charter. The former envisages the formation of a larger number of organs or institutions than were provided for in the OAU Charter. Whereas the OAU Charter provided for four 'institutions' (Article VII), the AU allows for the establishment of nine 'organs:' (i) the Assembly of the Union, (ii) the Executive Council, (iii) the Pan-African Parliament, (iv) the Court of Justice, (v) the Commission, (vi) the Permanent Representatives Committee, (vii) the Special Technical Committees, (viii) the Economic, Social and Cultural Council, and (ix) the financial institutions (see Article 5 of the Constitutive Act).

In the AU the OAU Assembly of Heads of State and Government has been replaced by an 'Assembly of the Union' and vested with some enlarged functions. The Council of Ministers of the OAU has been replaced by an 'Executive Council', with significant additions to its functions. The Executive Council under the AU shall coordinate and take decisions on policies in areas of common interest to member states, such as (i) foreign trade; (ii) energy, industry, and mineral resources; (iii) food, agricultural, and animal resources, livestock production, and forestry; (iv) water resources and irrigation; (v) environmental protection, humanitarian action, and disaster response and relief; (vi) transport and communications; and (vii) insurance (see Article 13 of the Constitutive Act). The OAU Council of Ministers was not vested with these functions; its only job was to implement the decisions of the Assembly and coordinate inter-African cooperation in accordance with the instructions of the Assembly of Heads of State and Government. Therefore, from the nature of its vast array of functions, it appears that the Executive Council, under the Constitutive Act, may turn out in the end to be the forerunner of the cabinet of the United States of Africa if and when it is established in the future. The Constitutive Act envisages seven technical committees, each in charge of a special technical function. They take the place of five Special Commissions in the defunct OAU.

The major innovation that the Constitutive Act of the AU can be credited with is the creation of a Pan-African Parliament. No similar organization or institution was provided for under the OAU Charter. The Constitutive Act stipulates that such a parliament will ensure full participation of African peoples in the development and economic integration of the continent (see Article 17 of the Constitutive Act). The Constitutive Act also provides for the establishment of a Court of Justice, in place of the Commission of Mediation, Conciliation, and Arbitration as provided for under the OAU Charter, which, as we know, was a non-starter. Another innovation in the Constitutive Act is the creation of a Permanent Representatives Committee, whose task is to help the Executive Council in the discharge of its functions. Such a Committee did not exist under the OAU. An Economic, Social, and Cultural Council has also been created. The AU has three financial institutions, namely, the African Central Bank, the African Monetary Fund, and the African Investment Bank (see Article 19 of the Constitutive Act). There was no such provision in the OAU Charter, although the Abuja Treaty, which stressed regional integration, did envisage the creation of such institutions.

It is hoped that these organs – the Pan-African Parliament, the Court of Justice, the African Central Bank, the African Monetary Fund, and the African Investment Bank – will help to achieve greater unity between African countries. As the AU makes progress, a common currency will be introduced for the continent and a common defence force will also be eventually established. The important thing is that the regional and subregional economic organizations that are functioning at present on the continent continue to function in their respective spheres, but the duty of the AU is to coordinate and harmonize their policies for the gradual attainment of continental unity.

An important feature of the Constitutive Act of the AU is that it vests the Assembly with power to impose sanctions on any member state that defaults in the payment of its contribution to the budget of the AU. The sanctions can be in the form of denial of the right to speak at meetings, to vote, to present candidates for any position or post within the union, or to benefit from any activity or commitments therefrom (see Article 23 of the Constitutive Act). It is also provided (in Article 23) that 'any member state that fails to comply with the decisions and policies of the union may be subjected to other sanctions, such as the denial of transport and communications links with other Member States, and other measures of a political and economic nature to be determined by the Assembly'. These provisions are expected to deter the member states from refusing to honor their financial obligations to the AU as well as to make certain that they refrain from acting contrary to the policies and decisions of the Union. This may be regarded as a major improvement over the provisions of the now defunct OAU, which was unable to punish recalcitrant members.

On the whole, the establishment of the African Union is a 'giant' step that may lead to greater unity among African states. It is certainly a bold initiative, full of promise, taken by African governments. It is a good sign that African leaders have begun to realize that the survival of their continent lies in increased levels of political and economic integration. It will be easier for them to meet these challenges if they act collectively rather than individually. Today, a growing number of Africans are recognizing that individual African countries cannot stand alone against the power of the transnational corporations that have exploited them and their resources since the colonial period for the benefit of the metropolitan economies. They need to come together in order to successfully defend their interests. An African trading bloc should significantly improve the ability of Africans to benefit from the new globalization. Politically, integration should enhance Africa's ability to participate in global affairs. This optimistic view, however, is only hypothetical. The reality on the ground so far indicates the opposite.

The AU: Challenges to its Objectives

Modeled on the European Union (EU), the AU seeks, among other things, to promote unity on the continent, to create a larger African market to make the continent more competitive in the international economy, and to find innovative ways of addressing the continent's galaxy of problems, including the crisis of governance, debt, corruption and HIV/AIDs (Salim 2001: 10–14). The achievement of these noble objectives requires the strengthening of intra-African ties and, in a sense, increasing the self-sufficiency of the continent.

However, analysts are already beginning to identify fundamental flaws in the AU agenda, which may render the union less effective in altering the current nature of Africa's international relations. Some observers argue that the AU is too ambitious a project to achieve real continental unity within a short space of time. The EU on which it is modeled took over three decades to materialize; attempting to achieve economic and political unity in years in a continent characterized by conflicts and mutual suspicion may therefore be too idealistic (Makgotho 2002: 1). Even admitting the rhetorical commitments by member states to unite, there still remain critical issues to be addressed. There are, for instance, the vast disparities in economic performance and income levels among African states, which continue to be sources of conflict. Such differences are certain to trigger other auxiliary and indeed undesirable developments, including migration from weaker economies to the more affluent countries. Moreover, in the midst of troubling economies marked by escalating external debts, it is unclear how member states will meet their financial obligations to the union. Similar questions also include the extent to which the AU can prevent conflicts and promote good governance on the continent. These are compelling questions that may be sources of pessimism about the ability of the AU to chart a completely new direction as far as the international relations of the African states are concerned (Akokpari 2002: 13). In terms of conflict resolution (which is the thrust of this chapter), how should the AU proceed?

AU Attempts at Conflict Resolution

An important organ responsible for conflict resolution is the Peace and Security Council (PSC), which was launched by the AU in May 2004 (Saxena 2004:184). This is necessary, given that Africa is beset by conflicts, political turbulence, and humanitarian disasters. The PSC has fifty elected members and its mandate includes recommending the deployment of AU peacekeeping missions to conflict areas where cease-fire deals have been signed. It is also charged with urging the AU to intervene militarily where cases of genocide or crimes against humanity have been reported. The council is supposed to be funded by contributions from the AU's fifty-three members and donors. This is critical, because, when an AU force was sent in 2003 to help implement cease-fire agreements aimed at ending the eleven-year civil war in Burundi, the force commanders and AU officials complained about the lack of resources to back the mission (Saxena 2004: 185).

The launching of the Peace and Security Council followed on the heels of the Pan-African Parliament, which was itself launched in March 2004 (*Daily Nation* 2004: 19). In a continent scarred by conflict and military activity in Burundi, Côte d'Ivoire, Democratic Republic of Congo, Liberia, Somalia, Sudan, and Uganda, among others, the Pan-African Parliament recognizes that, without peace, its plans are bound to be nothing but utopian. For years, Africans had been waiting for the West to solve their conflicts. However, with the establishment of the Pan-African Parliament and the Peace and Security Council, the AU seems to be on the way to reversing the trend. With the then AU Commission chairman, Alpha Konare, joining other world mediators in July 2004, in negotiations with parties involved in Western Sudan's Dar Fur crisis, the AU began to show that it was trying to solve its own problems (*Kenya Times* 2004: 9). This is notwithstanding the probability that the move was also intended to boost investors' confidence in the continent. The AU, trying to win increased Western investment in return for ending wars and despotism and curbing corruption, sent a few hundred soldiers to Dar Fur to protect 60 unarmed AU monitors and civilians. However, the protection of civilians, the Sudanese Foreign Minister Mustafa Osman Ismail contended, was the responsibility of the Sudanese government (*Saturday Nation* 2004:12).

After years of tension between nomadic Arab ethnic groups and African farmers, two groups rebelled in 2003, accusing Khartoum of arming the Arab militia known as the Janjaweed. Sudan's Islamist government denies the charge. Nevertheless, more than a million people have fled the fighting, thereby raising the concern of the AU, the United Nations, and the US State Department – all interested in trying to resolve the crisis. Both US Secretary of State Colin Powell and UN Secretary General Kofi Annan visited Khartoum in July 2004 with a view to finding a solution to the crisis. But Konare's presence in the Chadian capital, Ndjamena, where he met the Sudanese parties participating in the negotiations demonstrated that African leaders were playing an important role in pulling together the meeting, and that the resolution of the Dar Fur crisis was no longer a duet sung by the US and the UN.

Years of war and conflict in Africa have given the continent a sad stereo-type as a land riddled with the influx of refugees and insecurity. Coupled with the current instability in several African countries, all this acts as a drag on foreign investment in the continent. Perhaps not surprisingly, Africans who account for nearly 13 per cent of the world's population attract about 1 per cent of foreign direct investment, 1 per cent of world gross domestic investment and about 2 per cent of world trade (*Kenya Times* 2004: 9).

The AU, apparently aware of what its priority is, and probably disappointed with the inaction of the West during the 1994 genocide in Rwanda, has started to 'mind its own business'. Its moves include the establishment of the aforementioned Peace and Security Council and a proposed standby force. Although the latter exists only in official documents for the time being, the Peace and Security Council has already done concrete work, especially in resolving the Congolese-Rwanda row that arose from the Democratic Republic of the Congo's (DRC) deployment of troops on its eastern border areas with Rwanda in early 2004, as fears mounted internationally about the collapse of the DRC's fragile peace process. The AU did not wait for foreigners and played a major role in resolving the conflict with Presidents Joseph Kabila of the DRC and Paul Kagame of Rwanda meeting in the Nigerian capital of Abuja in late June 2004 under the auspices of the PSC chief, Nigerian President Olusegun Obasanjo, who was then chairman of the AU. According to AU spokesman Desmond Orjiako, 'After what happened in Rwanda, Liberia and Sierra Leone.... We do not want to sit and wait until the UN deploys its peace-keeping forces before we could do something', referring to the recent and not-so-recent conflicts in Africa (*Kenya Times* 2004:9).

The AU, therefore, seems determined to consolidate what it has already achieved. With the positive signs identified, Africans may one day really manage to contain conflicts in their own land. It is in this regard that foreign intervention in Sudan's Dar Fur region (and other 'trouble' spots in the continent) must be rejected. The AU itself should sort out such problems. This was the position taken by the leaders of Libya, Sudan, Egypt, Nigeria and Chad at their meeting in 2004 to discuss the Dar Fur crisis (*New Vision* 2004:10).

It is gratifying to see African governments standing up for themselves and taking ownership of the problems afflicting the continent. It is a welcome change in attitude that should eliminate what had become frequent unilateral foreign interventions in crises in postcolonial Africa. However, for this new determination to take root, real action must be seen on the ground. The reality now is that the humanitarian crisis in Dar Fur and Acholiland (in northern Uganda) is worsening. In the two cases, over 2 million people are in need of food, shelter, and medicines. Scores more are dying from either disease or even violence visited upon them by rampaging Janjaweed militiamen in Dar Fur and the Lord's Resistance Army (LRA) and the Uganda People's Defence Forces (UPDF) in northern Uganda.

The AU did take it upon itself to raise a force to help pacify Dar Fur; a great gesture in itself, but, then again, it has provided only 300 soldiers out of the desired four battalions. Moreover, the 300 soldiers took two months to assemble. Rapid deployment of AU forces (in their thousands) is, therefore, required in Dar Fur, northern Uganda, and now Somalia which has at last got a government. Somalia needs AU assistance to bring about and maintain peace following the collapse of the state in 1990 with the overthrow of Siad Barre (Saxena 2004:186).

Given the chronic shortage of funds of many governments, and even the AU itself, the better approach should be to seek logistical support from elsewhere while keeping the monitoring forces purely African. That would be a better arrangement for the many world powers and organizations that are weary of contributing peacekeeping troops. They could, instead, be asked to supply support such as transport, construction of airstrips, medicines, finance, food, and communications equipment. Africa's new-found resolve is welcome. However, it should be used pragmatically as the AU takes care not to dither while Dar Fur, northern Uganda, and other conflict areas burn.

Conclusion

Despite its large membership and influence on the African continent, the OAU played a surprisingly minor role in resolving conflict in Africa during the thirty-seven years of its existence. An explanation for this poor performance is evident in the examination of the limitations that its Charter and structure, and the few unsuccessful historical cases of intervention, placed on the organization. With the global changes stemming from the end of the Cold War, the OAU could not cope with the new threats, and so it was wound down. From its ashes emerged the AU.

Unlike its predecessor, the AU is a more professional, and a less toothless, outfit, attributes that place it in good stead to fulfill its objectives. If the AU is able to receive full cooperation from its member states, it should be able to play a significant role in resolving conflicts and other problems that have bedeviled the continent. We have noted that so far it has performed fairly well in that direction. For the greater success of the AU, two things are required from the member states. First, that they regularly pay their annual dues to the Union. As pointed out in this chapter, one of the most important impediments to the proper functioning of the OAU was the fact that the member states defaulted on the payment of their annual dues. Paucity of funds left the OAU unable to carry out its functions and hampered many of its activities, including those relating to peacekeeping. In addition, member states often acted in open defiance of the policies and decisions of the OAU, which had no power to take any action against such erring states. Second, member states need to comply with the policies and decisions of the Union. Of course, the AU must function democratically, providing all the relevant stakeholder groups with the facilities to participate fully in policy design so that the policies adopted reflect the interests and concerns of the member states. Such an approach to policy design can encourage compliance and minimize the chance that member states will adopt positions contrary to that of the union.

What is the guarantee that the AU will not be as cash-starved an organization as the OAU? After all, the economic conditions of African states have not improved significantly over the years. In fact, they have worsened in recent years. Unless economic conditions change dramatically for the better, the AU is likely to face the same financial problems that plagued the OAU. Since the AU is a continental organization, its costs would have to be borne by the African countries. The AU is expected to help Africans and African countries assert their independence, especially from the industrial countries of the West. It would be ironic if the same West that these countries are trying to get away from is asked to assume the costs of maintaining the AU and its activities. If African countries are serious about asserting their independence and taking their place in the global community and having other members treat them with respect, they must come up with the funds to finance the AU. For one thing, if they rely on external actors to finance the organization, these groups will invariably dictate policy to the union and, as a consequence, the programmes promoted by the AU are unlikely to be those that serve African interests.

References

Akokpari, J.K. 2002. 'Post-Cold War International Relations and Foreign Policies in Africa: New Issues, New Directions and New Challenges'. Paper presented at the Tenth General Assembly of CODESRIA on the theme: Africa in the New Millennium. Nile International Conference Centre, Kampala, 8–12 December: 1–25.

Andemichael, B. 1994. 'OAU-UN Relations in a Changing World', in El-Ayouty, ed., *The Organization of African Unity After Thirty Years*, Westview, CT: Praeger, 30–50.

Asante, S.K.B. 1987. 'The role of the Organization of African Unity in promoting peace, development and regional security in Africa', in E Hansen, ed., *Africa: Perspectives on Peace and Development*, London: United Nations University, 120–34.

Da Costa, P. 1995. 'Keeping the Peace.' *Africa Report*, May-June:5–11.

Daily Nation, 2004. 19 March. Nairobi. 'PanAfrican Parliament Launched', P. Oluoch:19.

El-Ayouty, Y. 1994. 'An OAU for the future: An assessment', in Y. El-Ayouty, ed., *The Organization of African Unity After Thirty Years*, Westport, CT: Praeger. 1–24.

Foltz, W. 1991. 'The Organization of African Unity and the resolution of Africa's conflicts', in F.M. Dengand and I.W. Zartman, eds, *Conflict Resolution in Africa*, Washington, DC: The Brookings Institution, 80–96.

Jonah, J.O.C. 1994. 'The OAU: Peace-keeping and Conflict resolution', inY. El-Ayouty, ed., *The Organization of African Unity After Thirty Years*, Westport, CT: Praeger, 1-30.

Kenya Times. 2004: 3 July, Nairobi. 'AU Transcends OAU in Conflict Resolution'. F. Macharia: 9–10.

Layachi, A. 1994. 'The OAU and Western Sahara: A case study' in Y. El-Ayouty, ed., *The Organization of African Unity After Thirty Years*, Westport, CT: Praeger, 1–17.

Makgotho, S. 2002. 'Beyond the African Union', in*side AISA* 14 (August): 1–13.

New Vision. 2004. 20 October. Kampala. 'Darfur Quagmire'. G. Opolot: 9–10.

Okoth, P.G. 1983. 'OAU: Forces of Destabilization.' *Ufahamu* XIII (1): 148–64.

Okoth, P.G. 1987. 'The OAU and the Uganda-Tanzania War, 1978–89.' *Journal of African Studies* (Special Issue on Tanzania) 14 (3): 151–62.

Salim, A.S. 2001. 'Towards the African Union.' *DPMN Bulletin* VIII (2): 10–14.

Saturday Nation. 2004. 10 July. Nairobi. 'Sudan in the New Era', Ahmed Babu: 1, 2.

Saxena, S.C. 1993. *Politics in Africa*. Delhi: Kalinga Publishers.

Saxena, S. C. 2004, 'The African Union: African Giant Step toward Continental Unity', in J. M. Mbaku. ed., *Africa at the Crossroads: Between Regionalism and Globalization*, ed. Wesport, CT: Praeger, 163–90.

Sesay, A. 1982. 'The OAU and Continental Order', in T. Shaw and S. Ojo, eds, *Africa and the International Political System*, Washington, DC: University Press of America, 15–32.

Weekly Review. 1998. 4 September. Nairobi. 'OAU and Conflict Resolution', R. Odek: 6–7.

3

The Continental Early Warning System of the African Union
What Role for Civil Society?

JAKKIE CILLIERS

Through its Constitutive Act and the Protocol on the Peace and Security Council (PSC), member states have mandated the African Union (AU) and its PSC with a substantially enlarged and much more robust role in the prevention, management and resolution of African conflicts than was the case with the Organization of African Unity (OAU). One of the instruments through which the Commission is to operationalize this mandate is with the establishment of a Continental Early Warning System (CEWS).

This chapter argues for a shared commitment to democracy, human rights and development between African leaders and African civil society organizations, and research institutes engaged in peace and security issues in particular. This would motivate a joint willingness to hold one another to the actual standards reflected in AU decisions and declarations as well as in legal documents such as the African Charter on Human and Peoples' Rights, on the basis that the nature of African governance is a key determinant of (in)security and (in)stability.

The chapter is divided into three sections. The first reviews the history of the OAU in early warning and conflict prevention. The second looks at the provisions on early warning as contained in the Protocol establishing the PSC and proposes a basic structure and costing. The chapter concludes by proposing key considerations for an operational early warning system, also commenting on the potential role of African research institutes in complementing the work of the CEWS.

A central theme running through the chapter is the close relationship between conflict prevention, democracy and good governance and an analysis that points to the fact that the OAU was restricted to conflict management and resolution – usually at the invitation of an affected government – rather than directed towards conflict prevention. As an organization built on consensus and the sanctity of the principle of non-interference in the internal affairs of member states, the OAU found it difficult to respond to emerging crises until such time as the clear warning signals became lost amidst armed conflict, widespread human suffering, and open hostilities. The AU has the potential to change this, although many of the expectations regarding the ability of the organization to undertake substantive conflict management and intervention activities, beyond basic and limited chapter VI observation missions, are probably exaggerated, except when undertaken by a lead nation such as Nigeria or, more recently, South Africa.

The OAU & Early Warning

The establishment of a unit for conflict early warning at continental level was formally initiated in June 1992 when, at its 28th meeting in Dakar, Senegal, the Assembly of the OAU decided to establish the Mechanism for Conflict Prevention, Management and Resolution. This decision was put into effect in June 1993 with the adoption of the 'Cairo Declaration' which established the Central Mechanism for Conflict Prevention, Management and Resolution (Organization of African Unity 1993). The Mechanism was charged with the anticipation and prevention of situations of armed conflict as well as with undertaking peacemaking and peace-building efforts during conflicts and in post-conflict situations. The Mechanism's operational arm, the Central Organ, was composed of 9 and later 14 member states that annually formed the Bureau of the Assembly,[1] plus the country chairing the OAU. As would later be the case with its successor structure, the Peace and Security Council, the Organ operated at summit, ministerial, and ambassadorial levels.[2]

The following year, in 1994, the Mechanism created a Division for Conflict Management and formalized an associated financial facility, the Peace Fund.[3] The Conflict Management Division was originally tasked with the development of policy options and the coordination of activities in support of the Mechanism's mission as described above. To this end, the Division was expected to: (a) collect, collate and disseminate information relating to current and potential conflicts; (b) prepare and present policy options to the Secretary-General of the OAU; (c) undertake or commission analysis and long-term research; and (d) support and manage political, civilian and military observer missions, and coordinate regional training policies to support peacekeeping operations.

The establishment of the OAU's Central Organ and its Conflict Management Division reflected the desire of the organization to focus on conflict prevention (those activities undertaken primarily to reduce the risk of the eruption of violent conflict), leaving the more expensive and complex task of conflict management, peacekeeping and post-conflict reconstruction to the United Nations.

Imbued by the independence struggle and free from the formal shackles of colonialism, Africa's post-independence leaders guarded their independence jealously. Hence the emphasis in the 1993 Cairo Declaration that: 'The Mechanism [on Conflict Prevention, Management and Resolution] will be guided by the objectives and principles of the OAU Charter; in particular, the sovereign equality of Member States, non-interference in the internal affairs of States, the respect of the sovereignty and territorial integrity of Member States, their inalienable right to independent existence, the peaceful settlement of disputes as well as the inviolability of borders inherited from colonialism. It will also function on the basis of the consent and the cooperation of the parties to a conflict.'[4] In effect, this constraint made it impossible for the OAU to meet the primary objective of the Mechanism outlined in the very next paragraph of the Cairo Declaration, namely, that the 'Mechanism will have as a primary objective, the anticipation and prevention of conflicts'. Bound by the principles and objectives of the OAU Charter, its focus on national sovereignty and the practice of solidarity politics, coupled with a critical lack of resources, the Organization could not give effect to its intentions.

In the aftermath of the US peacekeeping debacle in Somalia, the 1994 genocide in Rwanda and subsequent Western disengagement from peacekeeping on the African continent, the OAU expanded its proposed role from conflict prevention to include peacekeeping responsibilities – even if commensurate capabilities and actual contributions by the organization's member states did not keep pace.

Whilst the Cairo Declaration created most of the institutions (such as the Peace Fund) and practices (such as the use of eminent persons) that were subsequently included in the PSC, it did not explicitly provide for the establishment of a unit for early warning. This despite a vague and general authorization to the Council of Ministers, in consultation with the Secretary General (of the OAU), to 'examine ways and means in which the capacity within the General Secretariat can be built and brought to a level commensurate with the magnitude of the tasks at hand and the responsibilities expected of the organization'.[5]

It is unclear exactly how the General Secretariat came to agree on the need to formally establish an early warning unit but, in order to strengthen the OAU's capacity for conflict prevention and early warning, the Secretariat organized three consultations, in 1994, 1996, and 1998. The 1998 meeting proposed a rudimentary early warning system consisting of an Internet-linked situation room based in Addis Ababa and the development of a system of early warning focal points around the continent. The system that was discussed at that meeting included the use of non-governmental organizations, universities, journalists and others appointed by the OAU to act as providers of information. In addition, two sets of indicators were discussed, the first for the 'prediction' of impending conflict and the second to indicate ongoing conflict.

With the assistance of key donors, the capacity of the Conflict Management Division steadily expanded to eventually include a situation room, a small library and a documentation centre, regional desk officers and a 'Field Operations Unit' tasked with the organization of the deployment of military observer missions.[6] The situation room has not changed much in subsequent years and consists of a single large office with several work stations for interns, maps against the walls and a number of televisions to monitor CNN, BBC, and SABC Africa.

Although the Central Mechanism theoretically provided for a more systematic and institutional approach to conflict management, the Organization's performance remained, at best, uneven.[7] In fact, a 1999 OAU internal report entitled 'A Comprehensive Framework for Strengthening the Mechanism' summarized progress as follows: 'More than five years after the adoption of the Declaration establishing the Mechanism, the Central Organ still lacks adequate information to effectively predict, plan for, prevent and manage the complex and numerous conflicts that have plagued the region. It also lacks the capacity for in-depth analysis of strategic options on which to base its decisions.'

Despite these shortcomings the Conflict Management Division had, by 2000, become the most important arm of the OAU (Engberg 2002: 5), if inordinately dependent upon funding by non-African donors (with roughly 70 per cent of contributions).[8] By mid-2002, just before the transition process brought about by the Constitutive Act of the African Union, the Division had 41 staff positions (of which 15 were clerical and the rest professional). Of these, 13 were financed by the OAU, 11 by the UNDP and 16 directly by donors (Engberg 2002: 39).

At the July 2003 Summit of the African Union in Maputo, Heads of State approved a new staffing structure for the AU Commission in line with the changed mandate of the organization approved by the adoption of the Constitutive Act. The structure of the Commission now provided for ten Commissioners – the Chairperson, Deputy Chairperson and eight Commissioners including one for Peace and Security (Ambassador Saïd Djinnit) and for Political Affairs (Ms Julia Dolly Joiner).

The overall objective of the Department for Peace and Security is the maintenance of peace, security and stability through the coordination and promotion of African and other initiatives on conflict prevention, management and resolution within the context of the UN. Once fully established, the Department will have a staff complement of 53, including the Peace and Security Council secretariat and the PSO division. However, this number excludes the various Special Envoys, Special Representatives, AU Field Missions and other initiatives (such as the 32-person office for the AU mission in Dar Fur) that the Department will technically support (Cilliers 2002: 6).

Included in the staff complement of the Peace and Security Department are 3 professional staff,[9] a secretary and six interns (total of 10 staff) for the situation room. The interns provide an electronic clipping service and serve to staff the situation room after hours.

Early Warning & the PSC Protocol

The promotion of peace, security and stability on the African continent is a core objective of the African Union – detailed in Article 3 (f) of its Constitutive Act. Although the principle of non-interference remains a stated principle of the organization,[10] the AU now has the right to 'intervene in a Member State pursuant to a decision of the Assembly in respect of grave circumstances, namely war crimes, genocide and crimes against humanity', as well as in instances of 'threats to legitimate order' – a subsequent amendment to the Protocol.[11]

Having approved staff for the situation room, the Maputo Summit mandated the Commission of the AU to take the necessary steps for the establishment of the Continental Early Warning System (CEWS) as reflected in the Protocol on the Peace and Security Council, in anticipation of its

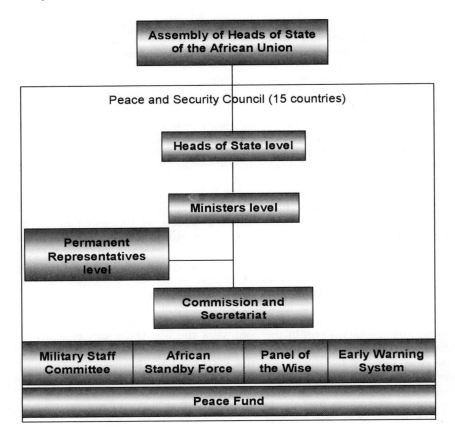

Figure 3.1 Broad structure of the AU and its Peace and Security Council

entry into force later that year. To this end, the Commission organized yet another expert workshop in Addis Ababa in October 2003 to 'brainstorm on the practical modalities and steps, drawing lessons from existing regional and international experiences on the establishment and functioning of an early warning system' (African Union. 2003). Despite coming up with a number of pertinent recommendations, the workshop, like the preceding ones in 1994, 1996 and 1998, found no practical implementation, and early warning at the AU remains limited to the small staff in the situation room.

In order to strengthen the AU's capacity in respect of the prevention, management and resolution of conflicts, the Constitutive Act provided for the establishment of a Peace and Security Council (PSC). Opened for signature during July 2002, the Protocol establishing the PSC entered into force during December 2003 when 27 of the 53 AU member states had deposited their instruments of ratification. The 15-member PSC was inaugurated on 25 May 2004 in Addis Ababa. Gabon, Ethiopia, Algeria, South

Africa and Nigeria are members of the Council for three years, while Cameroon, Congo, Kenya, the Sudan, Libya, Lesotho, Mozambique, Ghana, Senegal and Togo all serve for a term of 2 years.

The Protocol stipulates that the Commissioner in charge of Peace and Security will be responsible for the affairs of the PSC and that the Commission shall assist and provide support to the PSC with human and material resources. Furthermore, a Peace and Security Council Secretariat 'shall be established within the Directorate dealing with conflict prevention, management and resolution'.[12]

Article 2 (1) of the PSC Protocol defines its nature as '...a standing decision-making organ for the prevention, management and resolution of conflicts. The PSC shall be a collective security and early-warning arrangement to facilitate timely and efficient response to conflict and crisis situations in Africa.' Article 2 (2) thus provides that '... the Peace and Security Council shall be supported by the Commission, a Panel of the Wise, a Continental Early Warning System, an African Standby Force and a Special Fund.'

Article 12 (1) of the Protocol stipulates that a 'Continental Early Warning System to be known as the Early Warning System shall be established'[13] as 'one of the five pillars of the PSC'. The CEWS is tasked with providing the Chairperson of the Commission with information in a timely manner so that he/she can advise the Council on 'potential conflicts and threats to peace and security' and 'recommend best courses of action'.[14] '[T]he Chairperson of the Commission shall also use this information for the execution of the responsibilities and functions entrusted to him/her under the present Protocol.'[15] The PSC has a number of formal and informal systems and structures through which to effect preventive action including the Panel of the Wise and the Chairperson of the Commission, 'particularly in the area of conflict prevention.'[16]

Towards an Operational Continental Early Warning System

For the African Union early warning needs to consist of more than just the timely provision and sharing of relevant information. Effective early warning involves the collection and analysis of data in a uniform and systematized way and according to a commonly shared methodology within the CEWS. It requires the formulation and communication of analysis and policy options to relevant end-users (the Commission, relevant policy organs of the AU and the PSC) – information towards action. In this sense, the aim of early warning is to strengthen the capacity of the Commission and the Peace and Security Council to identify critical developments in a timely manner, so that coherent response strategies can be formulated to either prevent violent conflict or limit its destructive effects.

Currently the AU does not have a credible system that can perform early warning and, as argued below, the political obstacles to give effect to this requirement are significant.

The current practice within the AU is to combine the work of desk officers on specific areas/countries and the provision of information/analysis. In other words, early warning and conflict prevention/management are done by the same staff, thereby confusing analysis with action. Although there should be constant interaction between information collation/analysis/ interpretation and preventive action, there should be a clear separation between the two if the AU wishes to avoid being trapped in its own group think. Organizationally the CEWS should be a separate unit within the Commission, tasked with understanding, interpreting and providing analysis and policy options. Members of the CEWS should not be engaged in executing AU policy, although advice on policy options is an integral task of early warning. The primary resource for the provision of policy analysis within the CEWS is inevitably a team of highly qualified and competent analysts, each an expert in his/her field and dedicated to monitoring a specific geographical region and/or thematic area.

The current consultations that are occurring to amend the approved structure of the Commission and to bring it in line with the new vision and mission of the African Union do not appear to provide for the creation of an early warning system beyond the continuation of the current situation room. Yet early warning towards conflict prevention is a now a 'principle' of the Peace and Security Council ('...early responses to contain crisis situations so as to prevent them from developing into full-blown crises.'[17]) and the PSC is explicitly required to perform functions regarding '[e]arly warning and preventive diplomacy'.[18]

The Protocol further stipulates that the CEWS shall consist of 'an observation and monitoring centre, to be known as the "Situation Room", located at the Conflict Management Directorate of the Union, and responsible for data collection and analysis'.[19] As regards methodology, the Protocol determines that the collection and analysis of data must be based on the development by the Early Warning System of 'an early warning module based on clearly defined and accepted political, economic, social, military and humanitarian indicators'.[20]

The design of the CEWS that is reflected in the Protocol reflects the realities of a global village and is primarily designed to operate as an open system. Hence the CEWS is specifically mandated to collaborate with the United Nations, its agencies, other relevant international organizations, research centres, academic institutions, and NGOs,[21] Such collaboration is meant to 'facilitate the effective functioning of the Early Warning System.'[22]

Although the Protocol requires that meetings of the PSC are to be closed,[23] the PSC may decide to hold open meetings during which 'civil society organizations involved and/or interested in a conflict or a situation under consideration by the Peace and Security Council may be invited to participate, without the right to vote, in the discussion relating to that conflict or situation'.[24] The PSC may also hold informal 'consultations' with civil society organizations 'as may be needed for the discharge of its responsibilities'.[25]

Regional organizations such as the Economic Community of West African States (ECOWAS) and the Southern African Development Community (SADC) are considered an integral part of the overall security architecture of the Union, and the PSC is mandated to harmonize, coordinate and work closely with the conflict prevention and management mechanisms established at these levels.[26] Thus the situation room in Addis Ababa is to be linked to regions and the Protocol on the PSC creates the following obligations in this regard:

a) 'Observation and monitoring units of the Regional Mechanisms are to be linked directly through appropriate means of communications to the Situation Room, which shall collect and process data at their level and transmit the same to the Situation Room.'[27]

b) 'The Peace and Security Council shall, in consultation with Regional Mechanisms, promote initiatives aimed at anticipating and preventing conflicts and, in circumstances where conflicts have occurred, peace-making and peace-building functions.'[28]

c) 'The Chairperson of the Commission shall take the necessary measures, where appropriate, to ensure the full involvement of Regional Mechanisms in the establishment and effective functioning of the Early Warning System and the African Standby Force.'[29]

Whereas the OAU had sometimes been distracted by proposals for real time, three dimensional data display as an ostensible key requirement for effective early warning, the PSC Protocol is explicit in that the CEWS is to utilize an 'indicators module'.

Many commercial proposals have been made to the OAU and the AU over the years towards the use of cutting edge technology as a variety of consultants, often acting through NGOs, have sought to convince the OAU to go down a particularly commercial route. Common sense prevailed and the OAU resisted approaches that would have been patently inappropriate for an organization that only recently achieved a moderate level of external e-mail connectivity.

Gadgets and gimmicks aside, the political intent with such a module is clear. The use of some type of automated electronic process (as opposed to an approach based on human deductive reasoning) would provide a degree of objective automaticity to the work of early warning. Having decided on particular indicators of emerging conflict, an indicators module would, in theory, trigger some type of red light report and compel the provision of an alert to the Commission and possibly even the PSC. In this manner the inherent suspicion of the political manipulation of data as part of early warning could be averted and the staff of the CEWS will be provided with some level of 'technical protection'.[30]

Visualize, for example, the reaction should the CEWS 'warn' the PSC that it needed to consider preventive action on the basis that the 2005 general elections in Zimbabwe could trigger substantial internal violence. ZANU(PF) will inevitably react strongly to such a recommendation, rally its friends and allies, question the methodology and assumptions upon which the analysis is based and place substantial pressure on the Commission and its staff to desist from political meddling. And Zimbabwe does not even serve on the PSC at the moment. What would happen if the CEWS warns that violence in the Niger Delta region and amongst communities in the northern states threaten to push Nigeria over the brink into civil war? The reaction within the Commission and from President Obasanjo would hardly be a welcoming one. All of this merely makes the point, indicators module or not,

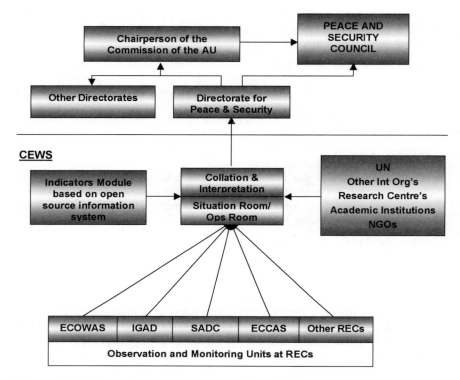

Figure 3.2 Schematic representation of the CEWS

that the CEWS would have to be politically astute and that all analysis would be informed by political judgement.[31]

Practically the AU could adopt any one of a number of off-the-shelf existing 'indicators modules' for violent conflict, and there is little objective reason to invest in the development of a complex new/tailor-made system. There is no absence of information on African governance and conflicts, and practical experience would indicate that the CEWS could avoid the establishment of more than a rudimentary database of its own. At best, the AU may need to subscribe to one or two selected existing databases and news services and outsource its current news clipping service.

In today's interconnected and globalized world there is very little that cannot be obtained through open sources – provided the researcher knows where to obtain his/her information, understands his/her area of analysis, has the opportunity to undertake field research and engages in the public discourse on issues under consideration. The biggest danger for any analysis unit is being locked into a particular system of information feed. The CEWS unit should therefore obtain its information from a variety of sources, and be able to test its analysis with others both governmental and otherwise. This study does not, therefore, take the view that the CEWS should be a closed, government-to-government system, dependent at the continental level on information provided only by member states. Obviously specific outputs of the CEWS for the Commission may be restricted in circulation even within the Commission.

The structure of the CEWS implied in the PSC Protocol is presented graphically in Figure 3.2 above. Although early warning touches upon many aspects of the work of the eight divisions within the Commission of the African Union,[32] prevention and response touches the Directorates dealing with Peace/Security and Politics most directly, reporting through the former. Figure 3.2 also makes a distinction between the situation room and the process of collation and interpretation. The latter should be undertaken by analysts and occurs through processes of desk research, fieldwork, networking, discussion and debate, facilitated by the necessary electronic systems.[33] For its part, the situation room is merely a common gathering place for discussions, meetings and briefings, complete with up-to-date maps and other graphical displays of information and could double as the operations room of the AU after hours.[34]

Conclusion

During the October 2003 workshop on the establishment of the CEWS, the then Director of Peace and Security at the African Union, Ambassador Sam Ibok, presented some of the difficulties encountered over the preceding years. These included: a) 'the barrier of national sovereignty, which often hampered efforts to collect reliable data and information, as well as timely intervention; b) the issue of data ownership, which often created problems on the flexibility of the use and dissemination of data collected; c) the issue of defining early warning modules and their ownership by the OAU; d) lack of adequate technological infrastructure; e) limited financial and human resources; f) lack of political will on the part of Member States.'[35]

That African leaders have a renewed determination to engage in conflict management is demonstrated by the robust engagement of the AU in the crisis in Dar Fur in Western Sudan and the unprecedented censure that has been applied to the Sudanese leadership in public and in private. Dar Fur reflects the nightmare of genocide – a repetition if not in scale, then in purpose – of events in Rwanda in 1994. The problem is that the AU sought to play a leading role in Dar Fur only at a time when the crisis had escalated beyond the means or the ability of the continental organization to effectively impact upon it (since the ASF does not practically exist), despite several months of intense media focus and reportage.

The obvious point is that the African Union should be in the business of preventing Dar Fur and crises such as that developing in Zimbabwe spiraling out of control. That, in turn, requires a commitment by the AU and African leaders to engage on matters of governance, human rights, and democracy.

Good governance and conflict prevention are two sides of the same coin – a linkage recognized by the OAU in the introductory paragraphs of the Cairo Declaration of 1995: 'We recognize and resolve that democracy, good governance, peace, security, stability and justice are among the most essential factors in African socio-economic development. Without democracy and peace, development is not possible; and, without development, peace is not durable'.[36]

The key early indicators of intra-state conflict and regional instability have repeatedly proved to be the abuse of power (often culminating in coups d'état), ethnic politics and exclusionary practices (such as those relating to citizenship in Côte d'Ivoire and eastern DRC), human rights violations, bad governance and institutional corruption (epitomized by the regime of Mobutu in the former Zaire), proliferation of small arms (possibly most evident in the West Africa conflict system) and the like.

The famous fact that democracies have seldom experienced a famine should remind us of the clear linkage between governance and insecurity. Thus poor governance dramatically intensified much of the starvation experienced at various times in countries such as Ethiopia and Sudan and the lack of food security in countries such as Zimbabwe and Malawi. Equatorial Guinea, a country notorious for its human rights record, has boosted gross domestic product (GDP) from $164m. in 1995 to $794m. in 2001, but without any improvement in living standards for the vast majority of its people who remain living in abject poverty despite the massive wealth being accrued by a small elite. It requires little analysis to predict that instability and insecurity will continue to characterize the domestic polity of the country until there are substantial changes in internal governance practices.

Having argued for the establishment of a CEWS within the Commission and commented on the probable nature of such a structure, this study has hinted at a number of complementary roles that African research institutes, NGOs, academia and others could play. These include complementing the work of the CEWS, working to strengthen the hand of the Commission, petitioning the Peace and Security Council and supporting the provision of information and analysis to prevention and amelioration efforts.

There are obvious strong caveats that need to be recognized in advancing this argument, including the massive capacity constraints, lack of common governance and oversight standards, and methodological and even ideological challenges faced by African NGOs, academia and researchers. Yet these are little different from those faced by many African governments, and the levels of dependence upon non-African funds is common to both African NGOs and many governments. Whilst the capacity constraints and the limits of research institutes in Africa are beyond this study, there are many networks such as the Organization of Social Science Research in Eastern and Southern Africa (OSSREA), the Council for the Development of Social Science Research in Africa (CODESRIA) and the African Human Security Initiative (AHSI) that could play a role as an information channel and a catalyst for accountability and transparency. The net result of expanding global citizen action has been to extend the theory and deepen the practice of grass-roots democracy. In Africa, where governance is thin, and states weak, it is the absence of governance that has sometimes necessitated and fueled the growth of civil society. There are many limitations to African capacity in this regard, but, similar to African governments, appropriate capacity will require substantial investment over time. None of this should obviate the potential constructive role that they could play in supporting the work of the African Union in conflict prevention.

References

African Union. 2003. *Report of the Workshop on the Establishment of the AU Continental Early Warning System (CEWS)*, Addis Ababa: AU, 30–31 October.

Cilliers, J. 2002. *From Durban to Maputo – a review of 2003 Summit of the African Union*, ISS Paper No 76. Pretoria: ISS, August.

Engberg, Katarina. 2002. *Impact Study of the OAU Mechanism for Conflict Management. Report written for SIDA*. Addis Ababa: Swedish Embassy. 25 June, p 5.

Organization of African Unity (1993). *Declaration of the Assembly of Heads of State and Government on the Establishment within the OAU of a Mechanism for Conflict Prevention, Management and Resolution*, Twenty-ninth Ordinary Session, Cairo, 28–30 June 1993. [Online] Available at www.iss.org.za.

Notes

1. Members of the Bureau draft the decisions of the Summit.
2. The Central Organ of the Mechanism consisted of the countries that were members of the Bureau of the Assembly of Heads of State and Government. The Bureau was elected annually based on the principles of equitable regional representation and rotation. In order to ensure continuity, the outgoing Chairman and the incoming Chairman were also members of the Central Organ. In between Ordinary Sessions of the Assembly, the Bureau assumed overall direction and coordination of the activities of the Mechanism. According to a 1995 Summit decision, the number of countries in the Bureau was increased from 9 to 14. (Resolution on the Increase in the Membership of the Bureau of the Assembly, AHG/Res.239(XXXI), 31st Assembly of Heads of State and Government, 26-28 June 1995, Addis Ababa).
3. 6% of the regular membership contributions of member states is currently allocated to the Peace Fund, up from the original amount of 5%. The annual budget of the OAU was roughly $42 million in 2003, indicating that the peace fund would receive about US$2 million per annum.
4. *Declaration of the Assembly of Heads of State and Government on the Establishment within the OAU of a Mechanism for Conflict Prevention, Management and Resolution*, AHG/DECL.3 (XXIX), para. 14, Assembly of Heads of State and Government, 29th Ordinary Session, 28–30 June 1993, Cairo, Egypt.
5. Para. 22.
6. The unit, staffed with a small core group of civilian and military officers, was subsequently equipped with communication resources.
7. For example, while the OAU was deeply involved with the UN, the US and the EU in attempts at the prevention of the war between Ethiopia and Eritrea, and with France and Senegal in Madagascar, it was largely absent from Somalia, Sudan (until Dar Fur), Angola, the DRC, Sierra Leone and Liberia.
8. The US was the largest contributor to the Peace Fund, particularly during the early years of the Clinton administration.
9. One P3 and two P2s.
10. See in this regard Article 4 (g) of the Constitutive Act, 11 July 2000.
11. Article 4 (h) of the Constitutive Act of the African Union, 11 July 2000.
12. Protocol Relating to the Establishment of the AU Peace and Security Council, 9 July 2002, Article 10 (4).
13. Article 12.
14. Article 12 (5).
15. Ibid.
16. Article 11.
17. Article 4 (b).

18 Article 6 (b) and (f). According to Article 3 of the Protocol, the PSC's objectives are to: 'Promote peace, security and stability in Africa, in order to guarantee the protection and preservation of life and property, the well-being of the African people and their environment, as well as the creation of conditions conducive to sustainable development; Anticipate and prevent conflicts ... promote and implement peace-building and post-conflict reconstruction activities to consolidate peace and prevent the resurgence of violence; Promote and encourage democratic practices, good governance and the rule of law, protect human rights and fundamental freedoms, respect for sanctity of human life and international humanitarian law, as part of efforts for preventing conflicts.'

19 Article 12 (2, b). The Conflict Management Division is currently a division within the Directorate of Peace and Security – on the same level as the Secretariat of the Peace and Security Council, the Peace Support Operations Division and the Strategic Issues Division. The latter falls under the Commissioner for Peace and Security.

20 Article 12 (4).

21 Art. 12(3)

22 Ibid

23 Art. 8(9)

24 Art. 8(10))

25 Art. 8(11).

26 Progress with the development of the various components of regional conflict prevention and management is most advanced in ECOWAS, SADC and IGAD, while the Economic Community of Central African States (ECCAS) is also busy operationalizing its plans. Also see Article 16 (1). As regards practical modalities of collaboration, Article 16 (4) postulates that 'in order to ensure close harmonization and coordination and facilitate regular exchange of information, the Chairperson of the Commission shall convene periodic meetings, but at least once a year, with the Chief Executives and/or the officials in charge of peace and security within the Regional Mechanisms'. Furthermore, Article 16 (8) states that: 'in order to strengthen coordination and cooperation, the Commission shall establish liaison offices to the Regional Mechanisms. The Regional Mechanisms shall be encouraged to establish liaison offices to the Commission.'

27 Article 12 (2, a, b).

28 Article 16 (2)

29 Article 16 (5)

30 Developing such a module is potentially a complex technical undertaking and, depending upon the approach adopted by the Commission, could be extremely expensive since most consultancies have viewed this as a *carte blanche* to propose the development of sophisticated databases that would demand substantive data coding and capturing.

31 A strong case could be made that CEWS reports should all be public since this would by itself serve as an important indication of possible PSC intent.

32 Including disputed elections, poor governance, large refugee movements, human rights abuses, crime, competition over natural and other resources, natural disasters, acts of terrorism and the like.

33 The AU will not succeed in translating its obligations on early warning into practice if it does not provide for sufficient, capable and interdisciplinary staff. In particular, the head of the CEWS should be a senior analyst/diplomat with the stature of director or deputy director within the AU staffing structure to enable him/her to adequately represent and present independent analysis within the context of an organization with a strong emphasis on hierarchy. In a recent submission to the Commission, the ISS proposed a structure orientated to work towards each of the AU's five regions. For each region we proposed the phased appointment of one military, political and socio-economic/ humanitarian analyst (i.e. 3 for each of the five regions) as an adequate and multi-disciplinary team for the undertaking of early warning activities. The political analyst would head up the regional section. The staffing structure proposed implies a total number of 21 staff members: the head, a deputy head, 2 secretaries, 2 clerks and 15 analysts, five of whom (the political analysts) serve as the head for the five regions. Based on these assumptions, the AU would require relatively modest means to establish the CEWS system based in Addis Ababa – less than US$1 million to establish (if building costs are excluded) and roughly US$1 million to run on an annual basis. This composition could be phased in over time, with the immediate priority being the establishment of the units for West, the Horn and Central Africa and one analyst each for North and Southern

Africa only. The remaining staff of the units for North and Southern Africa could be appointed during a second phase.

34   As the AU moves ahead with the operationalization of the African Standby Force (ASF) and becomes even more deeply engaged with peacemaking and peacebuilding, the requirement for an operations room that is staffed at all hours to refer urgent messages and information to key members of the Commission, becomes ever more relevant.

35   African Union, *Report of the Workshop on the Establishment of the AU Continental Early Warning System (CEWS)*, 30–31 October 2003, Addis Ababa, Ethiopia, p. 5.

36   *Relaunching Africa's Economic and Social Development: the Cairo Agenda for Action*, AHG/Res,236 (XXXI), para. 10, Assembly of Heads of State and Government, 31st Ordinary Session, 26–28 June 1995, Addis Ababa, Ethiopia.

4

The International Criminal Court
& the Lord's Resistance Army Insurgency
in Northern Uganda

KASAIJA PHILIP APUULI

In January 2004, the government of Uganda reached an agreement with the Office of the Prosecutor of the International Criminal Court,[1] to start investigating the activities of the Lord's Resistance Army (LRA),[2] with a view to indicting and bringing to trial all those who have wrought untold suffering on the civilian population of northern Uganda. Since 1986 when the government of the National Resistance Movement (NRM) led by Yoweri Museveni came to power, the people of northern Uganda have never known peace. 2004 marked the eighteenth anniversary of the start of the insurgency in northern Uganda. All this time, the insurgency has pitted the LRA of reclusive Joseph Kony against the national army of Uganda, the National Resistance Army (NRA) – later renamed the Uganda People's Defence Forces (UPDF) – supported by a myriad of local militias. The LRA insurgency, it should be noted, is the only one that has persisted against the NRM government, as all the others including those of the Uganda People's Defence Army (UPDA) of Brigadier Odong Latek, the Uganda People's Army (UPA) of Peter Otai, the Holy Spirit Movement I (HSM I) of Severino Lukoya, the Holy Spirit Movement II (HSM II) of Alice Lakwena, the West Nile Bank Front (WBNF) of Juma Oris, and the Allied Democratic Forces (ADF) of Jamil Mukulu, among others, have been defeated by the government.

The aim of this chapter is to spell out the international criminal offences with which the Prosecutor of the ICC might charge the LRA and the government forces within the limits of the Statute of the International Criminal Court (also called the Rome Statute) and international law in general.

The Roots of the Insurgency

There are multifarious explanations as to the root causes of the various rebellions in northern Uganda. The conflict between the government and the LRA has been variously explained: that it is a struggle of the predominantly Acholi population who have borne the brunt of violence involving indiscriminate killings and the abduction of children to become fighters, auxiliaries and sex slaves; that it is fuelled by animosity between Uganda and Sudan, which support rebellions in each other's territory; and that it is a continuation of the north-south conflict that has marked Uganda politics and society since independence (International Crisis Group 2004).

The north-south divide is explained in terms of the economic imbalance that was perpetrated by the colonialists. The north was seen as mainly a reservoir of labor for the army. Also, the British deliberately reserved the introduction of industry and cash crops to the south, for which the north became a reservoir of cheap manual labor. Successive postcolonial governments did not change this situation. The postcolonial Ugandan army continued to be heavily recruited from the north, while the south enjoyed relative economic prosperity. The Museveni rebellion against Obote has also been explained in the context of the north-south divide. For many, the rebellion was merely a continuation of the ethnic competition that has typified Uganda politics – a case of Bantu-speaking Southerners wanting to remove from power Nilotic-speaking Northerners (International Crisis Group 2004).

Broadly, therefore, all the insurgencies in northern Uganda, including that of the LRA, can be explained as an attempt by the people of that region to regain power that they lost in January 1986 following the victory of Museveni's NRM. Suffice it to note that from 1962 to 1986 the people of northern Uganda had ruled the country. However, the immediate cause of the rebellion against the Museveni government that started in 1986 can be found in the way the soldiers of the National Resistance Army (NRA) behaved when they reached the district of Gulu. The NRA captured Gulu town, which is predominantly inhabited by the Acholi people, in early March 1986 without a fight. Heike Behrend (1991: 165) has explained that,

> [S]oon afterwards, the 35th battalion of the NRA was sent to Kitgum. This included remnants of UNLA who had surrendered, and ex-Federal Democratic Movement (FEDEMO) troops who being mainly Baganda, had been formed to fight Obote. They took the opportunity to loot, rape and murder. To escape this, some of the Acholi ex-soldiers took up their weapons again and went into the bush to join the newly founded UPDA.

Clearly, it can be argued that the underlying cause of the LRA insurgency in northern Uganda can be found in attempts by the defeated northern forces that had presided over Uganda's affairs since independence to regain power. However, the immediate cause of the rebellion against the Museveni government in 1986 by the people of Acholi was the unbecoming and undisciplined behavior of the 35th battalion of the NRA (Simba 2000: 112).[3]

The Lord's Resistance Army (LRA)[4]

As the NRA seized power in Kampala in January 1986, the bulk of the former Uganda army, the Uganda National Liberation Army (UNLA), predominantly made up of people from Lango and Acholi Districts of the country, retreated north. When the NRA reached these areas, the defeated

UNLA attempted to stage a comeback. Their hope was that the people of the north would rise up against the invading southerners who predominantly made up the NRA. By late 1988, the NRA had already been able to defeat a number of northern rebel groups that had risen to fight against it in the north of the country, Prominent among them the UPDA of Odong Latek, and the Holy Spirit Movement I and II of Severino Lukoya and Alice Lakwena, respectively. By the early 1990s the rebellion in Teso region led by the UPA of Peter Otai had all but dissipated. However, from the ashes of the UPDA and HSM I and II, was to rise the LRA.

Joseph Kony, a former altar boy, started the LRA after the defeat by the NRA of Alice Lakwena's HSM II at Maga Maga in Jinja district in 1988. Kony is a nephew of Alice Lakwena, who herself is a daughter of Severino Lukoya. Kony proclaimed himself a messianic prophet (IRIN 2004a), and stated that he intended to overthrow the Museveni government and rule Uganda according to the Biblical Ten Commandments. However, as the rebellion lost popular support (among the people of the region) and was under pressure from both the UPDF and local resistance, the LRA and Kony fled to Southern Sudan, where he found fertile ground to operate as the area had been wracked by war since the Sudanese People's Liberation Army (SPLA) of John Garang began fighting the Khartoum government in May 1983. The Sudanese government found an ally in Kony as the government of Uganda openly supported the SPLA. Kony was able to obtain bases and much needed supplies of weapons to continue fighting the Uganda army. The LRA's tactic throughout its insurgency has been to attack and terrorize civilians, by killings and abductions. The LRA has been able to swell its ranks by means of child abductions and forceful recruitment.

Having been stung by the continued LRA presence in Southern Sudan, President Museveni, with the help of then President Daniel arap Moi of Kenya, reached a diplomatic agreement with President Bashir of Sudan in 1999 in Nairobi to cease their governments' support of the LRA and the SPLA, respectively. But this agreement did not put a stop to the LRA insurgency.

In March 2002, the UPDF launched what it called 'Operation Iron Fist', aimed at routing the LRA from its bases in Southern Sudan. This operation followed an agreement reached by the governments of Uganda and Sudan, allowing the former to send its troops on to the territory of Sudan below the 4th parallel in order to deal with the LRA insurgents. In July 2002, President Museveni moved to Gulu and at the time promised Ugandans 'that he would militarily end the northern rebellion by the start of the next rainy season (April 2003)' (*The Sunday Monitor* 2003: 8). The results of the operation have been mixed. Whereas the government and the UPDF claimed success from the fact that Kony no longer had permanent bases in the areas of Southern Sudan near the Uganda border from where he could launch attacks into the territory of Uganda, civil society groups like the Acholi Religious Leaders' Peace Initiative (ARLPI),[5] a group that has been seeking peaceful ways to end the conflict, noted that 'the operation was the biggest mistake of the government as it has doubled the numbers of the displaced and [has made the] security [situation] worse than ever'.[6]

The effect of Operation Iron Fist, among others, was to expand the LRA's operational area from its traditional bastions of Gulu, Pader, and Kitgum districts to the districts of Lira and Apach, and the two districts of Katakwi and Soroti in Teso region.[7] As a result of the LRA's invasion of Teso, the United Nations Office for Humanitarian Affairs (OCHA) has estimated that the number of internally displaced persons (IDPs) fleeing LRA terror rose from 800,000 to at least 1.2 million.[8] The IDPs, who are largely composed of malnourished children, live in squalid make-shift camps called 'protected villages', devoid of food or clean water, and with sanitation and medicine non-existent.[9] The concentration of people in IDP camps gives the LRA a chance to attack, kill, and abduct many people, despite the fact that local militias protect the camps. The United Nations Children Fund (UNICEF) has estimated that, in 2003, the rebels abducted a staggering 8,500 children. Many of the children once abducted, are never seen again.

The government's response to the increased LRA attacks has been to ask the local communities in the affected areas to raise militias, which it trains and arms ostensibly to protect the local populations from the marauding LRA. As a result, the Teso region has seen the rise of the para-military Arrow Group militia, while in neighboring Lango region there are the Amuka Boys. These para-military groups are ostensibly established to protect people while freeing the army to pursue the LRA. But some of these militias have been used in the army's offensive against the LRA. This has raised concerns among the local people and civil society groups about the long-term security of these regions. Suffice it to note that, many people who have joined the militias have been rebels in the past. For example, many members of the Arrow Group in Teso region were once part of Peter Otai's UPA which operated in the area between 1987 and 1993. The concern is whether, after defeating the LRA, these former rebels will disarm. The government and the army have given assurances that they will. Army spokesman Major Shaban Bantariza was quoted as saying that the army will ensure that they demobilize when eastern Uganda has been rid of terrorists.[10]

Government & International Response to the Conflict

Since the start of the LRA insurgency, the government of Uganda has always maintained that this was an internal matter, which had to be solved by Uganda.[11] It has always argued that the LRA rebels are fighting the constitutionally elected government of Uganda and they therefore have to be dealt with under domestic law. International law treats civil wars as purely internal matters (Shaw 1997: 798). In fact President Museveni calls the LRA 'bandits' and 'terrorists'. Article 2(4) of the UN Charter prohibits the threat or use of force in international relations, but not in domestic situations. Shaw notes that 'there is no rule against rebellion in international law. [Rebellion] is within the domestic jurisdiction of states and is left to be dealt with by internal law' (ibid.).

So far, the only foreign intervention that the government has allowed has been the provision of humanitarian aid to the IDPs by United Nations agencies, such as the World Food Program (WFP), the United Nations High

Commission for Refugees (UNHCR), and the United Nations Development Program (UNDP), among others. The conflict, much to the dismay of many Ugandans, has never found its way onto the UN Security Council agenda. President Museveni has claimed that he wrote to the Security Council alerting it to the situation, and it did nothing (Ryan and Wamboka 2004).

However, as the conflict entered its eighteenth year, the international community began to take notice. The international concern was in part aroused by the increased brutality of the LRA as a result of military pressure from government forces. Donor and senior diplomatic figures became increasingly vocal in their opposition to the government's military approach. Due to the concerns raised by the international community, the United Nations pledged US$128 million towards the emergency relief of the IDPs.

Despite increased international intervention in the conflict, President Museveni maintained that the conflict remained an internal affair and he did not welcome the intervention of the United Nations (*The Monitor* 2003).[12] Yet, he has called in the Prosecutor of the ICC to investigate the activities of the LRA. Uganda has ratified the Rome Statute and it is the first country to refer a case to the ICC since the court began operating (Human Rights Watch 2004). What led President Museveni to call in the ICC remains a matter of conjecture. However, two things can be noted. First, the leaders of the LRA, in particular Joseph Kony, remain beyond the jurisdiction of Uganda. In October 2005 Kony and the bulk of his LRA relocated from southern Sudan to Garambe National Park in the Democratic Republic of Congo where they have remained, although recent press reports have indicated that he has now moved to the Central African Republic. By inviting the ICC to investigate, Museveni probably hopes that it will be able to indict Kony, which will force the Sudanese government to hand him over. Secondly, the Rome Statute emphasizes the complementary principle.[13] This holds that the ICC can only assert its jurisdiction if the State Party is 'unable genuinely to carry out the investigation or prosecution'.[14] Clearly the government of Museveni has failed to either bring Kony and his henchmen to justice or take justice to them. Therefore, by invoking the powers of the ICC, the Museveni government is trying to achieve what it has failed to do all these years.

Jurisdiction *Rationae Materiae*

Since the start of the conflict, egregious punishable abuses have been visited upon the people of northern Uganda by the LRA.[15] This is not to say that the government forces have clean hands. Human Rights Watch has reported that the UPDF has committed extra-judicial killings, rape and sexual assault, forcible displacement of over one million civilians, and the recruitment of children under the age of 15 into government militias.

The jurisdiction *rationae materiae* of the Court under the Rome Statute is limited to serious crimes of concern to the whole international community.[16] The Court has jurisdiction with respect to crimes of genocide, crimes against humanity, war crimes and the crime of aggression.[17]

According to the formal agreement between the Uganda government and the Prosecutor of the ICC, the latter will be investigating with a view to bringing to justice those with the greatest responsibility for the crimes against humanity committed in northern Uganda. We should add that the offences that have continuously been committed in northern Uganda are a mixture of crimes against humanity and war crimes. Therefore, the ICC Prosecutor will have to investigate both.

The jurisdiction *rationae temporis* of the Court is limited to those offences that have taken place since 1 July 2002, when the Court legally came into existence.[18] This means that the Prosecutor will only investigate those offences committed in northern Uganda since that date.

Crimes Against Humanity

Crimes against humanity have been described variously as acts that trample underfoot the laws of God and humanity (Birkett 1947:317). Lord Browne-Wilkinson in the celebrated *Ex parte Pinochet Ugarte (No. 3) case* called them 'crimes *jus cogens*'.[19] Elsewhere, they have been called 'grave breaches of human rights' (Freeman 1999: 1072).

The term 'crimes against humanity' first appeared in the declaration of 28 May 1915 by the governments of France, Britain and Russia concerning the massacre of Armenians in Turkey (Hirsh 2003: 43). The declaration stated that all members of the government of Turkey would be held responsible, together with its agents implicated in the massacres, However, in the end it remained no more than a declaration. No Turk was ever prosecuted for killing the Armenians. Subsequently, the offence became 'positive law' with its embodiment in the Charter of the International Military Tribunal at Nuremberg in 1945 (Wexler 1999: 662). The Charter, under which the Nazi war criminals were tried, established crimes against humanity as a substantive offence to be punished. The offence was defined as 'murder, extermination, enslavement, deportation, and other inhuman acts committed against any civilian population, before or during the war; or persecutions on political, racial or religious grounds in execution of or in connection with any crime....'[20] When the Socialist Federal Republic of Yugoslavia imploded in the early 1990s and the UN Security Council decided to establish an *ad hoc* international criminal tribunal to prosecute persons responsible for serious violations of international humanitarian law in that country, the statute of the newly created tribunal included a provision outlining crimes against humanity.[21] Incidentally, for the first time the offence was applied to a conflict that was internal in character. When the International Criminal Tribunal for Rwanda was established, the offence was also included in its statute but with a slightly different construction from that of the Nuremberg Charter and the International Criminal Tribunal for the Former Yugoslavia (ICTY) statute.[22] The construction could have been different because of the genocidal context in which the Rwandese conflict took place.

The Rome Statute defines crimes against humanity as 'any of the following acts when committed as part of a widespread or systematic attack directed against any civilian population, with knowledge of the attack: murder; extermination; enslavement; deportation or forcible transfer of populations; imprisonment or other severe deprivation of physical liberty in violation of fundamental rules of international law; torture; rape, sexual slavery, enforced prostitution, forced pregnancy ... or any other form of sexual violence of comparable gravity; persecution of any identifiable group ...; enforced disappearance of persons; ...; other inhuman acts of a similar character intentionally causing great suffering, or serious injury to body or to mental or physical health.'[23] The Statute[24] goes on to explain what is meant by some of the terms that are used in defining the crime. It says that an attack against any civilian population means, 'a course of conduct involving the multiple commission of acts ... against any civilian population, pursuant to or in furtherance of a state or organizational policy to commit such attack'. Extermination includes, 'the intentional infliction of conditions of life, *inter alia* the deprivation of access to food and medicine, calculated to bring about the destruction of part of a population'. Enslavement means 'the exercise of any or all of the powers attaching to the right of ownership over a person and includes the exercise of such power in the course of trafficking in persons, in particular women and children'.

Deportation or forcible transfer of population means 'forced displacement of the persons concerned by expulsion or other coercive acts from the area in which they are lawfully present, without grounds permitted under international law'. Torture means 'the intentional infliction of severe pain or suffering, whether physical or mental, upon a person in the custody or under the control of the accused; except that torture shall not include pain or suffering arising only from, inherent in or incidental to, lawful sanctions.' Forced pregnancy means 'the unlawful confinement of a woman forcibly made pregnant, with the intent of affecting the ethnic composition of any population or carrying out other grave violations of international law ...' Persecution means 'the intentional and severe deprivation of fundamental rights contrary to international law by reason of the identity of the group or collectivity'.

War Crimes

Apart from crimes against humanity, war crimes have also been committed in the conflict in northern Uganda. Again, war crimes were established as an offence under international law under the Charter that established the Nuremberg Tribunal in 1945. The Rome Statute built on Nuremberg. War crimes under the Rome Statute[25] are defined as 'grave breaches of the Geneva Conventions of 12 August 1949, namely, any of the following acts against persons or property protected under the provisions of the relevant Geneva Convention ... when committed as part of a plan or policy or as part of a large scale commission ...: willful killing; torture or inhuman treatment ...; willfully causing great suffering, or serious injury to body or health; extensive destruction and appropriation of property, not justified by military necessity and carried out unlawfully and wantonly ...; unlawful deportation or transfer or unlawful confinement; and taking hostages'.

In the case of an armed conflict not of an international character, serious violations include, according to Article 3[26] of the four Geneva Conventions of 12 August 1949, any of the following acts committed against persons taking no active part in the hostilities: 'violence to life and person, in particular murder of all kinds, mutilation, cruel treatment and torture; committing outrages upon personal dignity, in particular humiliating and degrading treatment; taking of hostages; and passing of sentences and carrying out of executions without previous judgment pronounced by a regularly constituted court, affording all judicial guarantees which are generally recognized as indispensable'.[27]

Other serious violations[28] of the laws and customs applicable in armed conflicts not of an international character, within the established framework of international law, include any of the following acts: 'intentionally directing attacks against civilian population as part or against individual civilians not taking direct part in hostilities; pillaging a town or place, even when taken by assault; ... committing rape, sexual slavery, enforced prostitution; forced pregnancy ... and any form of sexual violence also constituting a serious violation of Article 3 common to the four Geneva Conventions; conscripting or enlisting children under the age of fifteen years into armed forces or groups or using them to participate actively in hostilities; and, ordering the displacement of the civilian population for reasons related to the conflict, unless the security of the civilians involved or imperative military reasons so demand.' This particular provision applies to armed conflicts that take place in the territory of a state when there is protracted armed conflict between governmental authorities and organized armed groups or between such groups.

The Range of Likely Offences

Since it started waging war against the government of President Museveni, the LRA has continuously wrought havoc on the civilian population of northern Uganda.[29] The LRA atrocities have been well documented by local and international NGOs operating in the region. However, for the Prosecutor of the ICC two attacks against the civilian population must be of special interest. First, on 5 February 2004, the LRA attacked an Internally Displaced People's camp at Abia, Lira District. In this attack, the LRA killed 50 civilians (*The New Vision* 2004a). Also, there was wanton destruction of property. The second is the attack on Barlonyo IDP camp that left close on 200 people dead (*The Monitor* 2004). The Prosecutor has already announced that he will be investigating the latter attack.[30] Again, there was wanton destruction of property, including the total destruction of huts that housed the civilian population, constituting a war crime under the Rome Statute.

Due to the LRA tactics of attacking the civil population, villages have been emptied of people, constituting a crime against humanity. By October 2003, an estimated total of 1.4 million people were living in IDP camps in northern Uganda.[31] These camps were a lot safer because the army protected them. However, they were not totally insulated from attack as the examples of Abia and Barlonyo showed. The living conditions in the IDP camps have been described as inhuman.[32] The camps lack infrastructure, adequate food and water, and medical care.

The LRA has been notorious for wantonly and systematically abducting people, particularly children. These abductions are aimed at accomplishing a number of things. The abducted boys and girls are forcibly recruited into the LRA ranks.[33] The girls are also married to the LRA rank and file.[34] It is reported that Kony himself maintains a number of these abducted girls as his wives.[35] In addition, the LRA uses the children as human shields, porters, and laborers (Human Rights Watch 2004). According to Human Rights Watch, an estimated 10,000 children had been abducted by the LRA by mid-2002. These children were forced to fight, to kill civilians, and to abduct other children. Those who failed to comply with the orders were murdered often by other children, who were forced to kill them. These actions clearly constitute crimes against humanity within the meaning of the Rome Statute.

The LRA is in clear violation of the international standards prohibiting the recruitment and use of children as soldiers. Additional Protocol II to the Geneva Conventions of 1977 prohibits all recruitment of children under the age of 15 or their use in hostilities.[36] This prohibition is binding on both governmental and non-governmental forces and is now considered customary international law. Under the Rome Statute, such recruitment is also considered a crime.[37] Furthermore, under the Optional Protocol to the Convention on the Rights of the Child in Armed Conflict (2000), the LRA is under obligation not to recruit in its ranks any person below the age of 18.[38]

The LRA has been known to rape, forcefully impregnate, and force into sexual slavery the women and girls its troops abduct. Many of the abducted women and girls are subjected to rape, unwanted pregnancies, and risk sexually transmitted diseases, including HIV/AIDS (Westcott 2003). According to officials of the Gulu Support the Children Organization (GUSCO), a local NGO that receives and treats trauma and gives counseling to returning abducted children, the girls who turn up at the center tend to bring with them three children whom they have had in captivity. The explanation given for this is that the abducted girls find it hard to escape because they are kept in close proximity to their 'husbands' – the commanders. Whereas the intention of the LRA is not to alter the ethnic composition of the population in northern Uganda by its policy of enforced pregnancies, this tactic is clearly a crime against humanity within the meaning of the Rome Statute.[39]

The brutality of the LRA is legendary. The only other comparable organization with tactics of a similar kind was the Revolutionary United Front (RUF) of the late Foday Sankoh in Sierra Leone. At the height of its insurgency, the RUF would attack villages, hacking civilians to death, while those who were abducted would have their arms and limbs hacked off. The LRA has used similar tactics on civilians. In order to terrorize the population, the LRA uses body mutilations, cutting off of arms and hands, ears, lips, and buttocks of villagers suspected of being government sympathizers (ICC: 2004). Clearly these LRA activities constitute torture within the meaning of the Rome Statute,[40] and therefore can fall under the categories of crimes against humanity or war crimes.

Government Forces in the Dock

Whereas it is the government of Uganda that has referred the situation in northern Uganda to the ICC, persistent reports have indicated that government forces are also in breach of the obligations of the Rome Statute, and other international law instruments.

Recruitment of Children into the Armed Forces
The government has been accused by international human rights and humanitarian organizations of recruiting children into the UPDF ranks to fight the LRA (Human Rights Watch 2003b, 2003c), although the government denies this.[41] Human Rights Watch has alleged that former LRA child soldiers are recruited into the Uganda army, often against their will.[42] These allegations constitute a war crime within the meaning of the Rome Statute,[43] but they are also a crime under other international legal instruments.

First, Uganda is apparently in breach of the Protocol Additional to the Geneva Conventions of 12 August 1949 and the Protocol Relating to the Protection of Victims of International Armed Conflicts of 1977 (called Protocol I), which it acceded to and ratified on 13 March 1991.[44] Also, the government is in breach of Protocol Additional to the Geneva Conventions of 12 August 1949 and Relating to the Protection of Victims of Non-International Armed Conflicts of 1977 (called Protocol II), which it also acceded to and ratified on 13 March 1991. [45]

Furthermore, Uganda has acceded to the Optional Protocol to the Convention on the Rights of the Child on the Involvement of Children in Armed Conflict (2000).[46] This instrument sets eighteen as the minimum age for all recruitment into the armed forces.[47] Under Article 3, Uganda, while acceding to the Protocol, made a binding declaration affirming eighteen as its minimum age for any voluntary recruitment into its armed forces.[48] The declaration states, 'the government of the Republic of Uganda declares that the minimum age for the recruitment of persons into the armed forces is by law set at eighteen (18) years. Recruitment is entirely and squarely voluntary and is carried out with the full informed consent of the persons being recruited. There is no conscription in Uganda.'[49]

Under the Protocol, state parties are under an obligation to take all feasible measures to prevent recruitment below the age of 18, including the adoption of legal measures necessary to prohibit and criminalize such practices.[50] The Protocol also places obligations on the government to assist in the rehabilitation and reintegration of former child soldiers.[51]

Lastly, Uganda is also a signatory – a State Party – to the African Charter on the Rights and Welfare of the Child. This regional treaty, which came into force in 1999, establishes that a 'child' is anyone below the age of eighteen. It also states that, 'States Parties ... shall take all necessary measures to ensure that no child shall take a direct part in hostilities and refrain in particular, from recruiting any child.'[52]

Rape and Sexual Assaults

The UPDF has perennially been accused of committing rapes and sexual attacks against the female population of northern Uganda. Human Rights Watch has documented and published torrid accounts of women who have suffered sexual attacks at the hands of the Ugandan army. Although these might not constitute a systematic attack, they are so widespread as to constitute a crime against humanity or a war crime under the auspices of the Rome Statute. The government has denied these allegations, just as it has denied allegations of recruiting children into its armed forces.

A 2001 survey found that, in Gulu district, girls identified 'rape and defilement' as their third most important concern after 'insecurity, abduction and murder' and displacement (Women's Commission on Refugee Women and Children (2001). Human Right Watch (2003c) has concluded that 'the apparent incidence of rape is associated with the increased presence of the UPDF and the vulnerability of the displaced population'. The Women's Commission on Refugee Women and Children (2001), while corroborating the rape claims, has reported that 'there are two young girls, one 12 years and another 17, who were returning from the garden and they found soldiers who intercepted and raped them. Both girls were tested for HIV and the result was positive.'

The Acholi Religious Leaders Peace Initiative (ARLPI), a civic group that brings together leaders of the various faiths in northern Uganda, 'received reports of more than twenty-seven women and girls [who] were raped by UPDF soldiers in Kitgum and Pader districts between June and December 2002'.[53] Among the incidents reported were; gang rapes of three different women by three different groups of UPDF in Kalongo on 25 August 2002; rapes of several young girls and women in Lagile Parish on 22 September 2002; the rape of a young girl by two UPDF soldiers at Puranga trading center on 28 October 2002; and rapes of several women by UPDF soldiers from Apatongo barracks on 21 November 2002.[54] These breaches clearly constitute war crimes and crimes against humanity under the Rome Statute. Also reported is the gang rape by twenty UPDF soldiers in Matere, Kitgum district, of a group of women who were visiting a mother and her newborn child on 16 January 2003.[55] The raped women were threatened with death if they reported the matter.

From these examples, there can be no doubt that the allegations of rape and sexual assaults against women in northern Uganda by the UPDF are not without merit. Suffice it to note that rape has been declared a crime against humanity.[56]

Other Allegations

Other allegations which are war crimes that have been leveled against the government forces include extra-judicial killings (summary executions), torture and forcible displacement of over one million civilians.[57] All these allegations fall under the war crimes or crimes against humanity within the remit of the ICC, and must be investigated. As a State Party to the Convention against Torture (1984), Uganda is under an obligation not to condone the crime of torture anywhere on its territory. There can be no doubt that the rule against torture has evolved into a *jus cogens* prohibition, which every state has a duty owed to the international community to outlaw and punish (Robertson 2002: 103) It has been reported that torture is used by the Ugandan army on suspected LRA combatants and sympathizers,[58] to elicit confessions or the whereabouts of the rebel hideouts. The Torture Convention clearly prohibits such kinds of activities.[59]

The force of the prohibition against torture as enshrined in the Convention against Torture was clearly stated in the International Criminal Tribunal for the former Yugoslavia (ICTY) in *Prosecutor v Furundzija*[60] as '[d]esigned to produce a deterrent effect, in that it signals to all members of the international community and the individuals over whom they wield authority that the prohibition of torture is an absolute value from which nobody must deviate'.

Before the LRA attacks on the IDP camps of Abia and Barlonyo, there had been an attack on the IDP camp of Paboo in Gulu district, one of the biggest IDP camps in northern Uganda. In this attack, over 6,000 huts were set ablaze, scores of people died, and many were arrested.[61] The UPDF was implicated in this attack and those who exposed it were threatened with deportation. This clearly qualifies as a war crime, which the Prosecutor needs to investigate. It would also appear that this was part of a large-scale commission of such crimes in this conflict.

The Amnesty Wrangle

As soon as President Museveni and the ICC Prosecutor reached agreement for the latter to start investigations into the activities of the LRA, religious groups and the Amnesty Commission (AC), an agency created under the Constitution, rose up in arms, arguing that the threat of prosecuting the LRA would worsen the situation in northern Uganda, and also that it would make the LRA more reluctant to surrender peacefully. As a way of encouraging the numerous rebel movements including the LRA to lay down their arms peacefully, Parliament passed the Amnesty Act (2000), under which the former rebel combatants were to end their rebellion, be pardoned and then be resettled by the state. This law was subsequently extended by Parliament a number of times after its expiration and is still in place. However, an amendment was brought in Parliament in 2005 intending to exclude the LRA indicted leaders from the amnesty. The Minister of Internal Affairs was supposed to provide Parliament with the names of those to be excluded from the amnesty (a requirement under the amended act). He has never done so, which means that the indicted leaders can still benefit from the amnesty.

As a self-help measure, the various religious leaders in northern Uganda came together and formed the ARLPI, a group which brought together the leaders of the Catholic, Anglican, Orthodox, and Islamic faiths in northern Uganda, with the primary aim of making contact with the LRA and initiating talks to end the rebellion peacefully. The AC and the ARLPI have been the main opponents of the government's agreement with the ICC Prosecutor to investigate the LRA. According to the Vice Chairman of the

ARLPI, Bishop McLeod Ochola, 'the probe is going to destroy all efforts for peace. People want this war to stop. If we follow the ICC in branding the LRA criminals, it won't stop' (IRIN 2004b). Ochola averred that 'the ICC probe must come after the war has ended'.[62] Another argument advanced by the Chairman of ARLPI, Archbishop John Baptist Odama, is that, if the ICC is to investigate, then it must probe both sides in the conflict,[63] – an argument that has been rejected by President Museveni, whose government has the remit to receive the rebels, document them, and resettle them in society.

The AC's position is no different from that of the ARLPI. It argues that the ICC probe into the LRA activities makes a peaceful settlement of the conflict impossible. Moses Saku, the AC spokesman, is quoted as having said, '[c]ertainly this is going to make it difficult for the LRA to stop doing what they are doing. They have already been branded 'terrorists',[64] which isn't going to persuade them to come'(Musinguzi 2004) The head of the AC, Justice Peter Onega, is also not in favor of the ICC probe. According to him, 'if the rebels – who come from the Acholi community – are prosecuted it would send a wrong signal to the people of the region that are still campaigning for a blanket amnesty' (ibid.). In his view, '[g]iven the history of Uganda ... reconciliation is the best option for us at the moment' (ibid.). Politicians from the region, who warn that calls to prosecute Joseph Kony, could trigger fresh violence, support this view. Reagan Okumu, a Member of Parliament from Gulu district, has stated that 'the debate is not healthy as it could scare Kony into killing innocent people. He should be arrested first before any prosecution can take place' (ibid.).

So the question is: should the ICC Prosecutor not proceed with the LRA probe because of the amnesty law in place? Cherif Bassiouni has opined that 'for the four *jus cogens* crimes of genocide, crimes against humanity, war crimes and torture ... there should be no general amnesty....' (Bassiouni 1996: 63–74). Under the founding treaty of the ICC, and generally international law, amnesties are not a bar to the prosecution of egregious crimes such as those that fall under the ICC's jurisdiction *rationae materiae*. It has clearly been stated that '[h]uman rights obligations are contracted on an international level... where these obligations are breached, the individual may be punished for such international crimes as a matter of international law, even if his or her own state, or the state where the crime was committed, refuses to do so' (Schabas 2000: 2).

Amnesties attempt 'to edit life's un-editable record' (Chigara 2002: 61). No government can legitimately deal with a victim's property rights as sacrifice for the purchase of national stability (ibid.: 38). With reference to the amnesty, two things should be pointed out under the Rome Statute regime.[65] First, there is the language used in the Statute's preamble, which suggests that deferring a prosecution because of the existence of a national amnesty would be incompatible with the purpose of the Court, namely, to ensure criminal prosecution of persons who commit serious international crimes (Scharf 1999: 522) The preamble's language is important because international law provides that 'a treaty shall be interpreted in good faith in accordance with the ordinary meaning to be given to the terms of the treaty in their context and in the light of its object and purpose'.[66]

Therefore, as has been noted, the preamble constitutes a critical source of interpretation because it indicates both the treaty's context and its object and purpose.

Second, there is the Prosecutor's discretion to initiate an investigation *proprio motu*. The Rome Statute provides that 'the Prosecutor shall, having evaluated the information made available to him or her, initiate an investigation unless he or she determines that there is no reasonable basis to proceed....'[67] In deciding whether to initiate an investigation, the Prosecutor shall consider whether 'taking into account the gravity of the crime and the interests of the victims, there are nonetheless substantial reasons to believe that an investigation would not serve the interests of justice'.[68] This means that the Prosecutor may decline to initiate an investigation and hence prosecution, if he or she believes that the investigation and prosecution would interfere with the purposes of a national amnesty. However, this decision of the Prosecutor is subject to review by the Pre-Trial Chamber.[69] In reviewing whether respecting an amnesty and not prosecuting would better serve the interests of justice, the Pre-Trial Chamber would have to evaluate the benefits of a particular amnesty and consider whether there is an international legal obligation to prosecute the offence.

In the current case, we have yet to see whether the ICC Prosecutor will determine that continuing the investigation into LRA activities and bringing prosecutions is inconsistent with the national amnesty that has been put in place, and that it will not serve the interests of justice.

Recent Developments

Towards the end of November 2004, the government announced a limited unilateral ceasefire in parts of northern Uganda,[70] with the aim of restarting peace talks with the leadership of the LRA. However, the talks broke down at the end of December 2004; nevertheless the chief peace mediator, Betty Bigombe,[71] pressed on in an effort to get the two sides to sign a comprehensive cease-fire agreement. It appeared that these efforts had begun to pay off when a number of top LRA commanders, including Chief Spokesman and Peace Negotiator, Sam Kolo, and Operations Commander, Onen Kamdulu came out of the bush.

The Bigombe talks broke down, however. In October 2005 the ICC unveiled its indictments of the five LRA leaders. In May 2006, the government of Southern Sudan announced that the LRA had contacted them to ask the Uganda government for talks, which subsequently began in Juba in July 2006. At the end of August 2006, the government of Uganda and the LRA signed a landmark Cessation of Hostilities Agreement (CHA). Under this the LRA were to assemble at two points: Ri Kwangba and Owiny Kibul in Southern Sudan. The LRA have failed to do this.

In December 2006, the Juba talks broke down. The LRA accused the Chief Mediator, Dr Riek Machar, of siding with the Ugandan government. In addition, the LRA asked for a change of venue for the talks from Juba to either Kenya or South Africa. The government has refused all the LRA demands. No one therefore knows when the talks will restart. Meanwhile the LRA has averred that it will not sign any peace agreement with the government unless the ICC withdraws its indictments. The government in turn has argued that it will only ask the ICC to reconsider the indictments when the LRA signs the peace agreement. There is thus an impasse.

Conclusion

The wheels of international justice have started turning in order to bring to justice the individuals who have visited untold suffering on the people of northern Uganda for a long time. If all goes according to plan, we might see the first warrants of arrests being issued soon. But while the ICC investigation has continued, political and civil society leaders from northern Uganda seem to favor amnesty for the rebels in order to promote reconciliation.

This chapter has attempted to expound on the range of likely offences that the ICC Prosecutor might want to investigate in the conflict in northern Uganda, which squarely offend the jurisdiction *rationae materiae* of the ICC and other international legal instruments. And as we have stated, there are a number of offences that have been committed by both the armed forces of the Republic of Uganda and the LRA. There is no doubt that these offences will attract the attention of the ICC Prosecutor, despite the differences that have come up as regards the whole enterprise of the ICC probe. The people of northern Uganda have suffered far too long. We can only hope that at last there is light at the end of the tunnel.

References

Bassiouni, Cherif M. 1996. 'Searching for Peace and Achieving Justice: The Need for Accountability', *Law and Contemporary Problems*, 59(4): 9–28.

Behrend, Heike. 1991. 'Is Alice Lakwena a Witch? The Holy Spirit Movement and its Fight against Evil in the North', in Holger Bernt Hansen and Michael Twaddle. eds, *Changing Uganda: the Dilemmas of Structural Adjustment and Revolutionary Change*, London: James Currey, 162–77.

Berhend, Heike. 1998. 'War in Northern Uganda', in Christopher Clapham. ed., *African Guerillas*, Oxford: James Currey, 107–18.

Birkett, J. 1947. 'International Legal Theories Evolved at Nuremberg', *Inernational Affairs* 23: 317–25.

Chigara, B. 2002. *Amnesty in International Law: The Legality under International Law of National Amnesty Laws*. London: Longman.

Freeman, M. 1999. 'Genocide and Gross Human Rights Violations in Comparative Perspective', *Ethnic and Racial Studies* 22 (6): 1072–3.

Hirsh, David. 2003. *Law against Genocide: Cosmopolitan Trials*. London: Glasshouse Press.

Human Rights Watch. 2003a. 'Abducted and Abused: Renewed Conflict in Northern Uganda.' [online] Vol. 15, No. 12 (A). July. Available at http://www.hrw.org/reports/2003/uganda0703

Human Rights Watch. 2003b. 'Stolen Children: Abduction and Recruitment in Northern Uganda.' Report Vol. 15, no. 7 (A). March. [Online] Available at http://www.hrw.org/reports/2003/uganda0303

Human Rights Watch. 2003c. 'Abducted and Abused: Renewed Conflict in Northern Uganda.' Report Vol. 15, no. 12 (A). July. [Online] Available at http://www.hrw.org/reports/2003/uganda0703.

Human Rights Watch. 2004 'ICC: Investigate all sides in Uganda.' Press Release, 4 February. [Online] Available at http://allafrica.com/stories/printable/200402040752.html.

International Criminal Court (2004). The Hague, Netherlands, Press Release, 29 January.

[Online] Available at http://allafrica.com/stories/printable/200402050214.html.

International Crisis Group. 2004. *Northern Uganda: Understanding and Solving the Conflict.* ICG Africa Report No. 77. Nairobi/Brussels: ICG, 14 April.

International Crisis Group. 2005. *Shock Therapy for Northern Uganda's Peace Process.* ICG African Policy Briefing No. 23. Nairobi/Brussels: ICG, 11 April.

IRIN (United Nations Integrated Regional Information Networks). 2004a. 'Uganda: The 18 year old that refuses to go away.' 28 January. [Online] http://allafrica.com/stories/printable/200401280410.html.

IRIN. 2004b. 'Uganda: Peace groups and government officials worried about the ICC probe into the LRA.' 30 January. [Online] Available at http://allafrica.com/stories/printable/200401300047.htlm.

Mulumba, Badru D. 2004. 'Museveni rejects World Court UPDF probe', *The Monitor*, 5 March. [Online] Available at: http://www.monitor.co.ug/news03054.php.

Musinguzi, Bamuturaki. 2004. 'Amnesty Group Rejects ICC Trial of Kony Rebels.' *The East African* 16 February, [Online].

Robertson, Geoffrey. 2002. *Crimes against Humanity: The Struggle for Global Justice.* Harmondsworth: Penguin Books.

Ross, Willy. 2003. 'Uganda army in "rights abuses",' BBC News Online, 16 July. Available at http://news.bbc.co.uk/go/pr/fr/-/1/hi/world/africa/3071421.stm.

Ryan, Orla and Nabusayi Lynda Wamboka. 2004. 'Museveni blames the UN for unending war.' *The Monitor* 25 February. [Online] Available at www.monitor.co.ug/news/news02257.php.

Sadat, Leila Nadya. 2002. *The International Criminal Court and the Transformation of International Law: Justice for the New Millenium.* Ardsley, NY: Transnational Publishers Inc.

Schabas, W.A. 2000. *Genocide in International Law.* Cambridge: Cambridge University Press.

Scharf, Michael P. 1999. 'The Amnesty Exception to the Jurisdiction of the International Criminal Court', *Cornell International Law Journal* 32 (507) [Online] Available in LEXIS-NEXIS Library.

Shaw, Malcolm. 1997. *International Law.* 4th edn Cambridge: Cambridge University Press.

Simba, Kayunga Sallie. 2000. 'The Impact of Armed Opposition on the Movement System', in Justus Magaju and J. Oloka Onyango. eds, *No-Party Democracy in Uganda: Myths and Realities,* Kampala: Fountain Publishers: 109–26.

The ICC (2004). *Background information on the situation in Uganda* [Online] Available at: http://www.icc-cpi.int/php/show.php?id=bginfo.

The Monitor. 2003. 'Museveni snubs UN hand in Kony war.' 13 February.

The Monitor. 2004. 'Rebels massacre 192 in Lira Camp.' 23 February. [Online] Available at: http://allafrica.com/stories/printable/200402130105.html.

The New Vision. 2004a. 'General Museveni orders Abia Death probe.' [Online] Available at: http://allafrica.com/stories/printable/200402090693.html. 9 February.

The New Vision. 2004b. 'Genesis Of Barlonyo Massacre'[Online] Available at: http://www.newvision.co.ug/ D/8/13/344422. 5 March.

The Sunday Monitor 27 April 2003: 8.

Tindifa, Samuel. 2004. 'The ICC and the Lords Resistance Army Insurgency in Northern Uganda: A Commentary.' (Personal communication) (On file with the author).

Westcott, Kathryn 2003. 'Sex slavery awaits Ugandan Schoolgirls,' BBC News Online, 25 June. Available at: http://newsvote.bbc.co.uk/mpapps/pagetools/print/news.bbc.co.uk/1/hi/world/a...

Wexler, Leila Sadat. 1999. 'A First Look at the 1998 Rome Statute for a Permanent International Criminal Court: Jurisdiction, Definition of Crimes, Structure and Referrals to the Court', in Cherif Bassiouni. ed., *International Criminal Law*, Vol. II. New York: Transnational Publishers, 655–91.

Women's Commission on Refugee Women and Children. 2001. *Against All Odds: Surviving the War on Adolescents, Promoting the Protection and Capacity of Ugandan and Sudanese Adolescents in Northern Uganda.* New York: Women's Commission on Refugee Women and Children.

Notes

1 ICC Press Release, ' President of Uganda refers situation concerning the Lord's Resistance Army (LRA) to the ICC', available at: http://www.icc-cpi.int/pressrelease_details&id= 16.html.
2 In accordance with Articles 13(a), and 14(1) of the Rome Statute of the International Criminal Court (1998) (*hereinafter* 'The Rome Statute (1998').
3 For example, it is reported that these forces massacred 40 civilians in former Head of State Tito Okello's village of Namokora, Kitgum District. Many Acholi and others believe that the NRA chose not to use its disciplined forces in the North, sending instead the most brutal and unruly elements of the 35th battalion, in a deliberate strategy of revenge and subjugation. Simba (2000) has noted that the conduct of the 35th Battalion re-inforced UPDM/A propaganda to the effect that the NRA, a southern army, was plotting to kill all male Acholi, leaving those men with no alternative but to defend themselves and their community.
4 The LRA has changed its name a number of times. It started as the Lord's Salvation Army (LSA), then it became the United Salvation Christian Army (USCA), and then finally LRA in 1994. For a detailed background about the group and the rebel movements in northern Uganda, see Human Rights Watch (2003a); Behrend (1998).
5 See *infra* for details on ARLPI.
6 The *Sunday Monitor*, 27 April 2003, p. 8.
7 The other districts that make up the Teso region are Kumi, Pallisa and Kaberamaido.
8 Human Rights Watch 2003a.
9 Ibid.
10 Ibid.
11 Article 2(7) of the UN Charter.
12 Museveni has been quoted as saying that he does not favor UN intervention in the conflict in northern Uganda.
13 Paragraph 10 of the preamble of the Rome Statute (1998) emphasizes that the ICC shall be complementary to national criminal jurisdictions. Again in Article 1 of the Statute it is emphasized that the Court '... shall be complementary to national criminal juris-dictions'.
14 Article 17(1) of the Rome Statute (1998).
15 Human Rights Watch (2003b, 2003c) has discovered that the LRA has committed widespread abuses against civilians in northern Uganda, including child abductions, summary executions, torture, rape and sexual assault, forced labor and mutilations.
16 Article 5(1) of the Rome Statute (1998).
17 Article 5 of the Rome Statute.
18 Article 11(1) of the Rome Statute.
19 *R v Bow Street Metropolitan Stipendiary Magistrate and Others, ex parte Pinochet Ugarte (no. 3)* [1999] 2 WLR 827, p. 841.
20 Article 6(c) of the Charter for the establishment of the International Military Tribunal (IMT) at Nuremberg, annexed to the London Agreement of 8 August 1945, reprinted in Cherif M. Bassiouni, ed., *International Criminal Law: Enforcement,* 2nd edn, Vol. 111, Ardsley, NY: Transnational Publishers, Inc, 1999, pp. 69–71.
21 Article 5 of the Statute of the International Tribunal for the Prosecution of Persons Responsible for Serious Violations of International Humanitarian Law in the Territory of the Former Yugoslavia, 1993.
22 Article 3 of the Statute of the International Criminal Tribunal for Rwanda, 1995.
23 Article 7(1)(a-k) of the Rome Statute (1998).
24 Article 7(2)(a-i) of the Rome Statute (1998).
25 Article 8 (2)(a) (i-viii) of the Rome Statute (1998).
26 Article 3 common to the Geneva Conventions of 1949 states that, in case of armed conflict not of an international character occurring in the territory of one of the High Contracting Parties, each Party to the conflict shall be bound to apply, as a minimum, the following provisions:
   1 Persons taking no active part in the hostilities, including members of armed forces

who have laid down their arms and those placed *hors de combat* by sickness, wounds, detention, or any other cause, shall in all circumstances be treated humanely, without any adverse distinction founded on race, colour, religion or faith, sex, birth or wealth, or any other similar criteria. To this end, the following acts are and shall remain prohibited at any time and in any place whatsoever with respect to the above-mentioned persons:

a) violence to life and person, in particular murder of all kinds, mutilation, cruel treatment and torture;

b) taking of hostages;

c) outrages upon personal dignity, in particular humiliating and degrading treatment;

d) the passing of sentences and the carrying out of executions without previous judgment pronounced by a regularly constituted court, affording all the judicial guarantees which are recognized as indispensable by civilized peoples.

2 The wounded and sick shall be collected and catered for. An impartial humanitarian body, such as the International Committee of the Red Cross, may offer its services to the Parties to the Conflict.

The Parties to the conflict should further endeavor to bring into force, by means of special agreement, all or part of the other provisions of the present Convention.

The application of the preceding provisions shall not affect the legal status of the Parties to the conflict.

There is no doubt that this provision applies to the LRA insurgency in northern Uganda.

27 Article 8(2)(c)(i-iv) of the Rome Statute (1998).

28 Article 8(2)(e)(i-xii) of the Rome Statute (1998).

29 In the worst massacre to date, in 1995, the LRA butchered 240 civilians at Atiak, Gulu District in a single day.

30 ICC Office of Prosecutor, Statement by the Prosecutor related to crimes committed in Barlonya camp in Uganda, 23 February 2004, available at: http://www.icc-cpi.int/press/pressreleases/78.html

31 This figure was given by President Museveni when addressing a press conference in Kampala at which he explained the genesis of the Barlonyo massacre. See *The New Vision* (2004b). It has been corroborated by humanitarian agencies operating in the region.

32 This description was given by John Baptist Odama, the Catholic Archbishop of Gulu Diocese. He said that 962,000 IDPs were living in 62 camps spread around the Acholi sub-region in unhygienic and inhuman conditions. Cited in Human Rights Watch 2003a.

33 According to reports, over 85% of the LRA forces are made up of children. As part of initiation into the rebel movement, abducted children are forced into committing inhuman acts, including ritual killing and mutilations. In order to evade capture, thousands of children have become 'night dwellers', walking considerable distances to regroup in centers run by non-governmental organizations, on the streets, on shop verandas, in church grounds, and in local factories, heading back to their villages at dawn. See the ICC, 'Background Information on the situation in Northern Uganda', available at: http://icc-cpi.int/php/show.php?id=bginfo.

34 Older female captives are forced to become wives of senior soldiers or are given as sexual rewards for obedient boy soldiers. See ibid.

35 Estimates put the number of his wives at 60. See Westcott (2003).

36 Article 4(3) (c) of Protocol Additional to the Geneva Conventions of 12 August 1949 and Relating to the Protection of Victims of Non-International Armed Conflicts (1977).

37 Article 8(2)(e)(vii) of the Rome Statute (1998).

38 Article 4(1) of the Optional Protocol to the Convention on the Rights of the Child in Armed Conflict (2000) states that, 'Armed groups that are distinct from the armed forces of the state should not, under any circumstances, recruit or use in hostilities persons under the age of 18'.

39 Articles 7(1)(g); 8(2)(b)(xxii); 8(2)(e)(vi) and 8(2)(c)(ii) of the Rome Statute (1998).

40 Also Article 8(2)(c)(i) of the Rome Statute (1998) would apply here.

41 President Museveni has rejected these accusations outright. He says that people who are accusing his army are 'supporters of terrorists'. However, elsewhere, he has blamed some parents who lie about their children's ages, just to get them into the army ranks so as to earn a salary, see Mulumba (2004). The Army Spokesman, Major Shaban Bantariza, has dismissed these accusations by calling them, 'rain in the desert'. See Ross (2003).

42 Human Rights Watch (2003b) cites an example of a boy who was badly tortured under interrogation by the Uganda Army about his LRA activities. When he was asked if he wanted to join the army he was threatened: 'If not, you will stay in this prison forever'. See Ross (2003).

43 Article 8(2)(e)(vii) of the Rome Statute (1998).

44 Article 77(2) (2) of the Protocol Additional to the Geneva Conventions of August 12, 1949 and Relating to the Protection of Victims of International Armed Conflicts of 1977 states, 'States Parties shall take all feasible measures to ensure that persons who have not attained the age of 15 years do not take a direct part in hostilities.'; Article 77(2)(3) states, 'States Parties shall refrain from recruiting any person who has not attained the age of 15 years into their armed forces...'.

45 Article 4(3)(c) of the Protocol Additional to the Geneva Conventions of August 12, 1949 and Relating to the Protection of Victims of Non-International Armed Conflicts (1977) states that, 'Children who have not attained the age of fifteen years shall neither be recruited in the armed forces or groups nor allowed to take part in hostilities'.

46 It did so on 6 May 2000.

47 Article 2 of the Optional Protocol to the Convention on the Rights of the Child on the Involvement of Children in Armed Conflict (2000) defines a child as 'anyone below the age of 18 without exception'.

48 Article 3(2) of the Optional Protocol to the Convention on the Rights of the Child on the Involvement of Children in Armed Conflict (2000) states that, 'Each State Party shall deposit a binding declaration upon ... accession to the present Protocol that sets forth the minimum age at which it will permit voluntary recruitment into its national armed forces and a description of the safeguards it has adopted to ensure that such recruitment is not forced or coerced'.

49 Binding Declaration deposited with the UN Secretary General at Uganda's accession to the Optional Protocol, 6 May 2000. Cited in, Human Rights Watch (2003b).

50 Article 4 (2) of the Optional Protocol to the Convention on the Rights of the Child on the Involvement of Children in Armed Conflict (2000).

51 Article 6(3) states that 'States Parties shall take all feasible measures to ensure that persons within their jurisdiction recruited or used in hostilities contrary to the present Protocol are demobilized or otherwise released from service. States Parties shall, when necessary, accord to such persons all appropriate assistance for their physical and psychological recovery and their social reintegration.'

52 Article 22(2) of the African Charter on the Rights and Welfare of the Child (1990), OAU Doc. CAB/LEG/24.9/49 (1990).

53 Human Rights Watch (2003a).

54 Ibid. See also ARLPI Official website at, http://acholipeace.org., for more documentation detailing the rapes.

55 Ibid. See also Human Rights Watch (2003a).

56 ICTR, *Prosecutor v Akayesu case*, 37 I.L.M 1399 (1998).

57 See Christian Aid, 'Background to the Crisis', at http://www.christianaid.org.uk/uganda/background.htm.

58 Human Rights Watch (2003a). Also see Ross (2003).

59 See especially Article 1(1) which defines torture.

60 Case No: IT-95-17/1-T (1998), Reproduced in 38 I.L.M 317 (1999), para. 154.

61 See Tindifa (2004) See also International Crisis Group (2004), p. 11, noting that the army wanted to have Father Carlos Rodriguez, a member of the Acholi Religious Leaders Peace Initiative (ARLPI), deported after he made a number of claims about the army's operations in this camp.

62 This seems also to be the view of Samuel Tindifa of the Human Rights and Peace Center (HURIPEC) of the Faculty of Law at Makerere University, Kampala. He suggests that 'the ICC should join the diplomatic bandwagon to put pressure on both parties to come to a negotiated settlement.' Personal communication, on file with the author.

63 Archbishop Odama has argued that Kony, the LRA leader, is committing crimes and the UPDF is committing crimes. The ICC should therefore investigate both. In Odama's view, President Museveni should accept the argument that, since both sides are committing crimes, the government should not invoke the ICC probe. See Mulumba (2004).

64 Uganda Anti-Terrorism Act 2001, schedule 1. Under this law, the LRA and another rebel group called the Allied Democratic Forces (ADF), which has now been defeated by the

Museveni government, were declared terrorist organizations. Any person dealing with them commits a criminal offence.

65 It has been observed that, although the issue of amnesty was raised at the Rome Diplomatic Conference, no clear consensus developed among the delegates as to how the question should be resolved. According to the Chairman of the Conference, the question was purposely left open by the framers, while the Statute does not condone the use of amnesties by its terms; presumably the Prosecutor has the authority to accept them if doing so would be in the interest of justice. See Sadat (2002: 67).

66 Vienna Convention on the Law of Treaties 1969, Article 31(1).

67 Article 53(1) of the Rome Statute (1998).

68 Article 53(1)(c) of the Rome Statute (1998).

69 Article 53(1) of the Rome Statute (1998).

70 The government extended the ceasefire up to 22 February 2005, to give the rebels a chance to assemble in the ceasefire area and wait for the rebel leaders and the government team to sign the Peace Talks Memorandum. *The New Vision*, 19 February 2005. See story, 'Museveni extends LRA ceasefire to February 22', available at: http://allafrica.com/stories/printable/200502210292.html.

71 Betty Bigombe was a Minister of State for the Pacification of northern Uganda in the Museveni government up to 1996. Having failed to become a Member of Parliament for Gulu Municipality after the 1996 parliamentary elections, she left to work for the World Bank in New York. Bigombe was appointed chief mediator by the government; her position was rendered redundant by the Juba talks in 2006.

5

How to Make Democracy Work?
Local Government & the Beneficial & Destructive Potential of Social Capital in Post-Apartheid South Africa

URSULA SCHEIDEGGER

Social capital is a widely discussed concept, and a multitude of approaches assess its meaning, qualities and usefulness differently. In certain circles, social capital is considered not only a critical factor in facilitating and sustaining development efforts but also the variable explaining democratic performance, because empirical evidence suggests a correlation between levels of social capital, good governance and economic development. Post-apartheid South Africa is no exception and the promotion of social capital in communities and local government structures is highly valued as a critical facilitator of progress. This paper argues that social capital is an ambiguous resource in segmented societies such as South Africa, because, among competing social structures, networks do not necessarily promote the common good but also particular interests not conducive to democratization and development. The paper examines three local government wards that cut across former segregation boundaries and include parts of Alexandra Township and its adjacent areas in a context where local government is not only an important agent of development and redistribution but also a structure providing for popular participation.

Social Capital – The Context Matters

Robert Putnam initiated the current debate on social capital by developing a theoretical framework to explain successful democratic dispensations in his seminal book *Making Democracy Work*: social capital is the variable explaining democratic institutional performance and the key to making democracy work (Putnam et al. 1993: 185). For Putnam, social capital is intrinsic to social functioning because it enables people to cooperate and achieve a common purpose. He therefore emphasizes the importance of a rich and vibrant associational life in shaping democratic structures based on continuing relationships of exchange between the state, communities, and citizens (ibid.: 63).

Levels of social capital are reflected in the density of social networks and associations and the degree to which people associate regularly with each other in these settings based on relative equality, trust, reciprocity and group-specific values (Hall 2002: 22). Associations and social networks are considered to contribute decisively to the development of citizen skills, political attitudes and participation, because civil society is involved in a wide variety of public and quasi-public functions such as charity, sports, education or neighbourhood activities. In addition, civil society has a representative function. Interest groups or associations promote the demands and concerns of individual citizens and civil society stimulates public debate and potentially exerts pressure on the government (Foley and Edwards 1998: 12). Thus, the success of democratic governments is related to the nature of civil society.

However, societies in modern states include a variety of people, and there are differences between the affluent and the poor, ethnic and racial groups, dominant and marginalized groups, and political winners and losers. Perceptions of personal realities depend on socio-economic positions, minority status, religion or age group, and they are more pessimistic among disadvantaged groups such as the less educated, low-income earners, marginalized and discriminated groups, crime victims, those in poor health and the unemployed (Foley and Edwards 1999:153). No form of capital is evenly distributed, and access to all forms of capital depends on one's social location, because social networks differ enormously in terms of ties, relations, social positions and the resources they are able to access (ibid.: 164).

The democratic aspect of social capital lies in the indispensability of networks to mediate between citizens and the state, and in the political realm social capital provides the necessary structural settings for interactions with the state. However, social networks are not necessarily democratic and might serve not only collective but also particular interests, and they can promote or constrain public participation. In addition, social networks also mirror and reproduce societal power relations, to the disadvantage of, for example, women, minorities or poorly educated people (Molyneux 2002:181), because values, norms and beliefs that influence social interactions are passed down from generation to generation in hierarchical structures such as religion or tradition with little bargaining space (McLean et al. 2002: 10).

The cooperation between unequal partners is a problem and tends to be dominated by the better equipped. In addition, beneficiaries of a particular political and socio-economic order do not have much in common with less privileged groups (Fried 2002:31). Collective decision-making processes are more difficult, because citizens in segmented societies are affected by these decisions in very different ways (Uslaner 2002: 255). There are incentives for the disadvantaged to challenge the existing order that is defended by those benefiting from it (Boix and Posner 1998: 688). Civil society is thus a space of competing interests where power is contested. It is not only a foundation of democratic governance, but is also potentially subversive to political arrangements (Whittington 1998:24). Within competing social structures the nature of public goods is contested and different social groups place a variety of demands on the state (Foley and Edwards 1999: 155).

South Africa's first democratic election marked the formal end of apartheid. However, the social, economic and political transformation is incomplete. Even if the new political and social order is widely accepted, values, beliefs, perceptions of other population groups and prejudices are more resilient to change and remain a latent source of conflict. The new government faces enormous challenges in addressing three patterns of fragmentation with different expressions of inequality: racial segregation, socioeconomic class divisions and multicultural disparities (Smith 2003: 18). In addition, the political transformation created a climate of uncertainty, an asymmetric distribution of risks and benefits and high emotions, because transition processes are characterized by a loss of trust, rising levels of intolerance, the struggle for power and popular mobilization around a variety of demands and grievances (Diani 2001: 209). The former social and political system increasingly lost legitimacy and, as a consequence, new values and belief systems were shaped. Changing hierarchies and positions of influence and power emerged in response to the new political and social order.

Due to the magnitude of inequality and insufficient economic growth, gains made by one group are at the expense of another. Thus, the new social, economic and political system does not work for everyone and is contested by new groups of dissidents, whose common experiences of opposition to mainstream society generate solidarity in response to lacking opportunities and social recognition (Portes 1998: 17). Discrimination, marginalization and exclusion are a fertile ground for anti-social behaviour, and social capital becomes a disruptive force, because social ties and networks that are not embedded in society advance particular interest at considerable cost (Woolcock 1998: 162).

Beneficial & Destructive Forms of Social Capital

The value of social capital depends not only on the societal context but also on forms of social capital, because a high density of social networks is not necessarily an indicator of democratic structures and the quality of relations between the state, institutions and civil society. Determinants of beneficial forms of social capital are networks cutting across social divisions and favoring public goods in contrast to narrow, particular forms promoting individual or exclusive group interests. In the South African context, it is not only a critical question how to generate and sustain beneficial manifestations of social capital but also how to contain or eliminate the destructive ones.

Trust is an important feature of social capital and it is considered to facilitate human interactions. As a cultural and moral resource, trust informally influences modes of cooperation. The absence of trust limits mutually beneficial relations. Nevertheless, trusting behavior also increases vulnerability to someone whose response cannot be controlled (Coleman 1990: 100). Considering the risks involved, the generation of trust takes time.

Trust is based on assumptions and beliefs members of society have about each other, in particular that other people share the same fundamental values and therefore adhere to common social arrangements. Trust is an egalitarian ideal, because taking the moral claims of other people seriously is only possible among people of the same moral community (ibid.: 2). The inclusiveness of moral communities is a critical factor, because people tend to have more trust in those like themselves who come from a similar socio-cultural context and are likely to share the same values (Uslaner 2002: 32). However, high levels of trust within particular, exclusive demographic groups come at the expense of trust between people of unrelated groups (Fukuyama 1995: 92). In contrast, inclusive more generalized forms of trust are an important condition for the adoption of cooperative values such as tolerance and solidarity. Tolerance values differences between people as a source and not a threat, and is reflected in the willingness to accom-modate other people's preferences (Simone 2002:302). Solidarity promotes awareness of the interdependence of all social groups and is an important condition of a more egalitarian society (Offe 2000: 6).

Liberal democracy is a highly demanding form of political organization and is no guarantee of trust. On the contrary, liberal democracies developed as a result of distrust in traditional or clerical authority and aimed at reducing the discretionary powers implied by trust relations; more democracy meant less trust in authorities (Warren 1999: 1). However, democracy works poorly in a divided society since people have particular preferences and prejudices, distrust others and act in isolation from each other (Warren 1996: 242).

Trust, tolerance and solidarity are important features of liberal democ-racies. Firstly, it is not only necessary to limit the power of rulers, but also between citizens regulations are necessary, because personal freedom might conflict with other individuals' freedom. Tolerance helps to overcome fears that anyone might abuse personal liberty at the expense of others (Offe 2000: 4). Secondly, anyone bound by democratic laws should also be involved in the creation of laws. This qualification excludes many people lacking representation in the legislature, and results in fears that democratic enfranchisement of representatives is used to promote particular demands or interests. Trust is critical to overcome tensions between desirable and frightening aspects of sovereignty (ibid.: 5). Finally, the institutionalization of welfare and social security is necessary to protect people from negative exposure to economic forces and to reduce levels of inequality. Solidarity enables people to overcome fears of social programmes being abused (ibid.: 6).

The distribution of income is a critical factor for the generation of cooperative values and inclusive, more generalized forms of trust, because economic inequality and the competition for resources and opportunities are divisive and limit cooperation. A social and economic environment that is precarious and unpredictable prevents high levels of trust. In addition, economic conditions together with levels of education influence perceptions of personal realities and an optimistic or pessimistic perspective on life. If people believe that improvement is possible, that they have choices and can control their environment, they are more likely to trust other people. Optimism is linked to agency, empowerment and the confidence to shape one's world, and is conducive to political participation (Uslaner 1999: 138). In contrast, pessimists distrust others; they presume that people are likely to take advantage of them, and consider cooperation outside their particular group a risk (Uslaner 2002: 80). People from extremely different socio-economic contexts do not have much in common; their associational life is not only segregated but also perceptions of injustice reinforce negative stereotypes, which prevent trust and incentives for cooperation (Boix and Posner 1998: 693). History, state ideologies, worldviews, socialization, personal experiences and emotional aspects shape the appreciation of other groups. Social capital emanates from these social relations, and in segmented societies not only fault lines but also collective reputation and social barriers have developed over time. Levels of generalized trust and the propensity for cooperation tend to be lower among populations historically discriminated against and economically disadvantaged groups. Consequently, the powerful, well informed and affluent can afford to trust in contrast to the less privileged who may suffer from the breakdown of trust relations (Offe 1999: 9). Thus, there is a strong correlation between equitable income dispersion and high levels of beneficial social capital (Uslaner 2002: 181).

Furthermore, the credibility of government influences civic behavior; continuity and reliability provide for stability and predictable social, economic and political arrangements. Institutions are important agents for regulating social relations in a transparent, consistent and unbiased way, enabling cooperation and trust within complex societies (Levi 1996: 51). Social cohesion and stability depend on the capacity of the state to mediate between competing social structures in order to lessen disparities and to strengthen social interactions and cooperation.

Political and institutional arrangements shape the context of civic activities by stimulating and sustaining the involvement and participation of civil society; decentralization is a current trend in political reform processes. Nevertheless, also in democratic dispensations the question arises as to whether participation is so attractive that people are willing to commit themselves. Often in democracies space for participation is narrow and agency-constrained, and opportunities to make a difference seem rare (Warren 1996: 243). The state has a critical role in motivating and facilitating participation, because civil society needs agency and politics have to be relevant for citizens (Newton 1997: 580).

In segmented societies, it is an important function of the state to act as unbiased facilitator and mediator. Social cleavages are reflected in strong networks and particular groups furthering their own interests in competition for resources and power. Inequality promotes and sustains these networks, which often oppose development or democratization efforts because they are a threat to privilege (Nordlund 1996: 74). If a state's political institutions are capable of providing reasonable economic conditions for all and addressing grievances properly, then civil society is interested in sustaining social and political arrangements. In contrast, for dissatisfied citizens and neglected minorities, who perceive the state as an ineffective, useless or illegitimate institution, civil society becomes an alternative, and their associations and networks undermine political stability and deepen social cleavages (Berman 1997: 569).

State capacity influences political arrangements and the space for popular participation, but is also constrained by economic forces outside its control (Harriss and De Renzio 1997: 926). As long as economic inequalities are increasing, civil society is a space of contestation, and in societies torn by conflicting interests the meaning of social capital becomes more complicated (Fine 1999: 14). The socio-economic and political context in which social capital is embedded shapes the way social assets are distributed and managed, and determines the value of social capital as a beneficial force reflected in a shared development vision and the awareness of the interdependence of all social groups (Foley and Edwards 1999: 146).

Political Participation & Development in Post-Apartheid South Africa – Trying to Make Democracy Work[2]

The three local government wards discussed in this study belong to the administrative Region 7 of Johannesburg's metropolitan area; Ward 81 and Ward 109 have Democratic Alliance (DA) councillors and Ward 92 has an African National Congress (ANC) councillor. In order to assess levels of social capital, different social structures and networks were examined and interviews conducted with the three Ward Councillors and three Proportional Representative Councillors (PRs) assigned to the wards. Both parties, the ANC and DA, have local ward branches, and interviews were conducted with the respective representatives. In addition, administrative support structures from the regional administration and the Alexandra Renewal Project (ARP) were approached. Community organizations included churches, Community Policing Forums (CPFs) and participatory structures in schools. The interviews for this study were qualitative and semi-structured and were based on open questions, which allowed interview partners to include whatever they considered important. All interviews were conducted in English. The study did not seek to obtain a representative sample.

The destructive and unjust nature of apartheid policies is reflected in detrimental economic and social consequences. More than 18 million South Africans, or 45 per cent of the population, live below the poverty line. Income distribution between different income groups has changed to the disadvantage of the poorest 40 per cent of households (Terreblanche 2002:31). In 1995, the Gini coefficient was 0.596; it rose to 0.635 in 2001, an indication that income inequality has worsened (UNDP 2003:43). The extent of poverty is frightening: The poorest quintile shares 1.5 per cent of total income compared with the richest quintile which aggregates 65 per cent (Marais 2001:193).

Living conditions are difficult in Alexandra Township, a historic neighborhood of African freehold settlement in northern Johannesburg. The end of the pass laws brought an influx of people to Alexandra, exacerbating the already precarious shortage of houses. At the end of apartheid, there were fifty times more people per square hectare in Alexandra than in neighboring affluent Sandton and four times more than in Soweto. Unemployment, violence and crime levels are high. The infrastructure is inadequate and service delivery a problem (Mayekiso 1996: 157). In this context, local government has a critical role of rebuilding the local community as the democratic and non-discriminatory society's basic unit (Republic of South Africa 1998). Local governments are closest to people and hence have to develop strategies that engage and interact with citizens and business and community groups. There is a strong linkage between development and democracy; at the local level, control over political processes is enhanced, which enforces accountability. Integrated development planning and local government reform aim at overcoming the legacies of the past, but in a context of prevailing spatial, socio-economic and cultural divisions, the nature of the public good is contested. This study examines how the different population groups in Ward 81, Ward 92, and Ward 109 communicate, interact and face the challenges of spatial, socio-economic and cultural integration; it assesses relations with the government and its administration and it looks at the cooperation towards shared development goals.

Judith Nxumalo, Operational Manager Council Liaison and Support in Region 7, states: 'integration is a challenge because people come from different socio-cultural backgrounds. There are community participatory efforts and there is good will to work together, but it is a process and a question of time. Expectations and development priorities are not the same for all population groups and areas' (Nxumalo interview, 2003).

It is difficult to overcome spatial segregation because the violence at the beginning of the 1990s and high levels of crime contribute to the negative image of Alexandra and the reluctance of outsiders to enter the township. However, the Spatial Development Framework of the Alexandra Renewal Project (ARP) promotes integration because the geographic separation still translates into racial segregation. Improved road linkages through Alexandra aim at opening up the township to the wider community for public and private transport routes (Letter interview, 2003). Nobody moves from former white areas into Alexandra. In contrast, areas bordering the township have an increasing number of former Alexandra residents and the number of black residents is high, in some areas between 80 and 90 per cent. It seems that white residents tend to leave the area as the number of black residents increases. David Mills, a DA member, argues that 'problems arise because black house owners rent their houses to many residents, one family per room, which results in overcrowded one family houses and the value of houses in the neighbourhood drops. Also street trading is taking over, and it affects shopping centres because parking space is used for informal structures' (Mills interview, 2003).

In general, the administration of Region 7 considers demographically mixed neighborhoods relaxed, and integration seems unproblematic. However, communities outside Alexandra are more reserved, and communication is different from Alexandra; people outside have less time to socialize in their neighbourhood (Nxumalo, interview, 2003). Contacts with neighbors are less personal and more instrumental, for example, to borrow something. The trend is for people who can afford it to move out of Alexandra into adjacent areas. There is still a considerable influx of urban migrants into Alexandra. Migrants and residents of Alexandra are black and many are unemployed and poor (Madondo interview, 2003).

In wards cutting across former segregation boundaries cooperation is difficult. Not all groups within the ward attend meetings; the areas are still separated, and it takes time to develop a culture of visiting each other, between groups that were forced not to interact at all. Alexandra residents do not attend meetings outside the township and outside residents are not coming to the township. It will take time for people to see themselves as a community (Chuene interview, 2003).

Many people consider churches places of integration. During apartheid churches were locations where people of all races and from different backgrounds could meet. Various South African denominations participated in the liberation struggle and their proclaimed ideals of freedom, dignity and human rights applied to everybody; church congregations and their ideals cut across social boundaries. According to Father Makhalemele from the Anglican Church in Alexandra, white people came to worship in the township until the violence erupted at the beginning of the 1990s (Makhalemele interview, 2003). However, in post-apartheid South Africa parish boundaries are still along former segregation boundaries; in addition, services of the Methodist Church, for example, are in indigenous languages (Madibo interview, 2003).

St. Catherine's in Bramley is a parish of the Anglican Church in the vicinity of Alexandra and according to Reverend Lynn Wyngaard, the number of black worshippers is increasing; however, they are people who have moved into the area. Alexandra residents are working-class and would have problems with a middle-class, literate congregation. St Catherine's has outreach programs in the township and the soup kitchen attracts many people from Alexandra (Wyngaard interview, 2003).

Schools in Alexandra have only an insignificant number of pupils coming from the township's surroundings. They are all children of domestic workers. In contrast, schools located outside Alexandra have a considerable number of pupils from Alexandra. There are no barriers between pupils and they socialize with each other irrespective of race and religion, visiting their friends at home or inviting them for afternoon activities or sleepovers. Alexandra pupils visit the homes of friends outside the township; however, pupils living outside Alexandra usually do not visit their friends in the township, unless they have family connections and know the environment. For birthday parties, some pupils from Alexandra invite their friends to a location outside the township, for example to McDonald's or to watch a movie (De Oliveira, Fargher, Rocky and Smith interview, 2003).

Crime affects everyone irrespective of race, and all population groups are concerned with security and crime prevention. Community Policing Forums (CPFs) are based on cooperation between the police and the population, and therefore help to improve the still historically strained relationship between them. People from different social backgrounds can get involved and contribute proactively to a safe and productive social environment. However, CPF boundaries run along old segregation lines separating Alexandra and its adjacent areas. Furthermore, crime affects trust. The general assumption is that the vicinity of Alexandra is heavily affected by crime and that perpetrators come from the township. Perceptions of crime are false because the kingpins of organized crime related to criminal syndicates are usually not black. It is important to break down these racially based prejudices because they prevent social integration (Stein interview, 2003).

In addition to the spatial segregation, a further challenge is to overcome socio-economic disparities Edwin Mokgwatsana (interview, 2003), Strategic Adviser of the Regional Director, states:

> everyone agrees upon the necessity to catch up with development deficits in Alexandra but in reality nobody is willing to contribute. People in former white areas complain about the Region's resource distribution. They argue that only Alexandra benefits and that the infrastructure is decaying in adjacent areas. There are widespread prejudices such as the assumption that all administrative personnel or at least Blacks in the administration are African National Congress (ANC) members favouring their constituency. As a matter of fact, more than 85 per cent of the region's population lives in Alexandra. People continue to challenge the administration and government in stereotypical ways; they are still trapped in the old order and, for example, local government is considered to be corrupt.

This perception cuts across racial boundaries.

Income distribution is a primary factor of social segmentation. For example, according to Councillor Chuene (interview 2003), there are extreme differences in living standards in Ward 92 and the past still affects relations; there are concerns about vulnerable population groups. However, the sharing of wealth is a difficult issue. Resources are limited and wealthier groups are reluctant to give up their privileges. There are also differences in living standards between black communities in the ward. The settlement in Klippfontein contains Reconstruction and Development Program (RDP) low-cost houses, which were provided to the poor, whereas Mayibuye has 'bond houses' for wealthier people. As a result, Mayibuye residents put up a fence to prevent negative externalities of the RDP settlement in their vicinity (Madondo interview, 2003).

The churches in Alexandra received donations from more affluent outside communities, but the ministers from the Methodist Church and the Rhema Ministries claim that charity is declining. However, in both churches activities concentrate around, and are dominated by, the respective clerics. The resultant lack of transparency might be a reason for the declining donations from outside. In contrast, the Anglican Church in the diocese of Johannesburg has five parishes, one of them Alexandra with the only black cleric. The other parishes involve wealthy communities and 'they donate a lot'. The church in Alexandra works also together with the state's welfare services. Five social workers are based at the Anglican Church Community Centre and are paid by the Department of Welfare (Makhalemele interview, 2003).

Socio-cultural integration is a further challenge in wards where boundaries cut through former social networks and, as DA councillors argue, it cuts them apart. Human beings do not work like that; they need time to adapt. Because of the different cultural background, there is a lack of integration. On the other hand, there are also common concerns affecting everyone, for example crime, safety, the economy, job creation and education. To raise standards of living is a necessary condition for true social integration; currently, there is still a lot of distrust and no common caring and tolerance between the different population groups (Wolder, Heim interviews, 2003). For example, residents' organizations outside Alexandra are mainly concerned with road closures, which polarize the population. Whites are mistrustful because they think that Blacks commit most violent crimes. Whites tend to see Blacks as 'all being the same'. They do not differentiate between good and bad people. There is a need for the white and black population to be assisted with integration and trust building; it would be a major social engineering project (Topic interview, 2003).

People tend to look after their own interest in a context of limited resources and opportunities, and uncertainty enforces imaginary boundaries. Heim (interview, 2003) argues 'the less one knows about others the less one trusts each other. Despite more interactions between different social groups, people are still suspicious about the unknown, in particular because of the high incidence of crime.' There are also doubts that integration is possible, because the history of the different social groups is 'utterly different' and questions the possibility of bridging these cultural divides. For example, there are a lot of complaints along the former segregation line. In particular, the residents of an Old Age Home often feel intimidated by music and other noise from the nearby recreation area, where black residents are celebrating in their different ways. It is difficult to find a compromise, and this conflict contributes to further polarization (Topic interview, 2003).

The councillor in Ward 109 considered it an opportunity that the ward boundaries cut across former segregated areas, and tried to encourage the cooperation between different population groups under the motto 'Breaking Down Barriers', but this initiative was a disappointing experience. Apparently whites disengage from political processes and are not willing to give time or resources to disadvantaged areas. The main organizational problem is that people from outside do not go into the township, even if transport is provided, because white people are afraid of the township. Planned activities were boycotted; for example, visits from schools outside Alexandra to schools in the township or from Alexandra to schools outside. The ward has two structures: Alexandra residents and those from outside (Fuchs interview, 2003).

The relationship between the government, the administration and the population is important, and it depends on institutional arrangements that provide space for political agency and regulate social relations in a transparent, unbiased, and consistent way. This is difficult in a situation where people are still trapped in stereotypical perceptions and prejudices. Participation is stimulated by politics that are relevant for people, and the perception that agency and community involvement can make a difference.

DA members claim that, since they have little common ground with the ANC, they are sidelined and practically all their suggestions are dismissed. In addition, due to the ratio between ANC and DA members of roughly two-thirds to one-third, there is no space for contributions or suggestions from the DA. It is more difficult today to be in opposition than during the National Party years. Differences are not clear, because previously there was a tremendous ideological divide and today many aims are the same. There is only dispute about how to do it. For the ANC, it becomes a matter of pride not to give in to the opposition's proposals. In addition, DA members claim that 'the structure of the ANC was never democratic; it was communist, based on authoritarian principles. However, many Afrikaners have forgotten how they changed everything in 1948 and now the ANC is doing the same' (Heim, Topic and Wolder interview, 2003).

There are DA claims that the administration in Region 7 is notorious for inefficiency and nepotism, favoring friends and family of ANC officials, and that the council's resources are used for party requirements. The focus of Region 7 is completely on Alexandra; outside areas are sidelined. The bottom-up, participatory approach does not work because decisions are made before the consultations. In addition, the information available at the People's Centre in Alexandra and in publications of Region 7 is biased and only relevant for the township's residents. Information booklets and also posters in the People's Centre and the Region 7 offices in Wynberg are incomplete and omit some of the councillors and PR councillors of the DA (Fuchs interviews, 2003). In contrast, in the opinion of the ANC councillor in Ward 92, the cooperation between the administration in Region 7 and the City Council is good.

Ward boundaries are also a disputed issue. The *Local Government: Municipal Structures Act 1998* regulates the delimitation of wards. Different DA interviewees argued that the criteria for the delimitation are vague and leave room for interpretation. Former segregation boundaries separate densely populated areas from those with a significantly lower population density. It is generally assumed that township residents vote for the ANC. Thus, the manipulation of ward boundaries for reasons of integration actually secures the ward for the ANC, because a small area of the township included in a ward brings a high number of voters. Such claims are difficult to prove, but they reveal a lot about attitudes, sensibilities and prejudices. More transparency would increase the state's credibility and trust in its role as an unbiased mediator. For example, DA members claim that the boundaries of Ward 109 were adjusted before the local elections in 2000. A larger part of Alexandra was added and it was expected that the ANC would win this ward. However, the DA had less than 200 votes more (Fuchs interview, 2003). ANC members reckon that, with a more appealing candidate, the ANC would have won this ward (Ebrahim interview, 2004).

Disparities between legal and organizational frameworks and their effectiveness in practice are common; Region 7 and its local government wards are no exception. There is not only the difficulty of integrating the varying expectations, priorities and development visions of the different population segments. Local government structures also depend critically on the commitment, effort and participation of the incumbents of office, the stakeholders and the population, but people are reluctant to get involved in their community (Mokgwatsana interview, 2003).

In particular, ward committee elections are a problem, and not only in wards with formerly segregated populations. There is little response to calls for nominations, and the competing political parties manipulate the system. According to administrative staff, the ward committee system is good in theory but does not work in practice. People are not interested in getting involved in the community, and it is questionable if they have any knowledge of how local government works. It is already difficult to find people willing to become involved in their community, let alone to find representatives for interest sectors such as youth, religion, business, safety or women. Ward committee elections take place every two years (Mbingeleli interview, 2004). The lack of interest in community affairs affects all racial groups. The high mobility in Alexandra and its adjacent areas is a critical factor reducing participation because new residents need time to settle before they are able to get involved in their community.

The DA claims that rules concerning ward committee elections are not clear. The administration of Region 7 announces meetings, nomination procedures, an election venue and dates. However, Heim (interview, 2003), a PR Councillor, argues, 'out of 50000 residents, 200 come and should then represent the community. If one is not a councillor, it is difficult to know about ward committee elections and their meaning. Ward committees work in theory, but in practice it is not possible to implement them.'

As well as the negative impact of high mobility levels, there is no civic culture of participation and as yet the new local government system is neither consolidated nor a well-known institution. Ward demarcations are relatively new, and apart from the ward branches of the ANC and DA, there are barely any other groups representing interest sectors at a ward level. Social networks are indispensable to mediation between citizens and the state.

In Ward 81 the first ward committee elections in 2001 resulted in six out of ten members elected coming from Riverpark, a small area of the ward in Alexandra. The election procedure was incorrect because there were nominations from the floor and the committee was dissolved before it had begun working. For the September 2003 ward committee elections, the administration of Region 7 informed voters and residents selectively. Despite interventions by the ward councillor, information about election procedures, nominations, date and venue was extremely unevenly disseminated, resulting in a ward committee of 10 people, all from Riverpark and all ANC members. This committee represents neither the population of the ward, nor interest groups from the different sectors; in addition, only about 30 to 40 people voted (Topic interview, 2003). Nevertheless, the venue was not in Alexandra, taking the reluctance of outsiders to enter the township into consideration. The ANC ward branch believes that the community is represented in this ward committee.

Ward 92 has a functioning ward committee, and there were no problems with the elections of the new committee in July 2003. The councillor does not know how people deal with the elections and whether they nominate themselves, are asked to stand for election, or suggest someone. Region 7 facilitates and supports ward committee elections. There are guidelines, such as that those nominated have to be resident in the ward and up to date with their service payments, they cannot have a criminal record and must be of sound mind. The challenge is to get a decent representation in terms that allow for choice and ensure that all interest sectors such as youth, health or sports and all areas of the ward are represented. Most committee members come from the Eastbank in Alexandra; however, residents from other areas were encouraged to participate. The councillor does not know the party political affiliation of ward committee members (Chuene interview, 2003). In contrast, DA members claim that they were not informed about the ward committee elections and that all committee members are ANC (Mkhonto interview, 2003).

In Ward 109, the first ward committee in 2001 had two members from Kelvin outside the township, while the rest of the members were all from Alexandra and all ANC supporters. However, four members never came to meetings and one member died. They were replaced, and the ward committee then had four ANC and four DA members. According to the DA chairperson, the 2003 elections were competitive. From an organizational point of view, the DA approached people to stand for election and managed to get ten people for the ten interest sectors. For the elections, the DA constituency was mobilized. The ANC also handed nominations in; however, the DA had the larger crowd and nine of the ten ward committee members are DA and only one ANC. There is one white DA member from Wendywood in the committee, the rest are Alexandra residents (Mijambo interview, 2003).

Ebrahim, the only ANC ward committee member, claims that the ANC had a list of nominated people, all valid candidates, to represent a certain interest sector. About 60 people attended the election meeting; the DA brought in Alexandra residents by taxi, because the meeting was held outside Alexandra. The DA had a majority of two or three votes. This ward committee is not representative, in terms of either interest sector or residents, because all members come from Alexandra. A huge problem is that ward committee members are not paid; a paid job would probably be taken more seriously. In addition, people lack the confidence and the knowledge to get involved (Ebrahim interview, 2004). Ebrahim is ignorant of the fact that one ward committee member comes from Wendywood.

Finally, there are common interests around which people can organize; however, there are not many established structures that cut across former segregation boundaries. Schools are considered to promote integration. In addition, there is a widespread assumption that children born in the 1990s have no experience of apartheid and have had no exposure to racially based ideologies; they therefore approach other individuals without racial prejudice.

All the schools contacted during my fieldwork have a high number of black pupils; in contrast, they all have predominantly white teachers. If they have governing bodies and Parent-Teacher Associations (PTAs), these do not reflect school demographics, but tend to have a higher number of white parents and are usually chaired by white parents. In none of the schools did the PTA or governing body include a parent from Alexandra; PTAs reflect social hierarchies. The involvement of parents in school activities differs. White parents are generally more involved than black parents; however, there is a significant difference regarding school involvement between black parents living in Alexandra and those living outside the township. In addition to transport problems, it seems that social class determines parental participation more than race.

Similar to the mobility behavior in residential areas, white parents tend to withdraw their children from schools where black pupils exceed a critical number; some schools around Alexandra have 100 per cent black pupils. Children from Alexandra are exposed to a different and difficult social environment compared with those living outside the township. Transport is a problem for pupils coming from Alexandra; they often arrive late, which is disruptive, and they are not fetched in time after school. Education is highly valued in a competitive economic environment, and parents are concerned about standards of education. Poor children tend to struggle with more problems; they come from a less stimulating background and sometimes lack fundamental skills, which is considered to have a negative effect on the learning environment, contributing to prejudices that, for example, educational standards drop if too many disadvantaged pupils are together. In view of the high number of African poor, class differences translate into racially based exclusions.

Community Policing Forums (CPFs) are based on cooperation between the police and the population; crime prevention affects everyone. Unfortunately, CPF boundaries run along old segregationist lines and do not provide for integration. According to Lionel Stein and Thomas Sithole (interview, 2003), CPF chairpersons, alcohol and social crimes constitute the biggest problem for the police, and the CPFs are involved in awareness campaigns and assistance to prevent alcohol-related offences. The second biggest problem is the high number of gun owners, in a socio-cultural context that sanctions the possession of a gun as a means of self-defence. It is easy to get hold of a gun; however, weapons influence the nature and consequences of crime. Types of crime in Alexandra include assault, murder, robbery, car hijacking and, in particular, domestic violence; incidences of assault and rape are high compared with outside areas. Often crime occurs between people known to each other; in many cases, the settling of personal disputes involves violence. Young people, in particular young women, are affected most by crime. Outside Alexandra, patterns of crime differ significantly. Robbery, housebreaking, and car hijacking are the most common crimes; levels of violence and incidences of rape are significantly lower than in Alexandra.

Crime prevention offers an opportunity for integration across social boundaries, if the emphasis is on community participation and not based on clichés regarding perpetrators and victims. A defensive approach to crime prevention aims at removing potential facilitators such as taxi ranks, cardboard collectors, hawkers or the closure of areas with fences and booms. Groups addressing the problem of crime reactively are not concerned if the reduction of crime in one area comes at the expense of another area, an attitude entrenching divisions. In contrast, a participatory approach to crime prevention stresses responsibility for one's neighborhood and provides a sense of agency; it includes different social actors and vindicates the interdependence of all social groups, possibly contributing to bridging social capital, cooperation and integration.

Conclusion

In South Africa the negotiated transition process resulted in a widely accepted new social, economic and political order based on a democratic constitution and represented by a democratically elected government.

However, values, beliefs and prejudices are more resistant to change and remain a latent source of contention. It is more difficult to overcome perceptions of other demographic groups and social barriers that were shaped by history, state ideologies, worldviews, socialization, personal experiences and emotional aspects. Social capital emanates from these social relations and, in a context of limited resources and opportunities, the adoption of cooperative values and the generation of trust cutting across social divisions are a challenge.

The socio-economic and political context in which social capital is embedded shapes the way social assets are distributed and managed in South Africa. Social capital is an ambiguous resource. In segmented societies, expectations and development priorities are not the same for all population groups, and public policies affect them in very different ways. Within these competing social structures, different groups place a variety of demands on the state. Social cleavages are reflected in networks and forms of particular groups furthering their own interests in competition for resources, opportunities and power. Development and democratization efforts are opposed when they become a threat to wealthier groups reluctant to give up their privileges.

In this context, it is a challenge to make democracy work, because in local government wards the cooperation between groups once forced not to interact with each other is difficult. The past still affects relations and it will take time to develop a culture of working together. Administrative boundaries cut across social networks that have not been replaced by more integrated social structures that cut across spatial, socio-economic and cultural divisions. However, social networks are indispensable to mediate between citizens and the state, and community mobilization works best if it can cut across social divisions, such as class, race and gender. There are modest beginnings of more integrated structures, for example around common concerns such as crime prevention and education. As an unbiased mediator between alienated populations, the state can encourage the strengthening of social relations and the reduction of disparities. However, due to the magnitude of inequality, the empowerment of one group comes at the expense of another. Inevitable biases in resource allocation and different expectations and priorities often enforce prejudices and the resort to clichés. A more equitable distribution of income is certainly an important key to making democracy work because it is a critical condition for the generation of trust, tolerance and solidarity, the sources of beneficial forms of social capital and a shared development vision.

References

Berman, S. 1997. 'Civil Society and Political Institutionalisation', *American Behavioural Scientist* 40 (5): 562–73.

Boix, C. and D.N. Posner. 1998. 'Social Capital: Explaining Its Origins and Effects on Government Performance', *British Journal of Political Science* 28 (4): 686–93.

Coleman, J.S. 1990. *Foundations of Social Theory*. Cambridge, MA: The Belknap Press of Harvard University Press.

Diani, M. 2001. 'Social Capital as Movement Outcome', in B. Edwards et al. eds, *Beyond*

Tocqueville: Civil Society and the Social Capital Debate in Comparative Perspective, Hanover, NH: University Press of New England, 207–18.

Edwards, B.and M.W. Foley. 1998. 'Civil Society and Social Capital Beyond Putnam', *American Behavioural Scientist* 42 (1): 124–39.

Fine, B. 1999. 'The Developmental State is Dead – Long Live Social Capital', *Development and Change* 30 (1): 1–19.

Foley, M.W. and B. Edwards. 1998. 'Beyond Tocqueville: Civil Society and Social Capital in Comparative Perspective', *American Behavioural Scientist* 42 (1): 5–20.

Foley, M.W. and B. Edwards. 1999. 'Is It Time to Disinvest in Social Capital?', *Journal of Public Policy* 19 (2): 141–73.

Fried, A. 2002. 'The Strange Disappearance of Alexis de Tocqueville in Putnam's Analysis of Social Capital', in S.L. McLean et al. eds, *Social Capital Critical Perspectives on Community and 'Bowling Alone'*, New York: New York University Press, pp. 21–49.

Fukuyama, F. 1995. 'Social Capital and the Global Economy', *Foreign Affairs* 74 (5): 89–103.

Hall, P. A. 2002. 'Great Britain, The Role of Government and the Distribution of Social Capital', in R.D. Putnam, ed., *Democracies in Flux*, Oxford: Oxford University Press, 21–57.

Harriss, J. and P. De Renzio. 1997. ''Missing Link' or Analytically Missing?: The Concept of Social Capital', *Journal of International Development* 9 (7): 919–37.

Levi, M. 1996. 'Social and Unsocial Capital: A Review Essay of Robert Putnam's *Making Democracy Work*'. *Politics and Society* 24 (1): 45–55.

Marais, H. 2001. *South Africa's Limits to Change: The Political Economy of Transition*. London: Zed Books.

Mayekiso, M. 1996. *Township Politics*. New York: Monthly Review Press.

McLean, S.L. et al. 2002. 'Inttroduction', in S.L. McLean et al., eds, *Social Capital Critical Perspectives on Community and 'Bowling Alone*,' New York: New York University Press, 1–17.

Molyneux, M. 2002. 'Gender and the Silences of Social Capital: Lessons from Latin America', *Development and Change* 33 (2): 167–88.

Newton, K. 1997. 'Social Capital and Democracy', *American Behavioural Scientist* 40 (5): 575–86.

Nordlund, P. 1996. 'Democracy and Social Capital in a Segmented South Africa, in Agora Project, 1996', in *Democracy and Social Capital in Segmented Societies*. Uppsala: Department of Government, Uppsala University.

Offe, C. 1999. 'How Can We Trust Our Fellow Citizens?', in M. Warren, ed., *Democracy and Trust*, Cambridge: Cambridge University Press, 42–87.

Offe, C. 2000. 'Political Liberalism, Groups Rights and the Politics of Fear and Trust'. Paper presented at the Conference on 'Challenges to Democracy: Peripheries as a Vantage Point', Ben Gurion University, Beer Shiva, Israel, 19–21 May 2000.

Portes, A. 1998. 'Social Capital: Its Origins and Applications in Modern Sociology', *Annual Review of Sociology* 24 (1): 1–24.

Putnam, R.D., R. Leonardi, and R.Y. Nanetti. 1993. *Making Democracy Work: Civic Traditions in Modern Italy*. Princeton, NJ: Princeton University Press.

Republic of South Africa. 1998. *Government Gazette*, Vol. 393, No. 18739, 13 March, Notice 423 of 1998, White Paper on Local Government.

Simone, A.M. 2002. 'The Dilemmas of Informality for African Urban Governance', in S. Parnell et al., eds, *Democratising Local Government: The South African Experiment*, Cape Town: UCT Press, 294–304.

Smith, D.M. 2003. 'Urban Fragmentation, Inequality and Social Justice: Ethical Perspectives', in P. Harrison et al., eds, *Confronting Fragmentation, Housing and Urban Development in a Democratising Society*, Cape Town: UCT Press, 26–39.

Terreblanche, S. 2002. *A History of Inequality in South Africa 1652-2002*. Pietermaritzburg: University of Natal Press.

United Nations Development Program (UNDP). 2003. *South Africa Human Development Report 2003*. Oxford: Oxford University Press for UNDP.

Uslaner, E.M. 1999. 'Democracy and Social Capital', in M.E. Warren, ed., *Democracy and Trust*, Cambridge: Cambridge University Press, 121–50.

Uslaner, E.M. 2002. *The Moral Foundations of Trust*. Cambridge: Cambridge University Press.

Warren, M.E. 1996. 'What Should We Expect From More Democracy?: Radically Democratic Responses to Politics', *Political Theory*, 24 (2): 241–70.

Warren, M.E. 1999. 'Introduction', in M.E. Warren, ed., *Democracy and Trust*, Cambridge: Cambridge University Press, 1–21.

Whittington, K.E. 1998. 'Revisiting Tocqueville's America', *American Behavioural Scientist*, 42 (1): 21–32.
Woolcock, M. 1998. 'Social Capital and Economic Development: Toward a Theoretical Synthesis and Policy Framework', *Theory and Society*, 27 (2): 151–208.

Notes

1 I wish to thank Professor Tom Lodge for valuable comments and advice. The research for this study was supported by funds from the Swedish International Development Agency (SIDA).
2 The following interviews were conducted:
Chuene, W. ANC, Councillor Ward 92, interviewed by author, 1 October 2003
De Oliveira, I. Principal Fairsand Primary School, interviewed by author, 5 November 2003
Ebrahim, G. ANC, Ward Committee Member, Ward 109, interviewed by author, 27 January 2004
Fargher, M. Headmistress St. Mary's School, interviewed by author, 14 November 2003
Fuchs, A. DA, Councillor Ward 109, interviewed by author, 28 July 2003
Heim, P. PR Councillor Ward 81, interviewed by author, 23 October 2003
Letter, N. Director Alexandra Renewal Project, interviewed by author, 31 July 2003
Madibo (Reverend), Methodist Church of South Africa, interviewed by author, 30 September 2003
Madondo, S. Independent Electoral Commission, Electoral Projects Coordinator of Region 7, interviewed by author, 22 August 2003
Makapela, L. ANC Branch Ward 81, interviewed by author, 11 November 2003
Makhalemele, S. Anglican Church in Alexandra, interviewed by author, 23 October 2003
Mbingeleli, M. Council Liaison and Support, interviewed by author, 8 January 2004
Mills, D. Chairperson of DA Branch Ward 81, interviewed by author, 20 October 2003
Mijambo, R. Chairperson DA Branch Ward 109, interviewed by author, 2 October 2003
Mkhonto, S. Chairperson DA Branch Ward 92, interviewed by author, 29 October 2003
Mokgwatsana, E. Strategic Adviser of the Regional Director, interviewed by author, 31 October 2003
Nxumalo, J. Operational Manager Council Liaison and Support in Region 7, interviewed by author, 4 August 2003
Rocky, A. Rembrandt Park Primary School, interviewed by author, 27 October 2003
Sithole, T. Chairperson of Alexandra CPF, interviewed by author, 10 October 2003
Smith, H. Principal Wendywood Primary School, interviewed by author, 22 October 2003
Stein, L. Chairperson of Sandringham CPF, interviewed by author, 9 October 2003
Topic, B. DA, Councillor Ward 81, interviewed by author, 25 July 2003
Wolder, R. DA, PR Councillor Ward 81, interviewed by author, 20 October 2003
Wyngaard, L. Anglican Church in Bramley, interviewed by author, 5 November 2003

6

Local Government & the Management of Conflict in Fragmented Societies
South Africa, Namibia & Mauritius Compared

CHRISTOF HARTMANN

One of the central questions of post-conflict societies is political: how to construct a stable form of power-sharing and government. Political science textbooks describe democracy as the only institutional mechanism for solving political and ethnic conflicts in a peaceful manner. Democracy allows society to deal with the various manifestations of conflict in a stable and consensual manner (Sartori 1987). A long tradition in political philosophy also maintains that for these internal reasons democratic states have been more peaceful in their external relations.

In Africa the processes of democratic change initiated in the early 1990s brought considerable hope of a reduction of violent conflict, both at the intra-state and the inter-state levels. If African governments were to become replaceable via the ballot box or amenable to change by peaceful means, there should be a corresponding decline in the resort to armed struggle. Thus the establishment of some basic democratic dispensation featured prominently in the peace accords that ended protracted civil wars in Angola, Mozambique or Liberia.

By the end of the 1990s the hopes of such a democratic peace dividend had been shattered. The various processes of political liberalization and democratization had indeed been accompanied by a rise in the number of violent internal conflicts and processes of state collapse. Nevertheless, some ethnically, racially and culturally fragmented societies such as Mauritius, South Africa, and Namibia did not follow this trend but consolidated their democratic institutions. A standard argument against multi-party democracy, articulated chiefly by representatives of non-democratic regimes, had always been that this system is a Western construct unsuited to the culture and ethnic diversity of African countries.

Demands for democracy that swept across the continent from the early 1990s were clearly linked to the massive popular frustrations caused by declining economies and the failures of incumbent governments. In many countries political liberalization resulted from uncivic behavior and was a symptom of massive internal social conflict. For the African popular movements democratization was not conceptualized in purely procedural or strategic terms, but rather in terms of the degree to which it challenged entrenched structures of social and political domination. The violent conflicts that accompanied liberalization and democratization were probably often an indicator of the real change taking place in settings unfamiliar with high degrees of open political competition. 'Electoral violence erupts particularly in situations in which elections offer a genuine possibility of changing existing power relations' (De Gaay 2000: 76; Quantin 1998).

As the institutional void of the transitional situation was eventually filled, did the new African democracies manage to develop peaceful routines for resolving political conflicts? Many analysts are pessimistic, noting the legacies of authoritarian systems and other structural obstacles to sustainable democratic rule (Snyder 2000). Perhaps the most salient feature of democratic openings in Africa remains their fragility. It seems that, in many countries, 'politics' is still seen more as a root cause of, and not as a solution to, crisis and conflict.

This chapter starts from the premise that the specific role of democratic institutions in conflict management is still not adequately considered in the African context, especially with regard to the analysis of structural root causes of conflict and crisis prevention. It will therefore explore what contribution social science has to make concerning the design of institutional arrangements that may help prevent violent conflict or rebuild post-conflict societies. It is thus concentrated less on managing violent conflict than on institutional strategies of preventing violent conflict.

I shall proceed in four steps: The next two sections introduce a theoretical statement concerning, first, the distinction between different levers of democratic intervention (the system of government, the electoral system, and the territorial structure of the state), and, secondly, a simplified model of general and specific contributions of local government to conflict management. The third section presents empirical evidence drawn from a comparative analysis of local government in three African countries with protracted socio-cultural conflict, i.e. Mauritius, Namibia and South Africa. The concluding section tries to develop some policy lessons for processes of institutional engineering.

Which Institutional Variables?

Comparative empirical research on democratization processes has enormously expanded our knowledge about the role of democratic institutions in shaping political outcomes. Much of this literature is based on the assumption that democratic governance and the conscious design of political institutions are key factors affecting the likelihood of democratic consolidation, political stability and the sustainable settlement of violent conflicts (Sartori 1994; Harris and Reilly 1998; Bunce 2000; Reynolds 2001). In stark contrast to the euphoria over institutional engineering in Eastern and Central Europe and East Asia and the long-standing belief of Latin American elites that institutional reforms may indeed improve democratic performance and the prospects of consolidation, the discourses on democracy in Africa tended to be concentrated more on the quality of leadership and political elites (i.e. actors), and on economic macrostructural conditions. Only recently did constitution-makers and scholars start to think about reforms of the institutional arrangements that had been put in place at independence or with democratization (Barkan 1996; Reynolds 1999; Bogaards 2003). Still, this body of literature has an exclusive focus on national institutions, such as presidentialism or the parliamentary electoral system (Nohlen et al. 1999; Cowen and Laakso 2002).

Although considerable debate still exists, most of this scholarship agrees that deeply divided societies can best be governed if they exhibit a number of basic institutional features at the macro-political level. First, divided societies are more likely to be stable if power is dispersed in a parliamentary rather than a presidential system. Multiple strong institutions are associated with the effective dispersion of power. Parliamentary democracies tend to promote multi-party systems and encourage the formation of coalition governments. Second, proportional representation electoral systems tend to be more consensual, as they try to limit, divide, and share power. Most important, they avoid winner-take-all results and promise that most groups will not be denied the opportunity to participate in the government. And, third, divided societies are more likely to be stable and conflict-free if power is decentralized to the sub-national level (Harris and Reilly 1998; Lijphart 1999). In ethnically or racially fragmented societies such as Mauritius, Namibia or South Africa the major conflict-mitigating role of devolution may consist in a better political representation of national minorities and more effective developmental services in favor of formerly marginalized segments of the population. And indeed, one of the motives that might explain the rise of decentralization policies in these three (but also other) countries is the conscious use of decentralization as a political mechanism by ruling groups to placate, neutralize, contain or seek compromise with regional or local elites.

These are admittedly general hypotheses but they have the advantage of moving the analysis away from the relationship between democracy and conflict management to specific sets and options of democratic institutions and their impact on crisis prevention and conflict management. According to this body of literature, one of the reasons for the conflictive character of democratization may thus lie in the specific institutional set-up of most African countries. Most political systems actually have centralist and presidential forms of government and provide for majoritarian electoral systems, and thus present a combination that is generally thought of as having particularly crisis-inducing effects.

A different school of thought draws our attention, on the contrary, to the mainly informal institutions (like clientelism, neo-patrimonialism, etc.) that 'work' or 'do not work' in the fabric of African societies, with all their negative and positive side-effects (Bayart 1993; Chabal and Daloz 1999). This emphasis on informal rules plays down the role that formal institutions may claim for shaping political behavior and outcomes, and would regard as futile any reforms of these formal rules. In this chapter, however, it will be argued that formal institutions and rules indeed matter, and make a difference to the democratic and crisis-preventive governance of African societies.[1]

In the following I shall concentrate on one of the three institutional variables mentioned above, the territorial distribution of political power and resources through decentralization and federal arrangements. Many conflicts in Africa centre on the role of the state in society and emanate principally from its structure and organization. The argument is that some of these conflicts could be prevented or mediated by restructuring the state: federalism, autonomy and local government institutions. The theoretical literature is mostly interested in the conflict-mitigating effects of federalism (Lijphart 1999). Local politics and local democratization have, on the contrary, rarely been discussed in terms of specific institutional settings and designs.

Why and When Local Government Matters for Conflict Management

It would hardly make any sense to assume that 'local government' generally matters for 'conflict management'. In order to produce testable hypotheses we need to operationalize both what dimensions of local government might matter as well as which types of conflict or aspects of conflict management might be influenced.

Table 6.1 Overview hypothesis

Local government	→	Conflict
Specific elements of local government	→	Specific aspects of conflict and conflict management

Types of Conflict

There are different ways to build conflict typologies. One (and probably the most frequent) is to distinguish according to the degree of violence involved in conflicts. While social conflict itself is regarded by most social scientists as unavoidable and even desirable, it is the violent escalation of conflict that needs to be prevented or ended or managed. The very idea of crisis prevention is to tackle the root causes of conflicts while these conflicts are still latent, i.e. violence has not yet erupted. Conflicts then pass through different steps or cycles with differing degrees of violent encounters including a post-conflict phase (which should actually be renamed a post-violent conflict phase).

Another way to make sense of the multiplicity of real-world conflicts is to order them according to the main root cause of conflict. We find competing typologies in the literature, with most authors distinguishing resource-based conflicts (competition for economic power, access to natural resources), conflicts over governance and authority (based on competition for political power and participation in the political process), ideological conflicts (involving different value systems), and identity conflicts (based on competition between rival ethnic, religious or other communal identity groups for both economic and political power and social justice (Rupesinghe 1998). Empirical work with these typologies is often hindered by the fact that most conflicts in Southern countries are characterized by a combination of these different root causes.

A third possibility for building a conflict typology, and one increasingly used in 'conflict management and resolution research', is to distinguish the individual and collective actors involved in conflicts. This idea is based on the premise that conflicts are the result of differences in the interests of actors and that the management or resolution of conflicts consists in reconciling the different interests by creating win-win situations for all relevant stakeholders. Paul Lederach's (1997) Track I-III actors are a prominent example of such an approach: different groups of actors have specific capacities and roles within conflict management independently of the precise public good that is contended among the parties to a conflict.

To what extent do these conceptual differences matter for our research question? We start with the last typology. Which are the actor constellations in conflicts at the local level? Three typical conflict situations may arise (Mehler 2001):

(i) Within a local government area different groups with contrasting political views or structural disparities in economic power or different ethnic or religious affiliations, may conflict with each other.
(ii) Conflicts may also arise between different local government units.
(iii) Finally, conflicts may exist between one (or several) local government units and the central government over the extent of political, financial and economic autonomy and authority.

Conflicts involving international actors are – on the contrary – rare in the local arena. Protracted violent conflicts see the emergence of various international actors at some point in time (warlords with international connections, arms traders, international humanitarian organizations), but these scenarios will be excluded from the comparison.

Combining these three different conflict constellations with our criteria on the root causes and the degree of violence, we arrive at the following overview:

Table 6.2 Overview: Conflict types and local government

Actors	Root cause	Degree of violence
Different groups within local government	Resources, governance, identity	Non-violent – violent
Different local governments	Resources, identity	Non-violent
Local government against central government	Resources, governance, identity	Non-violent – violent

As our analysis is primarily concerned with local government in fragmented societies, we most likely find a combination of identity with governance and socio-economic resources conflicts, depending on the specific contexts of the three countries. Whereas the population patterns in Mauritius and South Africa might lead different communities to clash within local government units, local government is more ethnically homogeneous in most other countries (except for the capital city). Likewise, conflicts between different local government units might have a more technical character (attribution of funds) or hide conflicts between different political parties or ethnic groups in control of different local government units. Conflicts between local government units and central government might also have an ethnic dimension, especially where ethnic minority groups or opposition political forces use the control of municipalities to defend their ethnic or political interests.

Institutional Dimensions of Local Government
Most African states experiment with some form of sub-national government, but decentralization policies and local government have remained poorly analyzed (and maybe also poorly developed) in African countries (Wunsch 1998; Reddy 1999; Olowu 1999; Wunsch and Olowu 2004), and we do not know much about the real impact of decentralization policies on the interests and strategies of local stakeholders.

The processes of decentralization are normally supposed to improve effective service delivery, the accountable use of resources, and tax collection. It is obvious that the successful management of conflicts dealing with access and control of natural resources might primarily consist in a 'good' and 'sound' public policy, and that some of these policies might or even should be (planned and) implemented at the local level. But politics is more than policy and a lack of sound local policies in most cases is neither the direct result of missing human capacities nor the simple result of scarcity of material resources. Local and national institutions provide a framework of rules (both written and unwritten) that decide the allocation of human and material resources to local government. Local institutions may provide (or not provide) the local society with channels of effective participation. Institutional theory summarizes these assumptions in the idea of incentives that influence actors' behavior in significant ways. The specific rules embodied in local government create incentives that lead local actors to engage in politics, to pursue sectional or community-wide interests, to perceive other local governments as allies or as competitors. They affect the distribution of political power and thus the likely output of the political system as well as the relative ability of different groups to influence that output. Institutions also afford a certain predictability.

Most analysis of decentralization and local government has been more concerned with administration than with politics, or, to put it differently, more interested in structures that can provide an effective 'output' (i.e. delivering benefits to local populations), than a representative 'input' (guaranteeing effective political participation). Leaving aside the thorny question of measuring the effectiveness of these outputs, it seems that anyone interested in the potential conflict-mitigating role of local government should also be interested in the input-side, i.e. the question of how different political, ethnic or social interests are represented in local government.

From an institutionalist perspective we have thus to look for specific input-variables of local government that may influence conflict management. From a wider array of institutions (Hartmann 2004) four of them were selected as particularly important for our research question (the list is not exhaustive):

Countries vary with regard to the number of tiers of sub-national government and the type of local government, i.e. a single unified model of government or different categories of local government across the urban-rural divide. This question is closely linked to the question of the size of municipalities, i.e. whether to opt for relatively big (consolidation) or small local government units. This may have direct consequences for the homogeneity or heterogeneity of local government.

First, legal provisions may provide for the inclusion or exclusion of relevant local stakeholders, such as traditional leaders and ethnic minorities, within councils and local administrations. With regard to the management of local resource conflicts, it matters a lot whether established power-holders feel their interests directly threatened by elected bodies or not. Concerning minorities, it is decisive who is in charge of appointing personnel.

Second, the electoral systems for local councils give different roles to political parties, may provide for a direct election of mayors, and allow for different degrees of popular participation in decision-making. For local elections, majoritarian electoral systems are generally favored as they allow a direct accountability of representatives to their voters. The reduced scale of territorial space in which elections are held implies that the voter is more familiar with the political problems of, and possible solutions to, public affairs.

Third, the characteristics of the candidate as a known person may have a greater influence on the voters' electoral behavior than in national elections. PR systems are, on the contrary, praised as the more consensual system, which is better equipped to suit the exigencies of ethnically fragmented societies. This system provides for party lists in constituencies of varying size, with voters voting for party lists instead of candidates. Seats are distributed to political parties according to the share of votes that the party receives in a given constituency.[2] Voting for party lists may strengthen the consolidation of viable political parties, but limits voters' direct influence on who may sit in council and blocks the election of popular independent candidates. At a more general level, elections are the primary formative act of political communities, and suffrage rules may decide whether minorities have a full right of participation in local affairs.

Finally, the relationship between national and local government is not only characterized by legally circumscribed functional divisions of authority (over personnel, resources, policies), but also by party-political considerations, the crafting of political careers and the geographical size of the country. The analysis of these linkages between local politics and national politics is generally lacking in accounts both of democratization and of decentralization processes. The major conflict-mitigating role of devolution may consist in the possibility that political interests excluded at the national level gain political representation and power at a local or regional level and start experimenting with assuming political management and responsibilities.

The discussion of these four institutions has been voluntarily narrowed down to their conflict-sensitive effects. It is very obvious that – to give an example – decisions about the size of local government units are motivated primarily by other considerations such as economies of scale, enhanced planning, and better qualified staff (Keating 1995). Such decisions may nevertheless have unintended effects on the management of social, political and cultural conflicts.

Preliminary Conclusion: A Set of Refined Hypotheses
Bringing together the discussions in the two previous sections we are now able to refine our general hypothesis and relate different institutions of local government to different types of conflict as shown in Table 6.3.

Table 6.3 Refined hypothesis

Local government	→	Conflict
Size of municipality	→	Conflict between local groups
Composition of councils and administrations	→	Conflict between local groups
Local electoral system	→	Conflict between local groups
Relationship between local and national government	→	Conflict between local governments Conflict between local and central government

As a final caveat it is important to bear in mind that institutions as introduced here do not possess any inherent normative positive role. The claim is that they matter, but not that their influence is necessarily beneficial for conflict management.[3] The very same set of institutions (electoral system, size) may produce different effects in different countries or even in different local governments within a country. Institutions interact both with structurally given conditions and with the contingent decisions of individuals.

Local Institutions & Conflict Management in Southern Africa

Instead of discussing the relationship between local institutions and conflict management separately for the three countries, the following presentation of empirical results is structured along the four local government institutions previously mentioned.

Number of Tiers and Size of Municipalities
Namibia and South Africa have popular elections for representatives at the local *and* the regional level. In South Africa, municipalities with elected councils exist side-by-side with provinces of a quasi-federal status charac-

terized by their own parliaments and executives. In the wake of independence, Namibia created new multi-ethnic regions bridging the former homelands and former exclusively white-controlled commercial areas. The Namibian population thus votes for both local councils (municipalities, towns, and villages) and regional councils. Due to the small size of the Mauritian island, regional government does not exist there.

The socio-economic and demographic disparities between urban areas, on the one hand, and scattered rural settlements, on the other, lead to differences in service needs as well as in the availability of resources. Cities and urban settlements have thus historically been provided with special arrangements for their governance. Most African countries therefore have two or more classes of local authorities, with the urban ones granted more power and responsibility than the rural ones. Mauritius follows this model, with the rural authorities being called *districts*, and the urban ones *cities*. There are important differences in the electoral constitution of these authorities: the rural population elects village councils that in turn elect indirectly the district councils and chairmen.[4]

Table 6.4 summarizes the differences. It accounts for the distinction along the vertical axis (whether elected councils exist only at the local level or at the local and regional level) and for the distinction along the horizontal axis (whether within the same tier a uniform approach to elected local government is applied, or whether elections are held only in urban areas).

We see that South Africa and Namibia have different elected institutions at the sub-national level. South Africa applies a relatively uniform classification of municipalities (following the transformation of local government in the late 1990s).[5] Except for the seven metropolitan cities and some sparsely populated District Management Areas (DMA), there is a single type of municipality governed by a single legal document.[6] Namibia, on the other hand, holds local elections only in municipalities, towns and villages. According to Namibian terminology, municipalities are urban areas that existed before independence in 1989, while the towns were created in the former communal areas after independence. The 'old towns' (municipalities) have thus established traditions of self-government and more administrative

Table 6.4 Sub-national government systems and elected councils

		Territorial scope (horizontal dimension)	
		Uniform approach	Urban approach
Intensity	2 sub-national tiers elected	South Africa	Namibia
(Vertical dimension)	1 sub-national tier elected	Mauritius	(Mozambique)

Notes: a) 'Uniform Approach' means that the whole national territory is divided into local governments, and all of these local governments have elected councils that are governed by the same legal instrument.
b) 'Urban Approach' means that elected local governments exist only in urban areas, while rural areas may have no local government at all or administrative sub-units without elected representatives.

staff. In the years since independence some of the new towns (Rundu or Oshakati) have grown much bigger (in terms of population and financial resources) than most of the municipalities, but the government has not yet regrouped the urban areas (Simon 1996; Toetemeyer 1999; Piermay and Sohn 1999). The rural population is represented exclusively at the regional level (in the form of the regional councillor for their constituency). These regional councils, in contrast to the district councils of the other SADC countries, are, however, not the exclusive representative institution of rural populations, but a separate tier of government and represent both the rural and urban population living in that region.

What lessons can we draw for conflict management? Namibia and South Africa, with a similar legacy of apartheid local administration, opted for contrasting models. While South Africa in 1998/9 substantially reduced the number of local authorities by consciously merging predominantly white and black areas to build a stronger local government, Namibia kept the original system. There is still a marked contrast between the rich and well-administered municipalities and the newly established towns, although Windhoek or Swakopmund has integrated the townships and been governed by SWAPO ever since the first local authority elections in 1992. Nevertheless, the differences between South Africa and Namibia have less to do with political considerations than with the socio-geographical context: the predominantly rural setting of Namibia keeps ethnic and racial groups much more in distinct and relatively homogenous areas than urbanized South Africa. The politics of ethnic conflict management was more concerned with the regional than with the local level. Previous homelands and communal areas were dismantled and new provinces (in South Africa) and regions (in Namibia) designed on the drawing board to foster inter-ethnic contact and block separatism.

Composition of Councils and Administrations

Who is allowed to run in local elections? Candidature provisions are often of decisive importance, as they define who is permitted to participate in the local political competition. Of major importance in some of the countries are formal educational requirements that have to be met before councillors are allowed to effectively participate in the council's decision-making. At the same time they may, especially at the local level, exclude the participation of popular candidates.

Elected local councils normally enter a political space which is already occupied by other established and relatively more powerful structures, such as local party organizations, members of parliament for that constituency in the national legislature, field agencies of various ministries, traditional leaders, or local development committees in which party members and field officers of various ministries predominate over the representatives, if any, from the elected councils. One type of political actor needs to be analyzed in greater detail, whose role in the local political competition differs considerably between SADC states: the traditional leaders.

In most of the Southern African countries elected local government structures are entrusted with the control and/or management of resources, including land, and the provision of basic services to the communities. At

Table 6.5 Candidature provisions for local councils

	Role of political parties	Formal role of traditional leaders
Mauritius	Independent candidates . allowed At village council elections no formal party affiliation	No traditional leaders
Namibia	Only political parties and local political associations	Allowed as candidates in regional elections, but not in local elections.
South Africa	Independent candidates allowed	Quota of up to 10% of elected members (only in provinces that include former homelands)

the same time, nearly all these countries also have traditional institutions operating at the local level. Both traditional and elected authorities have an interest in developing the local community. However, if their functions and duties are not harmonized, overlaps between their activities and resulting conflicts can be extremely detrimental to the local community. There are either laws in place or strong sentiments against allowing traditional leaders to combine traditional and competitive political leadership roles. Such prohibitions were generally meant to prevent traditional leaders from abusing their positions to gain unfair political advantage. Because traditional leaders are, by definition, linked to particular ethnic groupings, political cleavages along ethnic lines are likely to occur if traditional leaders were to be given the freedom to engage in party politics. But that has not resulted in their exclusion from politics altogether. They can be elected by their peers into the reserved positions or may be nominated to these positions, in countries where such provisions are in place (South Africa). Alternatively, they can abdicate their traditional leadership and compete as ordinary citizens. In Namibia the Traditional Authorities Act explicitly states that any traditional leader is prevented from allowing his political opinions or allegiance to influence members of his traditional community. There are no traditional authorities on the island of Mauritius.

Which lessons may we draw so far with regard to the role of these traditional institutions? Without a viable local political process in the relevant territory (that reflects community characteristics) or the inclusion of traditional authorities, decentralized entities will rarely have a role in conflict management. Forms of decentralization that devolve competences and resources only to existing municipalities or district capitals (sometimes with long-standing traditions of urban self-government) risk depriving the rural populations of any representation at the local level and create *de facto* two classes of citizens, thus creating new conflicts. In northern Namibia traditional leadership remains an important source of authority, often competing with elected local councils, especially where the jurisdiction of chiefs extends into the municipal territory. The balance is mixed in South Africa (Munro 2001; Williams 2004). While the politicization of chiefs may have put at risk their traditional legitimacy, they have been unable to hinder or even become the driving forces behind local outbreaks of violence between migrant communities, especially in KwaZulu/Natal.

Electoral Systems

Direct elections of mayors: In all three countries the traditional British type of local government prevails. Local elections are held in order to constitute a local council or representative organ, which at its first session (or at regular intervals) elects a mayor or chairman from among its members. The mayor or chairman is the political head of local government, while the management of the local administration is left to a professional manager (called town clerk or Chief Executive Officer/CEO). Political power and control resides with the Council, not with the Mayor or Chairman.[7] The three countries analyzed share a strong skepticism about the direct election of mayors (as practiced in Zimbabwe, Uganda, and Mozambique)[8] and ethnic and racial harmony is one major issue. While indirectly elected mayorship may be rotated among the ethnic-racial groups based on informal deals within councils (as is the case in the cities of Mauritius, especially Port-Louis and Curepipe, and in some municipalities of the South African Western Province), a popular election has a fixed mandate, and a single directly elected mayor will necessarily always represent a single ethnic or racial group. The direct election of a District V Chairman in the Western Ugandan district of Kibale was the main trigger for violent conflicts between autochthonous and migrant communities.[9]

Council electoral systems: In many Southern African countries, the need to operate transparent and simple electoral systems at the local level has led to the introduction of ward systems of representation with a plurality electoral system (i.e. the candidate who gets the greatest number of votes is elected, normally applied within single-member constituencies). In most cases this electoral system is also applied to elections for the national parliament. It is therefore no surprise that in Mauritius the plurality system in three-member constituencies implemented at the national level, is also applied at the local level, although in constituencies of variable size and without the unique best-loser system existing at national elections.[10]

In Namibia, different electoral formulas were applied for regional and local elections in the period following independence. While the government for many years advocated the general introduction of majoritarian electoral systems at sub-national level, the *status quo* has been maintained at least for the elections to come: plurality system for the regional councils, proportional representation for both the national elections to Parliament and for the local council elections. It has to be stressed, however, that the two PR systems are very different. At national level the system is applied in one national constituency with 72 MPs (and without any thresholds), whereas nearly all Namibian local councils consist of seven councillors, which strongly reduces the proportional effect of the PR system.[11] The

Table 6.6 Features of local government electoral systems in Southern Africa

	Term of office (years)	Electoral system for councillors	Same electoral system applied in national elections?
Mauritius	5	Plurality in MMC	Yes
Namibia	5	PR/Plurality in SMC[a]	Yes/No (PR)[a]
South Africa	5	MMP[b]	No (PR)

MMC = Multi-Member Constituency; MMP = Mixed-Member Proportional System; PR = Proportional Representation; SMC = Single-Member Constituency.
[a] For local elections a PR system is applied, for the regional elections a plurality system is applied in single-member constituencies. Namibia has thus the same electoral system for national parliament and local councils, but a different system for regional council elections.
[b] Mixed-member proportional system. Voters have two votes, one vote for ward candidates (50% of seats), and one vote for party lists (50% of seats). The total seat distribution is according to proportional representation. The constituency winners are then subtracted from the seat total of the respective party. Remaining seats are filled from the party lists. In local councils with fewer than 7 councillors, no ward candidates are elected, and voters have a single vote for a party list (PR).

'majority-prime' systems applied in some Francophone African countries – the party that wins most of the votes is automatically granted a majority of council seats, and the remaining seats are distributed among other parties on the basis of proportional representation – is unknown in Southern Africa.

In post-apartheid South Africa, a combination of plurality system in former township areas and proportional representation in former white areas was initially applied in the 1995 local elections. The transformation of local government before the second local elections in 2000 also brought with it a change in the electoral system. A so-called Mixed-Member Proportional System was introduced, where 50 per cent of the seats are elected from single-member constituencies by plurality system, and the remaining 50 per cent are filled from party lists.[12] The overall logic of the system is proportional representation, as the party seats compensate for disproportionalities caused by the plurality system (see note [b] to Table 6.6 and the detailed analysis of the South African local electoral system given by de Visser et al. 2000).[13] The seat calculation starts from the total share of votes that political parties and their candidates get in both the plurality and the PR election, and is thus different from the additional party lists applied in some African countries such as Senegal or Tanzania.[14]

What are the effects of the three different electoral systems for ethnic conflict management? In South Africa and Namibia MMP and PR allowed the parties to present ethnically mixed slates of candidates to the electorate. Mauritius shows how even majoritarian electoral systems may provide for a good solution of ethnic conflict management. In each constituency more than one candidate is elected and voters have as many votes as seats to be distributed (for local elections between three and eight per constituency), which allows parties to field candidates from different communities. While voters are free to follow the instructions of parties or not, the experience of the last thirty years does show that the councils of Mauritian towns are broadly representative of their ethnic and racial population, notwithstanding the majoritarian electoral system. In this case informal rules complement the written electoral rules to produce the socially desirable outcome.

Central-Local Relationships

If local government is to play any role in conflict management, it has to have effective powers and resources to make a difference in the eyes of the populations concerned. The problem, however, is that the empirical situation is highly complex and confusing: different local authorities appear to enjoy different degrees of authority over different policies at different times. Devolution is often not accompanied by an adequate transfer of resources, and municipalities have to shoulder debts from previous administrations (Namibia) or lack the adequate personnel to manage a wide array of functions effectively (South Africa). In these cases, decentralization may effectively increase conflicts as the central state ceases to provide services (say, pay electricity and water bills) and, on the other side, might not be legally entitled to solve local political conflicts. Still, for ethnic conflict management, even symbolic authority may have importance (such as political representation in a council that has no effective powers).

Local elections may be of importance in allowing the national opposition to control municipalities and regional councils (vertical power-sharing). In a context of dominant party systems (Bogaards 2000), opposition parties (representing ethnic and racial minorities) may get access to resources, prepare their personnel for assuming high public office, and present a more convincing challenge to the national government by having shown a certain degree of legitimacy and support at the local or regional level (Mauritius, Namibia, South Africa). The importance of local council domination may, of course, vary depending on the type of council. The local politics of the capital city is of crucial importance to the national government, especially where decentralization has given municipal councils competencies for the allocation of land and for the distribution of water and electricity.

The successful management of Cape Town by the national opposition Democratic Alliance (DA) hurt the ruling African National Congress much more than the DA presence in the national Parliament. On the other hand, any government is probably well advised to 'grant' the opposition such minor successes, thereby integrating it into the political process (and to some extent controlling it) without risking any loss of political dominance. In this regard, the lack of resources at the local level, underlined by donors and activists, may be the intentional outcome of incumbent central government strategies. Central-local relations are strongly influenced by the size of the country: In small countries like Mauritius, local government is strongly intertwined with national politics, while the rural and peripheral regions of Namibia are quite remote from the capital city, and hence from the political strategies of the main national actors.

Conclusion

The conclusions that we might draw from the experiments in local government in these three countries are not very clear-cut. Local actors are not necessarily more peaceful than national actors, and daily life in mixed neighborhoods may represent a continuous challenge for inter-ethnic harmony. Popular expectations of distributive policies by local authorities run high, especially in Namibia and South Africa. Both countries have a good record of managing potentially violent conflicts by allowing for far-reaching forms of regionalization and local control of opposition parties. Local government is, however, just one among different instruments of successful institutional conflict management.

The end of apartheid has created an institutional vacuum with a large window of opportunity for conscious institutional design, both at the national and the local level. The situation in other African countries is, however, different. It may be difficult to import or copy institutions that have proved to be successful in other places. Institutional reform of local government has to take into account the historical paths of institutional development that have shaped the expectations and interests of actors (Wunsch and Olowu 2004; Boone 2003). From the perspective of 'Do no harm', it has to be avoided that institutional reforms (by creating winners and losers) provide for new conflicts instead of successfully managing existing ones.

References

Atkinson, Doreen. 1998. *From a Tier to a Sphere. Local Government in the New South African Constitutional Order*. Sandton: Heinemann.
Barkan, Joel D. 1996. 'Elections in Agrarian Societies', *Journal of Democracy* 7 (1): 106–16.
Bayart, Jean-Francois. 1993. *The State in Africa. The Politics of the Belly*. London: Longman.
Bogaards, Matthijs. 2000. 'Crafting Competitive Party Systems: Electoral Laws and the Opposition in Africa', *Democratization* 7 (4): 163–90.
Bogaards, Matthijs. 2003. 'Electoral Choices for Divided Societies: Multi-Ethnic Parties and Constituency-Pooling in Africa', *Commonwealth & Comparative Politics* 41 (3): 59–80.
Boone, Catherine. 2003. *Political Topographies of the African State. Territorial Authority and Institutional Choice*. Cambridge: Cambridge University Press.
Bunce, Valerie. 2000. 'Comparative Democratization. Big and Bounded Generalizations', *Comparative Political Studies* 33 (6-7): 703–34.
Chabal, Patrick and Jean Pascal Daloz. 1999. *Africa Works. Disorder as Political Instrument*. Oxford: James Currey.
Cowen, Michael, and Liisa Laakso, eds. 2002. *Multi-party Elections in Africa*. Oxford: James Currey.
De Gaay Fortman, B. 2000. 'Elections and Civil Strife: Some Implications for International Election Observation', in J. Abbink and G. Hesseling, eds, *Election Observation and Democratization in Africa*, Basingstoke: Macmillan, 76–97.
Farrell, David M. 2001. *Electoral Systems. A Comparative Introduction*. Basingstoke: Palgrave.
Götz, Graeme. 1996. *The Process and the Product. The November Local Elections and the Future of Local Government*. Johannesburg: Centre for Policy Studies.
Harris, Peter and Ben Reilly, eds. 1998. *Democracies and Deep-Rooted Conflict: Options for Negotiators*. Stockholm: IDEA.
Hartmann, Christof. 2004. 'Local Elections in the SADC Countries: A Comparative Analysis of Local Electoral Institutions', *Journal of African Elections* 3(1): 160–84.
Humes IV, Samuel. 1991. *Local Governance and National Power. A Worldwide Comparison of Tradition and Change in Local Government*. New York: Harvester Wheatsheaf.
Keating, Michael. 1995. 'Size, Efficiency and Democracy: Consolidation, Fragmentation and Public Choice', in D. Judge. ed., *Theories of Urban Politics*, London: Sage, 117–34.
Keulder, Christiaan. 2002. *To PR or to Ward? Notes on the Political Consequences of Electoral Systems in Namibia*, Briefing Paper No. 14. Windhoek: Institute of Public Policy Research.

Lederach, J. Paul. 1997. *Building Peace: Sustainable Reconciliation in Divided Societies*. New York: United Nations Press

Lijphart, Arend. 1999. *Patterns of Democracy. Government Forms and Performance in Thirty-Six Countries*. New Haven, CT: Yale University Press.

Mathur, Raj. 1997. 'Parliamentary Representation of Minority Communities: The Mauritian Experience', *Africa Today* 44 (1): 61–82.

Mehler, Andreas. 2001. 'Dezentralisierung und Krisenprävention', in W. Thomi et al., eds, *Dezentralisierung in Entwicklungsländern: Jüngere Ursachen, Ergebnisse und Perspektiven staatlicher Reformpolitik*, Baden-Baden: Nomos, 287–99.

Munro, William A. 2001. 'The Political Consequences of Local Electoral Systems', *Comparative Politics* 33 (3): 295–313.

Nohlen, Dieter, Michael Krennerich, and Bernhard Thibaut, eds. 1999. *Elections in Africa. A Data Handbook*. Oxford: Oxford University Press.

Olowu, Dele. 1988. *African Local Governments as Instruments of Economic and Social Development*. The Hague: IULA.

Olowu, Dele. 1999. 'Local Governance, Democracy, and Development', in Richard A. Joseph. ed., *State, Conflict, and Democracy in Africa*, Boulder, CO: Lynne Rienner, 285–96.

Piermay, Jean-Luc and Christophe Sohn. 1999. 'Les municipalités namibiennes. Top Models ou Dinosaures.' *Politique Africaine* 74: 24–41.

Quantin, Patrick. 1998. 'Pour une analyse comparative des élections africaines', *Politique Africaine* 69: 12–28.

Reddy, P. S., ed. 1999. *Local Government Democratisation and Decentralisation. A Review of the Southern African Region*. Kenwyn: Juta & Co.

Reynolds, Andrew S. 1999. *Electoral Systems and Democratization in Southern Africa*. Oxford: Oxford University Press.

Reynolds, Andrew S., ed. 2001. *The Architecture of Democracy: Constitutional Design, Conflict Management, and Democracy*. Oxford: Oxford University Press.

Rupesinghe, Kumar. 1998. *Civil Wars, Civil Peace: An Introduction to Conflict Resolution*. London: International Alert.

Sartori, Giovanni. 1987. *The Theory of Democracy Revisited*. Chatham, NJ: Chatham House Publishers

Sartori, Giovanni. 1994. *Comparative Constitutional Engineering. An Inquiry into Structures, Incentives and Outcomes*. Basingstoke: Macmillan.

Schelnberger, Anna Katharina. 2005. *Decentralisation as a Means of Conflict Management: A Case Study of Kibaale District, Uganda*. Development Policy Working Paper No. 179. Bochum: Institute of Development Studies. (www.rub.de/iee).

Simon, David. 1996. 'Restructuring the Local State in Post-Apartheid Cities: Namibian Experience and Lessons for South Africa', *African Affairs* 95 (1): 51–84.

Snyder, Jack. 2000. *From Voting to Violence. Democratization and Nationalist Conflict*. New York: Schuster.

Toetemeyer, Gerhard C. K. 1999. 'Namibia: Democratic Empowerment through Centralisation or Decentralisation?', in P.S. Reddy, ed., *Local Government Democratisation and Decentralisation. A Review of the Southern African Region*. Kenwyn: Juta & Co., 179–99.

de Visser, Jaap, Nico Steytler and Johann Mettler. 2000. *Electing Councillors. A Guide to Municipal Elections*. Belville, University of the Western Cape: Community Law Centre.

Williams, J. Michael. 2004. 'Leading from Behind: Democratic Consolidation and the Chieftaincy in South Africa', *Journal of Modern African Studies* 42 (1): 113–36.

Wunsch, James S. 1998. 'Decentralization, Local Governance and the Democratic Transition in Southern Africa: A Comparative Analysis', *African Studies Quarterly* 2 (2), (http://web.africa.ufl.edu/asq)

Wunsch, James S. and Dele Olowu. 2004. *Local Governance in Africa: The Challenges of Democratic Decentralization*. Boulder, CO.: Lynne Rienner.

Notes

1   At the same time, the importance of informal institutions and the many varieties of their interaction with formal institutions is obvious, but space does not permit a detailed elaboration.

2   Sub-types of proportional representation are distinguished according to the size of the constituency, the specific mathematical formula applied (divisor or quota systems) and the existence of artificial thresholds that exclude parties from seat allocation having not reached a specified percentage of the overall share of votes. For a good introduction to PR systems see Farrell (2001).

3   The effectiveness of conflict management may, on the contrary, serve as a (normative) yardstick to assess the quality of the institutions.

4   This system is currently under revision and will most likely be modified in the sense of the general pattern of local government existing in Southern Africa, i.e. bigger districts with councillors directly elected by the population.

5   For a summary of the process of local government transformation in South Africa see Atkinson (1998); Goetz (1996).

6   In local elections all citizens living in the metropolitan cities and municipalities elect their local councillors, while the populations of DMA vote for their representatives to District Councils which are then filled up by representatives of the municipalities existing within that district.

7   For an introduction to different local government systems see Olowu (1988); Humes (1991).

8   The direct election of mayors was a substantial issue in the South African debate but the adherents of indirect election (and of party-political control) prevailed, and even in the metropolitan cities, such as Johannesburg or Cape Town, the mayor is therefore elected from among the councillors.

9   The traditional Banyoro establishment did not want to accept the election of an immigrant Bakiga politician as Chairman (see Schelnberger 2005).

10   The best-loser system is a device to guarantee the representation of ethnic minorities in parliament. Should the percentage of seats won by the different ethnic groups differ from the overall population share of these groups, the Electoral Commission will allocate up to 4 additional seats to those representatives of underrepresented minorities that won the highest percentage of votes in all constituencies without having been elected to parliament (therefore: best losers). For more details see Mathur (1997). The Mauritian parliament is currently considering a major reform of the electoral system. There is a general consensus to adopt the recommendations of an international expert commission headed by the South African Albie Sachs to complement the current plurality system and additional best-loser seats (62+8 seats) with 30 seats elected from national party lists (with a threshold of 10%). Details are still being discussed in Parliament, and the local elections (originally scheduled for 2004) might have been postponed to 2006 due to uncertainty with regard to the electoral rules to be applied (i.e. the extension of the new system also to the local level).

11   Due to the small size of constituencies the seat share of parties might not reflect their share of the votes, especially in the case of minority parties. For a more detailed discussion of the distorting effects of PR in small constituencies with examples from Namibia see the excellent contribution of Keulder (2002).

12   Councils with fewer than seven councillors are using a pure PR system.

13   The pure PR system currently applied for the national parliamentary elections in South Africa is deficient with regard to the accountability of parliamentarians (and has therefore come under criticism, see the Report of the Zyl van Slabbert Commission (Electoral Task Team) on the website of the South African Electoral Commission). http://www.elections.org. za/papers/27/ETT.pdf

14   In the additional party list system, a defined quota of seats is distributed according to PR to party lists in one national constituency, while the majority of seats is elected from single-member (or multi-member) constituencies according to the plurality system.

7

Managing the Process
of Conflict Resolution
in the Sudan

IDRIS SALIM EL HASSAN

After a long and protracted set of negotiations, the Government of Sudan (GoS) and the Sudan Liberation Movement (SPLM) have finally agreed to end in a peaceful manner the longest running war in contemporary Africa. The peace agreement signed on 26 May 2004 consists of six protocols covering: the Machakos general framework of guiding principles;[1] security arrangements; power-sharing; wealth-sharing; resolution of conflict in the states of Southern Kordofan/Nuba Mountains and Blue Nile; and, finally, resolution of conflict in the contested (between North and South) area of Abyei. The agreements are political and legal expressions of conflict settlement arrangements to achieve socio-economic development of a united Sudan based on equality, justice, non-discrimination and non-marginalization. If this does not work out as agreed (according to the Southerners), the agreement gives the right of self-determination – with the possibility of secession – to Southern Sudan. The legal and political nature of the protocols' framework leaves much to be desired in terms of the technicalities and socio-economic contexts that will condition the implementation of the agreement.

This chapter aims at explaining the implications of the above situation with particular regard to the public service. It is argued that the planned structures of public service and their levels, and the percentages suggested for the Southerners as civil servants, may turn out in reality to be different from what was originally envisaged in the protocols. This hinges on the realities of the socio-economic conditions and the availability and qualifications of those the SPLM names for its share in the public service, on the one hand, and the realities of the existing system of the public service in the Sudan, on the other. In short, the protocols, significant and important as they are for securing and protecting the rights of signatories, are not by themselves a guarantee of success of the execution of the agreement.

The Protocols of the Peace Agreement

The peace agreement between the GoS and the SPLM is unique in many ways, compared with other similar conflict situations. On the one hand, the

106

GoS by no means represents a united North (as there are many military and political opposition factions), nor does the SPLA for the South (there are numerous political bodies not in agreement with the SPLM; also there are 32 military militias not all of them with the SPLA). Nor is the agreement an outcome of victory by one of the two contenders; it is in fact the result of a common understanding of the two parties that the conflict cannot be won on the battle-field and that the cost has been very high for both of them in many respects. In the cases of, for example, Eritrea, Ethiopia, South Africa, Zimbabwe and Congo, the ruling military and political systems completely collapsed at the hands of 'rebels'. Hence, the GoS/SPLM agreement is a compromise of positions applying the principle of give and take, under regional and, most importantly, international pressures led by the United States to achieve peaceful resolution. Both sides came under extreme external, regional and international pressures to conclude the agreement and start implementing it as soon as possible. The agreement was finally signed in Nairobi, on 9 January 2005 (Sudan Government and SPLM/A. 2005).

Since the ultimate objective of the SPLM is to achieve full sustainable development in all the marginalized areas of Sudan, the agreement does not focus solely on political or security (military) issues. Power-sharing, especially in running the legislative, executive and judiciary systems, therefore occupies an important position in the protocols. In contrast, the 1972 Addis Ababa agreement was primarily concerned with the disarmament, demobilization and reintegration of the Anya Nya fighting groups in regional government and symbolic representation at the national political level. The present Naivasha protocol on power-sharing stipulates that the SPLM (and its nominees) are to participate at both levels of government, the national and in the South, as the full partner of the present regime in the North. Implementation of the accords in general and participating in the power-sharing in particular presuppose a strong and capable public service system. It is known that it is not possible to attain high standards of sustainable development without a well-founded, well-institutionalized, and harmonious bureaucratic system especially in 'post'-conflict situations.

The power-sharing protocol devotes a separate section to the civil service – article 2.6. It states that the national civil service should be representative of the people of Sudan without discrimination against any qualified Sudanese on the basis of religion, ethnicity, region, gender or political beliefs. But it also declares that existing imbalances must be redressed through affirmative action and training to achieve an equitable share of representation. To do this a commission is to be established with the task of formulating policies of training and recruitment. The commission also has to ensure that 20–30 per cent of the civil service, including middle and high-level positions, goes to qualified people from South Sudan over the 6-year interim period. This might appear to be simple and straightforward, but it has to be seen in the wider perspective of both the protocols and realities of the Sudanese situation in order to appreciate the possible difficulties to be encountered.

The protocols are premised on the complete restructuring of the executive, legislative and judiciary systems at all levels of government. It is intended that more powers and capacities be given to the states and local governments in all issues except matters of sovereignty (even these have been largely minimized by curtailing the powers of the president and the relevant ministers/ministries). There are to be four levels of government: the national government, the government of South Sudan, state governments, and local governments. Also, there will be a national assembly (parliament) and council of states (with representatives of the states) and a South Sudan Council. In addition to the national constitution (to be based on matters agreed upon in the protocols) every state will have its own constitution that should not be in opposition to the national one. Many commissions and committees (whose number has not yet been decided) will deal with matters mostly tackled at present by ministries, e.g., finance, natural resources, land, general and higher education, public service, etc. Equitable and fair representation of the people of South Sudan and other states of North Sudan in the commissions and other modalities should also include members of civil society as well. Needless to say here that management and facilitation implicit in the modalities mentioned require a good and high caliber administrative system.

The Sudanese Economy & Civil Service

Many social scientists know that the term 'power' in its general meaning implies both the political and the economic spheres, and that public service in modern society is the practical expression of that power by transforming economic and political policies into activities and executing them. Hence, matters pertaining to the public service are to be found in the power-sharing protocol as well as that on wealth-sharing in particular, and all other protocols in general. The present problems of the Sudan are not only the product of 'bad' politics, but are also due to the mismanagement, misuse and exploitation of economic resources by high-ranking administrative personnel. For example, large areas of rain-fed agriculture in Eastern and South-eastern Sudan and the Nuba Mountains have been allocated to retired senior civil servants (in addition to retired army officers and merchants from Northern Sudan). The civil servants' powers do not lie in the 'ownership' of resources, but in their manipulative abilities in enabling possession of government-owned resources; 'tampering' with paper work (taxation, customs, etc.); keeping and dispensing 'important' information to the general public, etc. The strong centralized system of government that has existed in the Sudan for decades resulted in one of the most important causes of civil strife, due to economic and political regional development disparities and marginalization of the people in Eastern, Western, and Southern Sudan.[2] Public service will be the heart of the proposed constitutional, economic and political restructuring contained in the protocols.[3] The new system of public administration should be capable of addressing issues of transformation and change in the 'post'-conflict period, and towards sustainable development in all parts of the country in a fair and equitable manner. To consider such a prospect it is important to discuss the external and internal socio-economic environmental arenas of public administration in the Sudan at present.

The Sudan economy is 80 per cent agro-pastoral, while the rest is divided between forests, industry, services and trade. Deterioration in all productive sectors (including agriculture, but with the exception of the oil industry) caused by the unstable political system, civil strife, drought and famine, mismanagement and so on, has resulted in mass migration to Khartoum, an increased rate of unemployment (20 per cent), increase in poverty levels (above 90 per cent of the population), the emergence of 4 million IDPs, and rising numbers of vagrants. This is compounded by an unfavorable international economic climate, lack of a clear development policy, and liberalization and privatization measures taken during the 1980s. The role of the government as a major employer has decreased in the urban areas, giving way to the expanding informal and private sectors (though the private sector is still weak). This situation has directly affected government revenues and, hence, the provision of vital social services (education and health) in a negative way. Another serious negative impact is the shrinking size and increased inefficiency of the public service, due to massive purges by the government on ideological/political grounds, and desertion of the service as it has no longer continued to be remunerative in terms of wages and privileges. Many top Sudanese civil servants have left the service for the Gulf countries, Europe, international or regional organizations, or simply the domestic private sector. Not only has government expenditure on services declined but also the quality has suffered a lot, leading to the vicious circle of more political instability especially in the regions (which are most affected as services expenditures are centrally controlled – the centre gets 67 per cent of the budget while all the other states receive 33 per cent). However, in recent years the economy appears to be improving noticeably compared with previous years. Inflation rates have dropped from 3-digit figures to one only (8 per cent)), and economic growth figures average 6 per cent. The balance of payments has improved with strongly increased exports and slightly decreasing imports. Oil revenues, it seems, will have an important impact on overall economic performance in future years – especially on poverty reduction.

Nonetheless, the destruction of the productive base of many parts of Sudanese society, and the breakdown of services will demand extensive efforts economically and on the part of the public service in the coming reconstruction stage on the finalization of the peace agreements. Education and health in particular will need high quality, efficient, transparent, and committed civil administration. This extends to the issue of the 4 million IDPs whom it is planned to settle, integrate, repatriate or allow to choose any voluntary plausible solution. Institutionally, the public service sector is itself characterized by inefficiency and underpaid and poorly motivated staff, resulting in weak law enforcement and poor provision of services. Shifting the responsibility for social services to poor localities without enough federal support only aggravates the situation.

The 1990 census (Ibrahim et al. 2003: 8) is the only comprehensive labor market and employment source. In 1983 and 1993 two labor force censuses were carried out (ibid.); however, their data quality is unsatisfactory. Sudan's population structure is quite young, with 44 per cent below the age of 15 in the mid-1990s. The labor force population ratio is 33 per cent, indicating a high dependency rate. The rate of population increase (at 2.6 per cent) exceeds the capacity of the labor market to absorb the increasing numbers of those who seek employment, with the consequence of rising unemployment rates (at 4.9 per cent per annum). General unemployment rates are higher for young people and women, and the prospect of unemployment increases with higher education (a trend expected to continue in the immediate future). Urban labor markets are unable to create jobs equivalent to the 6 per cent increase in the urban (mainly Khartoum) population. The decline in the agricultural and service sectors has led to the expansion of the private and informal sectors. By 1996 the informal sector accounted for 90 per cent of the total job opportunities created (1.6 million out of 1.8 million jobs); this represented 65 per cent of total urban employment (compared with 25 per cent in 1970) (United Nations Development Assistance Framework 2002)

Within the larger framework outlined above, 28.5 per cent of the work force in 1993 were salaried employees, the majority of them in the public sector (half a million workers). But declining real wages, despite apparent wage increases, have led many government employees to desert. For example, in 1995 the real value of the top grade civil servant's pay was only 28 per cent of its 1990 value – the minimum reduction in the wage scale was 72 per cent (Ibrahim et al. 2003). As already mentioned, this has hit the health and education professions in particular. The number of registered doctors is 19,000 (actual need 35,000) of whom only 4,000 are actually practicing; 15,000 have either left the Sudan for the Gulf and European countries, or shifted to other professions or the private sector. Government expenditure in the services sector has been severely curtailed and working conditions have worsened. Basic education has been hard-hit with reduced expenditures worse than the average for other social services.

As already noted, the adverse consequences of the Sudan's highly centralized public service system are manifested in regional development disparities leading to economic, political and social marginalization and, ultimately, civil strife. However, because of global, regional and local political and economic conditions of restructuring, the efficiency of the public service sector has deteriorated tremendously. Moreover, corruption has spread widely as a coping mechanism to compensate for the reduction in real wages and privileges. Though this takes many forms, the most prominent mechanism is through the government corporations involved in production, distribution, building and other services. These corporations enjoy a full monopoly, while at the same time they are not subject to regular government auditing and other financial or administrative controls. Though seen as 'investments' to augment revenues to keep the public service running, they have in fact been used for the benefit of the 'officials' who are running them by means of immense financial incentives and other material gains. In its present condition the public service sector is completely incapable of meeting the challenges of developmental goals in the 'post-conflict' stage in the Sudan.

The protocols, according to Mansour Khalid (2004), actually represent a 'paradigm shift' in the administration, politics and economy of the Sudan. The vision embodied in the protocols and encoded in the guiding principles suggests the creation of organizational frameworks, with the legislation to be set out later – all of it agreed upon by the GoS and the SPLM/A to be part of the new national constitution. However, these broad issues need to be translated into specific development strategies and plans based on technical expertise that is able realistically to evaluate the situation in the Sudan. A Joint Agreement Commission (JAM), constituted by the GoS and the SPLM/A, and to be supported by the World Bank, has been established and entrusted with the latter task and was expected to be launched immediately after the signing of the Comprehensive Peace Agreement. The JAM process is clustered around eight teams of international experts in addition to the GoS and SPLM/A teams. The cluster themes are: institutional development and capacity-building; governance and the rule of law; economic policy and management; productive sectors; basic social services; infrastructure; livelihood and social protection; information.

The above long-term vision implies economic, social and political reforms not only for the 'post'-conflict period but for future set-ups that will move the country beyond the reconstruction and rehabilitation phase. Such an ambitious programme requires a responsible and accountable government with capable institutions to lead and regulate the development process. Hence, government institutions, especially the civil service, must be reconfigured or reconstituted to be viable. As noted earlier, the civil service, like other institutions in the Sudan, has suffered from mass lay-offs, political interference, policy changes, and a massive brain drain. This, under the circumstances we show below, poses a real challenge for the implementation of the peace protocols – especially that on power-sharing.

The challenges of rebuilding after war, if not properly addressed, could threaten the stability of the peace agreement, as many experiences elsewhere in the world have shown. It is essential that appropriate measures, strategies and mechanisms be instituted concerning: the performance of basic government functions, the establishment of the civil administration, the execution of processes of receiving returnees, reconciling communities, returning, and resettling them, the rehabilitation and reconstruction of the social and physical infrastructure, and enabling citizens to participate effectively in the national, state, and local government institutions.

The reconstruction of the civil service structures in a 'post'-conflict situation needs to address the following issues:

(i)   The statutory basis under which civil servants function – including rights and duties;
(ii)   the scope and comprehensiveness of the civil service;
(iii)   its management;
(iv)   the composition of categories and grades;
(v)   salary structure and benefits;
(vi)   recruitment and promotion;
(vii)   disciplinary procedures and termination; and
(viii) the appropriate boundary between the political and administrative spheres.

If the above basic conditions are not duly met, long-term security cannot be guaranteed, which might lead to the collapse of the whole peace process and the efforts exerted towards its achievement. This also needs an atmosphere conducive to nurturing a healthy and effective 'post'-conflict administration. Public service must be depoliticized; the support of international organizations and national and foreign NGOs secured; the collaboration of civil society organizations and the private sector ensured; and every effort made to regain and sustain confidence and trust between the new partners themselves, on the one hand, and between them and the general public on the other. Mistrust, if left unchecked, could result in the paralysis of functions at the work-place due to rivalry, fragmentation of decision-making and policy development, increase in the national budget, reduced efficiency in service delivery, lowered morale among civil servants, increased rates of crime and corruption, and loss of confidence by the general population.

The ultimate aim of the above precautions is to install a small, flexible, less costly and highly efficient civil service structure that will not burden the national government budget by spending funds that would otherwise go to other development areas. In the case of the 'post'-conflict stage in the Sudan harmony and cooperation with common understanding of development issues and how they should be addressed are integral to a smooth interim period that might culminate in a peaceful and unified country. To achieve this a realistic picture must be painted for the situation of the public service both in North and South Sudan regarding the personnel, their qualifications, experiences, working conditions and expectations.

Unfortunately, there are no confirmed statistics or solid studies on the precise numbers of civil servants in the whole of Sudan, nor of those in the South. For example, the official figures range between 450,000 and 700,000 government employees in the country as a whole; in the South, the matter is more complicated as there are no official pay-rolls for all civil servants as many of them combine military with civil positions, others work on a voluntary basis and the majority of services are delivered by donors driven or run by NGOs. Again, the information on civil servants in the Sudan as a whole does not indicate ethnic, regional or other such bases of affiliation.

However, it is generally believed that control of the national public service is in the hands of the educated urban elites of central and northern Sudan, who dominate the cultural, social, political and economic spheres through many cross-cutting ties, especially of kinship, from their base in Khartoum. Here, the national politicians, high-level bureaucrats, senior military, educated professionals and wealthy merchants and entrepreneurs live, work and socialize. Now, more religious and ethnic leaders have their residence and sphere of activities in Khartoum. The latter, though not part of the professional or bureaucratic elite, have strong ties and associations with them. Due to historical developments all those who have been for decades in the three capital towns have Arabic/Islamic tendencies at least as cultural orientations, despite their real ethnic or geographic backgrounds. In the last few years as a result of developments in the Sudanese economy, politics and society in general, some of which have been spawned by wider regional and global changes, the elite groups have become susceptible to external factors and pressures to the extent that they no longer exhibit the same former cohesiveness and solidarity. Other emerging regional elites, some of whom are operating from Khartoum, while others work from outside the Sudan altogether, have started to compete with the already disintegrating former elites. This could have some positive impact on the public service formation if it were not for the fact that the public service structure itself is ailing, shrinking, and no longer attractive. So, the question is how the newcomers from South Sudan will fit into the new administrative set-up in the 'post'-conflict stage.

South Sudan's population is estimated at 6 million, 2 million of them are internally displaced in Khartoum, and around one million dispersed as refugees in neighboring countries or in the American or European diasporas. Apart from the dispossessed, largely illiterate and with few skills among the Khartoum IDPs, there are small groups of elites who are politicians, professionals (lawyers and doctors, for example), technicians and middle-ranking civil servants. Others work as operatives, security personnel, administrators, and the like, with international organizations, foreign and local NGOs and similar positions in the private sector. Very few, if any of them are big businessmen or investors. What binds them as elite groups is mainly their grievances and 'struggle' against northern domination; in Marxist terms they are an elite group 'of themselves' not 'in themselves'. It is the ethnic base, as well as political affiliation, which binds them in distinct social categories, and not, for example, professional or economic or intellectual factors.

Moreover, as things stand now in the South, the war-ravaged areas consist of depopulated, shattered communities, with no systematic public administration structures or amenities, and very few educational and health facilities. Southern Sudan, which is one-third of the land of Sudan and one-third of its population, has no more than 86 doctors and 600 nurses. The economy is largely subsistence-orientated, with agriculture as its backbone. There are practically no formal economic structures or processes with monetary or financial facilities. The private sector is also rudimentary with minimal significant investment. The economy is generally informal and limited to the exchange of a few basic commodities, implying the circulation of only small amounts of cash.

Socially and politically, inter-and intra-ethnic cleavages and armed conflicts among Dinka, Nuer, Shiluk, and other ethnic groupings over local grazing or political positions are quite frequent. The imposition of military administration on areas where the army personnel are not from the same ethnic groups as the local population has created serious tensions between the two. In some areas the army/administration depends for its subsistence on extortion from the local population rather than on regular and legitimate taxes and legitimate revenue sources. The presence of militias, whether supported by the GoS or the SPLA, is expected to be an impediment to normalization of the situation even after the signing of the peace agreement. The security arrangement protocol states that there shall not be any militias on the GoS or SPLA side; they have to be integrated into the regular forces or incorporated in the civilian structures run by each side. In any case, if their concerns and demands are not duly addressed they are prone to cause problems in the 'post'-conflict phase.

In other words, the South is incapable at present of reproducing itself economically or politically in a modern way; to do this will require a lot of effort. For the purposes of this chapter, the virtual non-existence of a competent civil service or other means of governance poses the most important challenge to the implementation of the power-sharing protocol at the national, South, state and local levels of government. However, for the SPLM/A the national level in particular is the locus of contention in its bid for a 'New Sudan'. In the light of the above discussion, the rest of this chapter is devoted to the examination of this aspiration from a realistic point of view.

The Challenges of Creating a New Sudan

Though the figures of Southerners occupying positions in the national public service are not readily available or verifiable, it can safely be stated that there are only very few of them working as doctors, public administrators, in the army, police force or security, judges and the like. Negligible numbers can be encountered in clerical posts or in positions that deal with the public directly. But the numbers increase as one moves down to menial jobs (World Bank 2003; Nyaba 2004).

To reiterate, we have discussed how the centralization of public service in the Sudan in the past has impeded the development of administration in the regional and local areas. Globalization and privatization have also played a negative role by pushing towards reduction of the government's expenditures on social services – particularly education and health. The chapter has also discussed the causes and symptoms of deterioration in the public sector and the consequences of that. Again, the study hinted at the expansion of the private sector and the possibility of this trend continuing in the future. So, even if we accept that persons from South Sudan will fill 30 per cent of public service positions, will they be effective in a context where the economic supersedes the administrative and the political? Given the conditions of Southern Sudanese as depicted above, it is most unlikely that they will be in a position to compete in the private sector of the economy. Having very few middle-ranking officials, their most suitable option will be the informal sector with its petty economic activities at present and minimal power. The few privileges of the public service post and the former glamor associated with it are progressively eroding; the only remaining benefit worth mentioning is through corrupt practices, as alluded to earlier. Therefore, the representation of South Sudanese people will be to a considerable degree somewhat symbolic.

Even this symbolic representation will be more or less inoperative in view of certain social and organizational aspects. In Khartoum, the seat of power, the networks of urban educated and family-connected elites make it (through the conventions and practices they have developed over time) rather difficult for outsiders to challenge them. On paper, Arabic and English should enjoy equal status in business, administration and higher education; however, in practice one expects that civil servants with few or no Arabic skills will lose out in terms of efficiency. However, it is unfair to treat all Southerners expected to be integrated into the national public service as a single category. There are those who have been in Khartoum for more than three generations; there are the displaced; thirdly, there are the combatants who have spent most of their youth in the military; fourthly, these are the well educated who have been resident in East African, European or American urban settings; and, finally, there are the refugees in neighboring countries. Those socialized outside the Sudan will come with varying practical experience but few Arabic language skills. Their work ethic and traditions will be derived from the societies they have come from. Such returnees might not choose to work as government officials but might find better opportunities with foreign investment firms or organizations. The lot of the displaced who may choose to stay in Khartoum will not change much during the immediate 'post'-conflict period and they will have to wait for a couple of generations before this is achieved. Those who have been in Khartoum for some time will fare relatively better as most of them are education-motivated and make use of evening classes and other forms of extra-mural studies while working in low-standard jobs.

In current social science theory modern societies are examined using the concepts of state, civil society and the market (private sector). Bureaucracy cuts across the three spheres as their raison d'être. Public service is the bureaucratic apparatus of the state *par excellence.* According to Weber bureaucracy in its ideal form is formal and impersonal. In Sudanese society in general the social overrides all other forms of human activity. Social relations are given priority over work, politics and economics to a large extent. Those whom you know (as relatives, affines, friends, school mates, neighbors etc.) are given priority in treatment over others in pushing paper work and rendering services in government offices. Work laws and regulations are bent where kinship and friendship relations are involved. For Southerners who have remained inside the Sudan, ethnic connections may be more important in terms of consolidating social relations. This could be an area of misunderstanding and potential conflict between old-time civil servants from the North and newcomers from the South. The question arises as to the criteria of who should be given preferential treatment.

Again, the power-sharing protocol stipulates that, as already mentioned, neither Arabic nor English should be discriminated against in business, institutions of higher education or government offices. In practice, how will dealings with the Arabic-speaking general public be conducted (or for that matter even with the majority of uneducated Southerners)?

Networks usually develop their own standards of behavior and means of judging what is acceptable, laughable, recommendable, and what is not. Frictions can easily erupt over misinterpretations of certain incidents or situations because of the differing cultural backgrounds of co-workers in different networks. These days, ethnic jokes are rife in Khartoum and might easily result in angry – and sometimes violent – responses. Since networks are part of larger sets of associations it can be imagined how such a slight misunderstanding could flare up to engulf many others outside the work-place altogether.

Conclusion

I would like to end this chapter by stressing the fact that, whatever the challenges, the drive for peace in all sections of Sudanese society in the North and the South is positively stronger than those challenges and difficulties. 'Post'-conflict experiences in other parts of the world indicate that the decisive factor in the make-or-break situation is trust between the former contending parties. In a war between North and South which has taken half a century (with unstable years of peace) and the loss of millions of lives on both sides, and (in some cases) the total destruction of whole shattered communities, it is not easy to forgive or forget. However, many people in the Sudan count on the inherent, and most valued, quality the Sudanese possess, namely, tolerance. Though the message in the chapter agrees with the optimistic spirit surrounding the majority of the country, yet it cautions against unrealistic optimism. Realities have to be faced and overcome, not overlooked; otherwise the seeds of conflict will grow again and transform into a full-fledged war once more.

References

Akol, L. 2001. *SPLM /SPLA: Inside an African Revolution*. Khartoum: Khartoum University Press.

Alier, A. 1990. *The South Sudan : Too Many Agreements Dishonored*. Exeter: Ithaca Press.

Beshir, M.O. 1968. *The Southern Sudan: Background to Conflict*. Khartoum: Khartoum University Press.

Deng, F. 1995. *War of Visions : Conflict of identities in the Sudan*. Washington, DC: The Brookings Institution.

El-Battahani, A. 2001. 'Democracy , Economic Growth and Poverty in Sudan', in *Proceedings of the Conference on Democracy, Sustainable Development and Poverty: Are they compatible?* Addis Ababa: Development Policy Management Forum (DPMF), 157–76.

Government of Sudan. 2001. *Proceedings of The National Conference on Public Adminstration*. 3 volumes. Khartoum: Ministry of Labor and Administrative Reform.

Ibrahim, I., A. Elobodi and M. Holi. 2003. *Poverty , Employment and Policy-making in Sudan: A country profile*. Cairo: ILO Office.

Khalid, M. 2004. 'Am I Pessimist or Optimist?', *Al-Rayalam Daily*, 25 June.

Niblock, T. 1987. *Class and Power in the Sudan*. Albany, NY: State University of New York Press.

Nyaba, P. 1997. *The Politics of Liberation in South Sudan*. Kampala: Fountain Publishers.

Nyaba, P. 2004. 'We Will Only Declare Our Wealth: Evening out social and economic disparities in post-war South Sudan.' Paper presented to Reconstruction of War-torn Communities in the Middle East and Africa (RWCMEA) workshop, Ahfad University, Omdurman.

Sudan Government and SPLM/A. 2005. *The Comprehensive Peace Agreement*. Nairobi, 9 January.

United Nations Development Assistance Framework. 2002. *Sudan: Common Country Assessment (CCA) 2002 – 2006*. Khartoum: UNDP, Sudan.

Voll, J. and S Voll. 1985. *The Sudan: Unity and Diversity in a Multicultural State*. Boulder, CO: Westview Press.

World Bank. 2003. *Sudan Stabilization and Reconstruction: Country Economic Memorandum*. Washington, DC: World Bank.

Notes

1 The government of Sudan and the Sudan People's Liberation Army had been engaged in continuous negotiations before concluding the final Comprehensive Peace Agreement (CPA) in January 2005. These negotiations were held in different parts of Kenya (Karen, Machakos, Nairobi, Nakuru and finally Naivasha) between 2002 and 2004. In Machakos the guiding principles for the subsequent negotiations were agreed on 20 July 2002 and became known as the Machakos Protocols, which later constituted an integral part of the final CPA.

2 There is a vast literature on the roots and development of the Sudanese conflict. For some useful texts, see (Beshir 1968; Voll and Voll 1985; Niblock 1987; Alier 1990; Deng 1995; Nyaba 1997; Akol 2001; El-Battahani 2001).

3 For a detailed survey of the civil service see Government of Sudan (2001)

8

Elections
& Conflict
in Southern Africa
KHABELE MATLOSA

The past two decades have witnessed far-reaching developments that could arguably be said to be revolutionary in both form and content (Huntington 1991; Hyden and Bratton 1992; Ake 1996, 2000; Bratton and van de Walle 1997; Luckham et al. 2003). These developments have been marked, in the main, by a deliberate transition from authoritarianism towards democratic governance. Equally significant has been the transformation towards economic liberalization throughout the globe. Equally important has been a global shift from the pervasive trend of violent inter-state conflict towards intra-state conflicts with implications for both democratization and economic liberalization. Harris and Reilly (1998:1) capture this trend poignantly:

> The nature of violent conflict in the world has changed in recent decades, both in its actual subject-matter and the form of its expression. One of the most dramatic changes has been the trend away from traditional inter-state conflict (that is, one between sovereign states) and towards intra-state conflict (that is one which takes place between factions within an existing state). Whereas most violent conflicts over the course of the twentieth century have been between states, in the 1990s almost all major conflicts around the world have taken place within states.

Thus, the world is undergoing both political liberalization and economic liberalization in tandem, and these have to be understood within the changing conflict dynamics at both the macro-level of the globe and the micro-level of the nation-state. As Luckham et al. (2003:1) argue persuasively: 'nearly everywhere, it has been argued, liberal representative democracy has been accepted as the best method of managing political affairs.' This global sea change towards both liberal democracy and market-propelled economic systems has been given added impetus by the ending of the Cold War in the early 1990s. The southern African region is no exception to this world-wide political transformation. Internal dynamics in individual countries have helped drive this process of political transition. Equally important has been the impact not only of the ending of the Cold War, but also of the collapse of apartheid in South Africa (Matlosa 2001),

118

during which the region had been enmeshed in protracted conflicts, which had not allowed its states to enjoy sustainable development, democratic governance, stability and peace. It was therefore expected, by many keen observers of the region's political development, that the post-Cold War and post-apartheid era would bring about the stability and peace so crucial for democratic governance and economic development (Baregu and Landsberg 2003; Matlosa 2004).

Elections are currently perceived as the central, albeit not the sole, condition for both the transition to and the consolidation of democracy and stability in the region. In essence, elections are an important, but not the only, ingredient for democratic practice and culture. If well managed, they are also crucial instruments for conflict management in war-torn societies. Conversely, elections can also accentuate existing conflicts among belligerent parties. This is not surprising, for elections themselves are, by their very nature, conflict-ridden, given that they present a contest over state power (Sisk and Reynolds 1998; Matlosa 2001; Lodge et al. 2002). For elections to add value to democratic governance, stability, peace and reconciliation, and clear rules, procedures and systems that bind all the contesting parties are required. Often the debate on elections and conflict tends to focus mainly on the general elections, thereby downplaying other levels of the electoral process more by default than by design. It is worth noting that primary elections within political parties are as (if not more) contentious as the general elections themselves. They have led to or accelerated intra-party power struggles, faction fighting, and splits of parties into fragmented political fiefdoms (Olukoshi 1998). In essence, primary elections could either stabilize or destabilize the party machinery, depending on the degree of inner-party democracy in each of the Southern African Development Community (SADC) states. On the whole, internal party democracy is weak; hence the fragmentation and relative ineffectiveness of opposition parties throughout the region.

Furthermore, it is worth emphasizing that local government elections are as important in southern Africa as general elections and, in much the same way, are as conflict-ridden. Whereas much of the conflict around general elections is primarily among political parties, the principal conflict in local government elections revolves around the power struggle between modern and traditional institutions of governance, although inter-party strife also marks local-level conflicts. It is interesting that, although many SADC countries have embraced the idea and practice of holding legislative and presidential elections on a fairly regular basis, almost all of them, bar three, namely, Angola, the Democratic Republic of Congo and Swaziland, exhibit a poor record in terms of regular local government elections. We are as yet not able to proffer a solid and convincing argument as to this glaring discrepancy or democratic deficit (to borrow Luckham's phrase), save to note that this is testimony to the level of political centralization of the current systems – itself a relic of the one-party/one-person rule of the yesteryears. Devolution of power to local areas in the form of democratic local government is yet to be institutionalized in the SADC region. This still remains one of the major challenges of democratic consolidation in the region and in the entire African continent.

Conceptualizing Governance

It is fairly easy to explain the embrace of democratic culture and practice in the SADC region. It is a little more difficult, however, to conceptualize these developments. Explanation of phenomena entails simple narration and description of what is happening, while conceptualization transcends narration and description as it seeks to unravel deeper meaning and ramifications as to why and how things happen the way they do. Thus a more plausible discussion of problems, progress and prospects for democratic governance, stability and peace in southern Africa, and the role of elections in this regard, has to grapple with some common understanding of critical concepts. These include the state, government, democracy and democratization, authoritarianism, conflict and conflict management, elections and electoral systems.

The concept of the 'state' usually invokes heated debate among social scientists. The state could be perceived as either the territorial entity which is home to a specific people sharing a common culture even if ethnically or racially diverse, or as an institutional entity. This chapter adopts the latter definition, which conceives of the state as a set of permanent institutions of government comprising decision-making structures (the legislature), decision-enforcing organs (the security establishment), and policy formulating agencies (the bureaucracy) (Chazan et al. 1988; Dunleavy and O'Leary 1987; Hall and Ikenbery 1989). The state therefore comprises permanent institutions, which do not change despite periodic elections and changes of government over time, and is thus crucial for the running of national affairs (Matlosa 2001).

In contrast, 'government' refers not to institutions but rather to officers who staff state institutions for the effective and efficient running of national affairs. Unlike state institutions, governments come and go, changing over time either through the smooth transition brought about by elections (ballot-propelled changes) or through the violent overthrow of regimes by way of military coups (bullet-propelled changes). A simple distinction between a state and a government, therefore, is that (a) the state refers to institutions, whereas government denotes people in charge of these institutions, and (b) the state is permanent whereas government is by its very nature temporary and ephemeral. The manner in which the state institutions are run defines the extent to which a political system in a given country could be classified as either democratic or authoritarian.

Governance denotes the process by which the state and government machineries are set in motion. The mode of governance determines the manner in which power is exercised in the public realm (Hyden and Bratton 1992). It simply refers to the method and art of governing a given country. Whereas the state refers to permanent institutions for running national affairs and government refers to officers who staff state institutions, governance defines the modality and process of governing. Governance can be either democratic or authoritarian (Jackson and Jackson 1997). Democratic governance derives its mandate, legitimacy, credibility and acceptability from consensus and persuasion, whereas authoritarian governance draws its value from threats, coercion and patronage. Elections play a more important role in democratic governance in present-day southern Africa. During the period of one-party and personal rule in the region, when authoritarian governance was the order of the day, elections were insignificant and had a minimal bearing on the political system as a legitimizing factor. The governance process in southern Africa has undergone a major transformation since the ending of the Cold War and the demise of apartheid in South Africa, away from authoritarian rule of civilian and military varieties towards politics of consensus and persuasion upon which legitimate rule is anchored.

Various authorities have defined democracy differently (Ake 1996, 2000; Jackson and Jackson 1997; Luckham et al. 2003). It is not far-fetched to surmise that there are as many definitions of democracy as there are writers on the subject. For this study, democracy is taken to mean a political system that allows all citizens to freely choose their government over time through elections, that is accountable to the electorate, and that accords people adequate participation in the running of national affairs. It is a system that is transparent in driving processes of nation-building and economic development, that respects fundamental human rights, and that strives towards a fair distribution of national resources. Only by meeting the above conditions is a government likely to enjoy both domestic and international legitimacy and credibility, which are needed for its moral title to rule. The three known forms of democracy throughout the world are (liberal democracy, social democracy and popular democracy. According to Jackson and Jackson (1997:77),

> an essential characteristic of democracy ... is the reconciliation of the need for order and stability with a degree of influence for competing political interests. Representatives are elected by a form of majority rule to make legislation, which has the force of law. They are allowed to do so because success in elections accords the winners the *legitimacy* required to govern. A *majority principle* is required so that decisions can be taken by the people and their representatives even when division continues to exist.

Authoritarianism, on the other hand, is a concept used to denote a political system which relies upon obedience, coercion and fear as its key legitimating factors to sustain continuity and reproduction of the governing elite. It is no wonder, therefore, that such regimes

> impose one political group or interest over everyone else. They restrict pluralism and limit public participation, calling for obedience and no dissent.... In authoritarian countries, power is organised by the elites through the military, bureaucracy, religious leaders, or similar authorities.... Usually little effort is made in such regimes to mobilize the population to political action because the leaders prefer apathy.... Parties are frequently banned and opponents imprisoned. The threat of state violence is never far behind significant political activity. (ibid.: 81)

Varieties of authoritarianism include mono-party states, military regimes, dynastic or monarchic oligarchies, and theocratic regimes.

Part of the limitation of the democratization project in southern Africa today has to do with its form and content. A majority of the states are following liberal democracy and in most cases it seems that the dominant party is the preferred mode of party system after the long years of a mono-party system. Under these circumstances, stability has not really taken root. Consequently, democratic governance and sustainable development remain elusive goals and elections make little sense to ordinary voters. What other scholars have observed recently is that, under the current process of political liberalization, there is an enormous amount of focus on the democratization of high politics revolving around the state with less focus on the democratization of 'deep politics of society' (Luckham et al. 2003:5). Even under the new democratic dispensation in southern Africa today, which Thandika Mkandawire (cited in SAPES/UNDP/SADC 1998) aptly terms a 'choiceless democracy' (and which we could also qualify as 'voiceless democracy'), evidence abounds that, first, both leaders and the electorate have little say in terms of choice of the democratic model in place; second, people vote not so much for real national issues as for individuals or parties on the basis of 'pork-barrel' or patronage politics; and third, democratization currently tends to amount to regular circulation and self-reproduction of a small coterie of the elite, thereby excluding the majority of poor people who are remembered only at election time – a trend that Patrick Bond, in the case of South Africa, terms an elite transition, suggesting that, despite the democratic transition in the country, politics tends to amount to elite circulation devoid of popular voices and choices (Bond 2005).

Although conflicts have been inherent in all societies since time immemorial, the concept 'conflict' remains both nebulous and elusive in social science discourse (Schellenberg, 1982; Ohlson and Stedman 1994). For this study, the concept is used to denote incompatibility of interests, choices and goals over the distribution of resources, ideological orientation, and power among various political actors. Thus three factors are important in defining a conflict situation, namely, resource distribution, ideological contestation, and power struggles. Conflict arises from interaction among two or more actors in the political system with incompatible interests, choices and goals wherein the ability of one actor to gain depends to an important degree on some loss on the part of others. Politics is therefore a conflict-ridden game. When all is said and done, conflict, in and of itself, is not necessarily a negative phenomenon, as much of the discourse in peace and security studies would make us believe. Conflict could also be perceived as part of the social transformation of societies in a positive direction, and as such cannot be wished away or detested, as it were. It is not conflict that presents a big problem for our societies but what is actually done with it, how belligerent parties strive to resolve it in a constructive manner. Constructive resolution of conflict revolves around the political settlement of disputes rather than pursuing a military course of action, since the latter naturally leads to conflict escalation rather than its resolution. It is worth noting that, following protracted liberation wars that were followed, in some countries such as Angola and Mozambique, by internal wars among parties with external support within the context of the Cold War and apartheid, all the violent conflicts in the region were resolved by way of political settlement involving multi-stakeholder dialogue and negotiation.

It should also be noted that the SADC Electoral Commissions Forum, established in the early 1990s, has a specific Conflict Resolution Programme, which aims at creating sustainable and effective capacity for member countries to manage election-related conflicts. The specific objectives of this programme are as follows: first, to facilitate collective exploration by SADC electoral commissions of the nature and manifestation of election-related conflicts, and the systems and capacities required to manage them; second, to facilitate the design of conflict management systems appropriate to each national context; third, to develop capacity, through training of designated persons in each country, to manage conflicts; and fourth, to establish a resource panel of experts who can be drawn upon to assist conflict-related crises during elections.

An election refers to a process whereby a people belonging to a particular territorial state and under the authority of a single institutional state, variously referred to as either the electorate or voters, choose their government periodically as a clear expression of representative democracy (Matlosa 2001). Elections, therefore, are an important ingredient of democracy. However, elections on their own do not guarantee democracy nor are they synonymous with it. As Jackson and Jackson (1997: 366) persuasively argue, 'without some form of elections, there is no democracy. Citizens have no choice, no say in who will govern them. But it is equally true... that elections themselves are far from a guarantee of democracy.'

Elections serve various functions including political education, recruitment and selection of political leadership, orderly succession of government anchored upon the ballot rather than the bullet, periodic review of the performance of the government, and an opportunity for renewal of mandate or replacement of the incumbent government by another. They ensure domestic and international legitimacy and credibility of government and, in war-torn societies, are a mechanism that assists in conflict resolution. Whereas an election is a process, an electoral system refers to a method or the rules of the process (Matlosa 2005). It is a method that a particular country adopts for choosing national leaders to represent the electorate in the legislature. Its primary *raison d'être* is to match votes with seats in Parliament (Reynolds and Reilly 1997; Reilly 2001; Reynolds et al. 2005). There are various electoral systems throughout the world and each country adopts a particular model on the basis of its culture, political history, and party organization, the three main types being the single member plurality system, the single member majority system and proportional representation. Different countries variously apply these systems and their application may include a mixture of any of the three. Evidence now abounds suggesting that the single member plurality system is more conflict-inducing and conflict-prone than proportional representation. With the exception of Botswana and Mauritius, almost all the SADC countries that have adopted the first-past-the-post electoral system have tended to experience much more profound violent and non-violent conflicts threatening their political systems as it generates instability.

Elections & Conflict: Ballots versus Bullets

For most of the 1980s, southern African states steered their political systems away from mono-party and military rule towards multi-party and pluralist political systems (Giliomee and Simkin 1999; Matlosa 2004; Matlosa 2005). Of all the SADC countries, only Angola, Swaziland and the Democratic Republic of Congo have not embraced multi-party rule and regular party-based elections as a vital form of contestation over state power. Despite these three exceptions, a consensus is emerging within the region that multi-party systems are better political arrangements than single-party systems (SAPES/UNDPP/SADC 1998; Luckham et al. 2003). Currently, the region is faced with the challenge of consolidating the new-found democratic practice and culture as well as institutionalizing the culture of peace and reconciliation after long years of both violent and non-violent conflict. As one writer aptly observes:

> Post conflict elections are supposed to transform a violent conflict into a non-violent one: *ballots take the place of bullets.* They are expected to enable the former warring parties to pursue their conflicting ideologies and programs in a peaceful fashion. Elections give all factions an opportunity to present their agendas to the citizens, debate with their opponents, and mobilise public opinion to capture political power. Like other elements of a democratic system, *elections contribute to the institutionalisation of a conflict resolution mechanism* in the body politic. (Kumar 1998:7, emphasis added)

Within the current process of political liberalization, multi-party elections have become firmly entrenched in the political system of a majority of southern Africa states. Botswana and Mauritius are the longest-enduring stable multi-party systems anchored upon regular elections over the last three decades of political independence, and they have experienced few, if any, violent conflicts (Matlosa 2001, 2004; Molomo 2004).

The region's recent electoral record and the degree to which elections resolve major conflicts show great variations. On the basis of the 1991 Bicesse Agreement, Angola held its presidential and legislative elections in September 1992 in the middle of a major violent conflict. The election result delivered a victory for the Popular Movement for the Liberation of Angola (MPLA). In the presidential race, Jose Eduardo dos Santos of the MPLA secured 49.67 per cent and the Union for the Total Liberation of Angola (UNITA's), Jonas Savimbi, 40.07 per cent of the total votes cast. In the National Assembly race, the MPLA won 53 per cent of the votes as against UNITA's 34.10 per cent. Instead of the electoral process acting as a catalyst in the transition to and consolidation of democratic rule, it accentuated and invigorated the armed conflict (Ottaway 1998; Matlosa 1999a). Like Mozambique, Angola operates the proportional representation electoral model which is highly regarded as enhancing broader participation and thereby contributing to political stability in post-conflict societies (Matlosa 1999b; Reynolds et al. 2005). The Angolan situation provides sufficient evidence that in some instances elections alone are insufficient to bring about political stability, reconciliation and peace. As Kumar (1998) and Ottaway (1998) remind us, there is little doubt that in many instances elections leave a bitter legacy, aggravating existing tensions and cleavages. The Angolan conflict is one of the most protracted and costly conflicts in Africa, and it is encouraging, indeed, that since the death of the UNITA leader, Jonas Savimbi, in early 2002, considerable progress has been made towards resolving this conflict constructively, with a likelihood of elections being held in 2005.

In contrast, Mozambique experienced a smooth political transition based on the 1992 General Peace Agreement signed in Rome by the belligerent parties (Lundin 2004). This culminated in the holding of presidential and legislative elections in October 1994, which resulted in a coalition government incorporating the Front for the Liberation of Mozambique (FRELIMO) and the Mozambican National Resistance (RENAMO). This suggests that, under certain conditions, elections could be useful in transforming war-torn societies into stable political systems. Furthermore, the Mozambican experience suggests that power-sharing is crucial for the credibility of the elections outcome and for sustainable peace in war-torn societies.

Mozambique's fledgling democracy was given a further boost by the second elections of 1999, which consolidated the coalition government. In the presidential contest, Frelimo's Joachim Chissano won 52.3 per cent and RENAMO's Alfonso Dlhakama 47.7 per cent of the votes cast, thereby ensuring the continuity of the government of national unity in a country slowly recovering from a severe war. In the legislative contest, FRELIMO won, by capturing 48.5 per cent of the votes, to RENAMO's 38.8 per cent. About 11 minor parties secured far fewer votes in the legislative elections and did not field candidates in the presidential race. As with the presidential elections, the outcome of the national assembly elections further consolidated the government of national unity, so crucial for both the political and the economic recovery in Mozambique.

Although the major opposition party RENAMO complained bitterly about what it perceived as irregularities and fraud in the electoral process, the outcome was accepted by all parties, thereby according the new government legitimacy and political integrity (Turner et al. 1998; Lundin 2004). This highlights the importance of acceptance of the results by all political players if stability is to prevail in a country, especially a war-torn one. Like Angola, Mozambique operates a proportional representation system, but the political effects of the elections on violent conflict in the two countries present sharp contrasts. In general, the proportional representation system lends itself to the constructive management of conflicts, especially when they are violent, as the experience of South Africa since 1994 clearly indicates. Mozambique's 2004 election was the third since its peace agreement of 1992. This general election was preceded by local government elections in 2003. President Joachim Chissano did not stand in the 2004 election, given that he had served his two terms in office, and this again is a positive sign for Mozambique's fledgling democracy.

In between the polar opposites of Angola and Mozambique lies a mixture of experiences with regard to the degree to which elections accentuate or contain conflicts. Quite obviously, elections have helped in the process of political settlement of the South African conflict. The South African example is instructive for the conduct of protracted negotiations among the belligerent parties; the signing of peace accords and the establishment of peace panels preceded the 1994 elections (Matlosa 2001). Although violence is still a major problem in South Africa, relative stability has been achieved and the country's electoral system permits broader representation of political actors in the legislature. In South Africa, therefore, elections contributed to the wider peace and reconciliation process to bring about stability, which still prevails today.

Although Namibia's political settlement of its long-drawn-out war of liberation also involved elections, which turned SWAPO into the ruling party, the international community, especially the United Nations, was heavily involved in the process. This demonstrates that, in war-torn societies, international assistance is often essential as there is usually a lack of institutional, financial and technical capability to hold and run elections (Kumar 1998). The same was true for the 1992 elections in Angola and in Mozambique in 1994 and 1999.

The Zimbabwean elections of June 2000 also attracted overwhelming international attention and more than 500 international observers and domestic monitors witnessed the electoral process. Given its entrenched mono-party political culture and heavy centralization of power, political liberalization presents a daunting challenge to Zimbabwe. Preparations for the June 2000 elections were marred by sporadic and violent conflicts, which were accelerated by the land invasions spearheaded by war veterans from February 2000. Dialogue and negotiation among the belligerent parties did not mark the road to the Zimbabwean elections and, as a result, there was little possibility that they would play a significant role in securing the country's long-lasting stability. In addition, there were no well-defined conflict resolution mechanisms to manage the conflict, leading to counter-productive accusations and counter-accusations regarding its root causes (Makumbe and Compagnon 2000; Sachikonye 2004; Matlosa 2002).

The Zimbabwe elections of 2000 were both interesting and intriguing in many respects. They were interesting, primarily because after years of hegemonic hold on power in a mono-party atmosphere, the ruling ZANU-PF faced a real political challenge from an emergent opposition formation, the Movement for Democratic Change (MDC). They were intriguing because, despite the political violence and intimidation that marked the campaign process, large numbers of ordinary Zimbabweans braved the political turbulence and went to the polls to exercise their democratic right to choose their national leaders. Of the 5.29 million registered voters, 65 per cent turned out at the polls, far exceeding the 32 per cent in the 1996 presidential elections, or the 57 per cent and 54 per cent respectively in the 1995 and 1990 parliamentary elections. There was a clear ideological divide between the ruling party, which espoused a land reform redistribution programme with a view to deepening the nationalist project of expanding or broadening political liberation into the economic sphere, on the one hand, and the opposition which espoused the idea of employment creation and upheld liberal democratic values (Matlosa, 2001, 2004, 2005; Sachikonye, 2004).

The outcome was fascinating too. Of the directly elected parliamentary seats (i.e. 120 seats) ZANU-PF won narrowly by securing 62 seats. The MDC put up an unprecedented political battle against ZANU-PF's long established hegemony and gained 57 seats, becoming the first-ever significant opposition. ZANU-Ndonga led by the Reverend Ndabaningi Sithole secured only one seat. Both ZANU-PF and the MDC face enormous challenges. The MDC has to prove that its electoral support translates into effective oppositional politics rooted in well-defined constituencies. Upsetting a hegemonic force such as ZANU-PF, albeit no mean task, is one thing, and sustaining the opposition momentum and avoiding internal fragmentation is quite another. Effective and meaningful opposition is a quintessential element of democratic transformation in Zimbabwe. The 2000 electoral process was perceived by many international observers as having been transparent, credible and acceptable to the majority of Zimbabweans, thus giving unequivocal legitimacy to the newly established two-party legislature. The outcome was also conducive to the resolution of major conflicts in Zimbabwe mainly around the land question and the constitutional review process. The former was at an advanced stage (Moyo and Matondi 2003) and the latter certainly had to be revisited in the post-election period following a pre-election referendum in which a majority of Zimbabweans rejected the draft constitutional amendments (Mandaza 2000).

Zimbabwe's most recent parliamentary election took place on 31 March 2005. Keen observers of the Zimbabwean political scene watched closely how the election unfolded and the extent to which the electoral authorities and other key stakeholders adhered to various regional electoral norms, guidelines and principles, particularly the SADC principles outlined earlier in this paper. The broader context within which we are able to understand the complexities surrounding the 2005 election is the history of one-party rule that had been entrenched in the country between 1980 and 1987 and the culture of centralization of power and curtailment of diversity of opinion and political tolerance as part of the one-party political trajectory of the past two decades. Although the one-party era is clearly over and has been replaced by a multi-party political regime marked by regular elections since the 1990s, the vestiges of the old order still linger on and, as the English aphorism goes, 'old habits die hard'. It is thus no surprise that the behavior of the ruling ZANU-PF towards both opposition parties, especially the Movement for Democratic Change (MDC), and other non-state political actors such as civil society organizations bears the hallmarks of a one-party political culture whereby criticism of or political challenge towards officialdom is considered heretical at best and treasonous at worst. This political culture tends to depend for its survival upon coercion and the 'conspiracy of silencing' rather than persuasion and public dialogue. One of the net effects of political coercion and silencing has obviously been the entrenched and all-pervasive polarization of the Zimbabwe polity, especially since the 1999 constitutional referendum and the 2000 parliamentary election.

The Role of Elections in Post-Conflict Societies: Healing Old Wounds?

As has been observed in the previous sections, elections serve an important function in the process of democratization and conflict management. This is more so in a situation where a country has just emerged from armed conflict. Elections following armed conflict serve at least three objectives. First, they compel the belligerent parties to bury their hatchets and seek a political settlement of their ideological differences. They remind them that ballots rather than bullets are a preferred method of contestation for the efficient transfer of state power. Second, they aim to bestow legitimacy and credibility on new democratic governance after a protracted conflict. The worst-case scenario is when one party wins outright, thereby marginalizing the others (as in Lesotho in 1993 and 1998). The best-case scenario is one where the election outcome leads to broadly based representation in the legislature, as was the case in South Africa after the 1994 elections. This then compels all parties to commit themselves to building a democracy by transforming the culture of the politics of coercion and embracing the politics of consensus. Virulent opposition in parliament is far better than violent opposition in the streets. Third, they serve to give practical meaning to the peace accords and reconciliation programme, as was the case in Mozambique (1992), Namibia (1994) and South Africa (1994).

The Angolan elections of 1992 failed to deliver stability precisely because the belligerent parties, in particular the opposition, did not abide by the Bicesse Accord and various other peace agreements made since the 1985 Lusaka Accord. Even the 1994 Lusaka Protocol failed to deliver peace and stability to Angola until the death of Savimbi in 2002. Although the elections are generally regarded to have been a technical success under the prevailing climate, they are considered to have been an utter political fiasco, as the losing party refused to accept the outcome, and preferred to resort to the bullet for resolving political differences and settling scores in the contest for state power (Turner et al. 1998).

Another interesting case of violence-ridden elections over the years is the small mountain kingdom of Lesotho. Although the 1965 pre-independence election did not really trigger a violent conflict as such, the 1970 election almost plunged the landlocked nation into a civil war. This was then followed by the military coup of 1986, which dislodged the authoritarianism of a civilian type and replaced it with one of a military variety. Following eight years of military rule, Lesotho returned to a multi-party political system on the liberal democratic model in 1993 through a general election that was resoundingly won by the Basutoland Congress Party (BCP) which had been denied its legitimate victory by the then ruling Basotho National Party (BNP) in the aborted 1970 election. Various types of violent and non-violent conflicts marked Lesotho's young democracy between 1993 and the general election of 1998, which was immediately followed by a much more profoundly violent conflict in which the ruling Lesotho Congress for Democracy locked horns in a fierce and bitter war with elements of the opposition parties. These not only caused enormous damage to the economy but also the military intervention of South Africa and Botswana (Vale 2003). Given the consensus that emerged following the 1998 election that much of Lesotho's problems stemmed from the nature of the electoral model, the country took the deliberate decision to abandon the purely first-past-the-post system for a mixed-member proportional system that combined elements of both. This system was first put into effect during the May 2002 election and the outcome has been quite impressive as Lesotho for the first time boasts a highly inclusive multi-party parliament conducive to general political stability.

There are several preconditions for elections after armed conflict. Eleven can be mentioned. First, all belligerent parties must commit themselves to peace and reconciliation. To this end a peace accord and a clearly defined reconciliation programme are required, as both the Mozambican and the South African situations vividly illustrate. Second, post-conflict elections can be held only if the parties have signed a peace agreement and devised an achievable reconciliation programme, which must also be accompanied by the signing of a justiciable code of conduct for political parties. Without this, it is a gamble to hold elections under conditions of violent conflict (Matlosa 2001), as the Angolan situation so amply demonstrates. Third, as Kumar (1998) and Ottaway (1998) point out, there must be a capable and functional state system in existence before elections are conducted under conditions of armed conflict. As these authors rightly observe, if the very existence of the state is in doubt, as is the case with many failed states such as Somalia, international assistance is unlikely to fill the gap, and elections cannot bring political stability or resolve conflicts.

International assistance is highly valuable when elections are held in conditions of armed conflict. This constitutes the fourth precondition. War-torn countries have severely ravaged economies and a constrained resource and production base from which to finance electoral processes. The involvement of international monitors and observers contributes immensely to the credibility of the elections and the acceptance of their outcomes by the political parties concerned. Moreover, it reduces the probability of large-scale fraud and cheating. Kumar (1998) and Ottaway (1998) identify three critical forms of international assistance: (i) financial assistance for planning and holding elections; (ii) technical assistance and expertise in election administration, rules and procedures; and (iii) political assistance in the form of support to political parties, and civil organizations, voter education, monitoring and observation.

The fifth precondition is the need to demobilize troops or warring factions, and the integration of the armies into a national army, as well as peacekeeping operations, are vital before elections can be held. This process of demilitarization is crucial in transforming the culture of politics of violence and coercion and embracing the politics of dialogue and con-sensus. Although demilitarization and integration of armed formations has been relatively successful in Namibia, South Africa, Zimbabwe and Mozam-bique, it has not been successful in Lesotho and Angola. This partly explains why elections have not really deepened and consolidated political stability and democratic governance in these countries. Sixth, prior to elections, following violent conflict, returning refugees and displaced persons must be settled and allowed sufficient time to register as voters. Refugees and displaced persons are 'often the worst victims of civil wars, and therefore their active participation in elections tends to strengthen the peace process' (Kumar and Ottaway 1998:230). This could prove a difficult and costly task, but one that is crucial for democracy to emerge from the debris of a protracted war (Matlosa 2001).

Seventh, the clearing of landmines and the banning of military supplies from external sources is also an important precondition for elections after armed conflict. This was very important in the cases of Angola and

Mozambique, two countries whose belligerent factions have received massive amounts of external military supplies and which are also heavily mined. It is easier to ban the external supply of weapons under conditions of peace, but it is quite difficult and costly to clear landmines. Such mines continue an atrocious attack upon an innocent civilian population years after hostilities have ceased and make life miserable for ordinary people in the villages. The fear that landmines instill among rural populations triggers migration to the urban areas with its well-known social ills.

Eighth, elections following violent conflict must be run and administered by credible, autonomous and competent institutions that are not in any way linked to any of the belligerent parties in a partisan fashion. To this end, the establishment of independent electoral commissions is essential. These institutions require sufficient financial, technical and political support, not only from the international donor agencies but also from such institutions as the Electoral Commissions Forum of the SADC countries and the SADC Parliamentary Forum. The ninth precondition is the need to provide adequate time for preparations for elections after armed conflict. In fact, all elections require a long time to prepare, but this is more so for those following violent conflict. Various important tasks for such elections, such as the signing of peace accords, the demobilization and integration of troops, the settlement of returning refugees and displaced persons, agreement on the electoral model, voter education, voter registration, the establishment of the Independent Electoral Commission (IEC), etc. require a lot of time. The tenth, institutionalization of inner-party democracy is also crucial, so that the democratic practices and cultures within parties help them to see the value of dialogue and politics of consensus when dealing with their adversaries. It has been found that, in the majority of African states, parties lack internal democracy and this in part accounts for the current disintegration and fragmentation of opposition parties. Although the incumbent rulers work hard to undermine the opposition and the electoral system, weak opposition parties are also hindered by the first-past-the-pos system and internal leadership squabbles not necessarily based on ideological or policy differences. All these factors have wreaked havoc upon the opposition parties in southern Africa (Olukoshi 1998).

Eleventh, there is need for constitutional reform in countries that have experienced a violent conflict before elections are held, so that the belligerent parties engage in dialogue and negotiation around a new social contract regarding the forms of state, political system and electoral model they would prefer. This is important for building a minimum program that binds the belligerent parties together, and is different from a peace agreement. The Convention for Democratic South Africa (CODESA) negotiations achieved this objective for South Africa (Maphai 2000). Zimbabwe attempted this strategy with its recent constitutional review, which culminated in a referendum that, to the chagrin of the ruling party, received a 'No' vote (Makumbe and Compagnon 2000; Sachikonye 2004). Lesotho underwent some constitutional reform, which led to the adoption of the mixed member proportional system, and prospects for peace, reconciliation and stability in this country look very bright indeed. Mauritius has just undertaken electoral reform in which adoption of the mixed member proportional system has been recommended in place of the plurality system. Unfortunately, in Mauritius the proposed new electoral model was not used during the recent general election of July 2005.

It is crucial that the rules of state and electoral administration are agreed upon as a basis for all parties to accept the outcome of the elections. In this manner, the view of politics as a zero-sum game is likely to be replaced by one that conceives of it as a positive-sum process. This is important for the tolerance of opposing and divergent views in multi-ethnic and multi-racial societies. It is worth heeding Tekle's advice that 'mutual appreciation of opposition views must be accepted and the conviction that losers lose everything while winners take it all can no longer be the norm. It must be recognised that in a democracy winners and losers are partners and not enemies who must destroy each other' (1998: 175).

Conclusion

It is important to recognize the stark reality that the world has experienced a major sea change since the collapse of the Cold War and apartheid in the 1990s. Whereas violent inter-state conflict marked the Cold War era, the 1990s ushered in a new era of intra-state conflict. This era coincided, for better or for worse, with a two-pronged transition: from authoritarian regimes towards multi-party democracy and the entrenchment of economic liberalization. These various transformative developments have their own distinctive implications for democratization in southern Africa and specifically for the role and significance of elections in this delicate process. This chapter has investigated the interface between elections and conflict in southern Africa. The edge of the argument is that, although elections may in certain contexts assist in healing old wounds, in others they have, in fact, helped to aggravate the pain and poured pepper on the often open wounds of previous conflicts. It is succinctly evident that elections have, of course, combined with other complex arrays of factors, contributed to healing the wounds of old conflicts in, say, Namibia (1989), Mozambique (1994) and South Africa (1994). There is abundant evidence pointing to the stark reality that these are in fact some of the countries in which appreciable progress has been made towards nurturing and consolidating democracy, although serious challenges still remain. We have also discovered that elections have aggravated the pain and intensity of old wounds in countries like Angola (1992), Lesotho (1998) and Zimbabwe (2000 and 2005 parliamentary elections; 2002 presidential elections). It is important to note here that the critical challenge facing the Electoral Management Bodies (EMBs), the political parties and the electorate alike, is precisely how to ensure that an election does not worsen insecurity and instability, but rather adds value to existing institutional mechanisms for the constructive resolution of conflicts. To this end, we have observed that post-conflict southern Africa needs to take concrete steps towards realization of this important goal. We have identified eleven distinct, albeit intertwined, steps to be followed in order to make sure that elections make a meaningful contribution to peace, reconciliation and stability in the SADC region.

Thus, ideally elections have great potential to heal wounds, although they do also have the unintended effects of accentuating old conflicts. There is no straightforward causal relationship, therefore, between elections and conflict in the SADC region.

References

Ake, C. 1996. *Democracy and Development in Africa*. Washington, DC: The Brookings Institution.

Ake, C. 2000. *The Feasibility of Democracy in Africa*. Dakar: CODESRIA Books.

Baregu, M. and C. Landsberg. 2003. *From Cape to Congo: Southern Africa's Evolving Security Challenge*. Boulder, CO: Lynne Rienner Publishers.

Bond, P.2005. *Elite Transition: From Apartheid to Neo-liberalism in South Africa*, Scottsville: University of Kwazulu-Natal Press.

Bratton, M. and N. van de Walle. 1997. *Democratic Experiments in Africa*. New York: Cambridge University Press.

Chazan, N., R. Mortimer, J. Ravenhill, and D. Rothchild. 1988. *Politics and Society in Contemporary Africa*. Boulder, CO: Lynne Rienner Publishers.

Dunleavy, P. and B. O'Leary. 1987. *Theories of the State: The Politics of Liberal Democracy*. London: Macmillan Press.

Giliomee, H. and C. Simkins, eds. 1999. *The Awkward Embrace: One-party dominance and democracy*. Cape Town: Tafelberg.

Hall, J. and J. Ikenberry. 1989. *The State*. Minneapolis: University of Minnesota.

Harris, P. and B. Reilly, eds. 1998. *Democracy and Deep-Rooted Conflict: Options for Negotiators*. Stockholm: International IDEA Handbook Series.

Huntington. S. 1991. *The Third Wave: Democratisation in the late twentieth century*. Norman, OK: University of Oklahoma Press.

Hyden, G. and M. Bratton, eds. 1992. *Governance and Politics in Africa*. Boulder, CO: Lynne Rienner Publishers.

Jackson, J. and D. Jackson. 1997. *Comparative Introduction to Political Science*. Upper Saddle River, NJ: Prentice Hall.

Kumar, K., ed. 1998. *Postconflict Elections, Democratization, and International Assistance*. Boulder, CO: Lynne Rienner Publishers.

Kumar, K. and Ottaway, M. 1998. 'General Conclusions and Priorities for Policy Research', in K. Kumar, ed., *Postconflict Elections, Democratization and International Assistance*. Boulder, CO: Lynne Rienner Publishers 229–38.

Landsberg, C. 2004. *The Quiet Diplomacy of Liberation: International Politics and South Africa's transition*, Johannesburg: Jacana.

Lodge, T., D. Pottie and D. Kadima, eds. 2002. *Compendium of Elections in Southern Africa*. Johannesburg: Electoral Institute of Southern Africa.

Luckham, R., A. Goetz, and M. Kaldor. 2003. 'Democratic Institutions and Democratic Politics'. University of Sussex (mimeo).

Lundin, B. 2004. 'Elections, Constitutionalism and Stability in Mozambique', *African Journal on Conflict Resolution* , 4 (2), 97–118.

Makumbe, J. and D. Compagnon. 2000. *Behind the Smokescreen: The politics of Zimbabwe's 1995 general elections*. Harare: University of Zimbabwe Press.

Mandaza, I. 2000. 'Constitution-Making in Southern Africa: the Zimbabwe Experience'. Paper presented at a Conference on Constitution Making in Southern Africa hosted by the Southern African Regional Institute of Policy Studies (SARIPS), Harare, 26-28 July.

Maphai, V, ed. 2000. *South Africa: The Challenges of Change*. Harare: SAPES Books.

Matlosa, K.1999a. 'Electoral System, Stability and Democratic Governance in Southern Africa: A case study of Lesotho', SADC/EU Conference on 'Strengthening and Consolidating Democracy in SADC through the Electoral Process', Gaborone. 20–22 June.

Matlosa, K. 1999b. 'Angola: can structural adjustment lead to peace?' in G. Harris, ed., *Recovery from Armed Conflict in Developing Countries: An economic and political analysis*, London: Routledge, 258–71.

Matlosa, K. 2001. 'Ballots or Bullets: Elections and Conflict Management in Southern Africa', *Journal of African Elections* 1 (1): 1–16.

Matlosa, K. 2002. 'Election Monitoring and Observation in Zimbabwe: Hegemony Versus Sovereignty', *African Journal of Political Science*, 7 (1): 129–54.

Matlosa, K. 2004. 'Electoral Systems, Constitutionalism and Conflict Management in Southern Africa', *African Journal on Conflict Resolution*, 4 (2): 11–54.

Matlosa, K. 2005. 'Elections and Democracy in Southern Africa: Progress, Problems and Prospects for Electoral System Reforms'. Paper prepared for regional conference on 'Electoral Systems and Reform in Representation', Sun and Sand Lodge, Mangochi, Malawi, 29 June-1 July.

Molomo, M. 2003. 'The Need for Electoral Reform in Botswana', *African Journal of Conflict Resolution*, 4 (2): 55–78.

Moyo, S. and P. Matondi. 2003. 'The Politics of Land Reform in Zimbabwe', in M. Baregu and C. Landsberg, eds, *From Cape to Congo: Southern Africa's Evolving Security Challenge*, Boulder, CO: Lynne Rienner Publishers, 73–95.

Ohlson, T. and S. Stedman. 1994. *The New is Not Yet Born: Conflict Resolution in Southern Africa*. Washington, DC: The Brookings Institution.

Olukoshi, A. 1998. *The Politics of Opposition in Contemporary Africa*. Uppsala: Nordiska Afrika-institutet.

Ottaway, M. 1998. 'Angola's Failed Election', in K. Kumar, ed., *Postconflict Elections, Democratization, and International Assistance*, Boulder: Lynne Rienner Publishers.

Reilly, B. 2001. *Democracy in Divided Societies: Electoral Engineering for Conflict Management*. Cambridge: Cambridge University Press.

Reynolds, A. and B. Reilly. 1997. *The International IDEA Handbook of Electoral Systems Design*. Stockholm: International IDEA

Reynolds, A., B. Reilly, and A. Ellis, eds. 2005. *Electoral System Design: The New International IDEA Handbook*. Stockholm: International IDEA.

Sachikonye, L. 2004. 'Zimbabwe: Constitutionalism, the Electoral System and Challenges for Governance and Stability', *African Journal on Conflict Resolution* 4 (2): 171–95.

SAPES/SADC/UNDP. 1998. *Regional Human Development Report on Governance and Human Development in Southern Africa*. Harare: SAPES Books.

Schellenberg, J. 1982. *The Science of Conflict*. Oxford: Oxford University Press.

Sisk, T. and A. Reynolds, eds. 1998. *Elections and Conflict Management in Africa*. Washington, DC: United Nations Institute of Peace Press.

Tekle, A.1998. 'Elections and Electoral Systems in Africa: Purposes, problems and prospects', *International Commission of Jurists Review* .60:167–78.

Turner, M., S. Nelson, and K. Mahling-Clark. 1998. 'Mozambique's Vote for Democratic Governance', in K. Kumar, ed., *Postconflict Elections, Democratization, and International Assistance*, Boulder, CO: Lynne Rienner Publishers, 153–76.

Vale, P. 2003. *Security and Politics in South Africa: The Regional Dimension*. Boulder, CO: Lynne Rienner Publishers.

9

The Somali Peace Process
from Arta to Eldoret to Mbagathi
Opportunities & Challenges

KIZITO SABALA, AISHA AHMAD
& EDWIN RUTTO

For fifteen years, Somalia has endured state failure and political anarchy, allowing a culture of warlord rule and civil conflict to become entrenched. Since the establishment of the Transitional Federal Government in November 2004 the Somali peace talks have made significant progress, particularly in the area of political reconstruction. The newly established Transitional Federal Government (TFG) has the opportunity to rebuild the country and re-establish security within its borders, if the brokered cease-fire holds and the warring factions maintain their commitment to the central government. Only through the process of centralizing authority and eliminating social and military fragmentation can the country move into a phase of post-conflict peace-building and reconstruction.

Insecurity, poverty and social fragmentation have not only worsened the political anarchy in Somalia but also exacerbated regional instability and cross-border illicit and criminal activities in the Horn of Africa. With respect to security considerations, the proliferation of small arms and light weapons ensuing from the decade-plus civil war requires a government-run Disarmament, Demobilization, and Reintegration (DDR) program, aimed at demilitarizing the Somali economy. Domestic security considerations also have regional implications, as the absence of government has resulted in cross-border arms trafficking and smuggling activities with neighboring Kenya and Ethiopia. Criminal activities have dominated the economy, resulting from the collapse of traditional farming and pastoralist activities. Economic failure and environmental degradation have resulted in a humanitarian disaster, with poverty, starvation, disease and mortality across the country and scarcity problems exacerbating the conflict and corruption.

The social fragmentation of Somalia results from a culture of clanism, which has formed the basis of the ongoing civil war. Human rights abuses and war crimes have been pervasive throughout the conflict. A period of post-conflict peace and reconciliation is now required urgently. Past grievances must be resolved and mechanisms must be put in place to resolve future disputes between antagonistic factions.

The challenges to post-conflict peace-building are numerous, ranging from physical reconstruction to social reconciliation. The purpose of this

134

chapter is to identify the opportunities for the new government in post-conflict peace-building, such as demilitarization and the development of national security, to address specific challenges to post-conflict reconstruction, specifically in the areas of domestic security, social cohesion, economic development, and regionalism. The research addresses the question of social cohesion among the country's many clans and factions, and how the TFG can promote nationalism as a viable alternative to clan and sub-clan loyalties. Finally, it analyzes the key role that the regional security architecture within the framework of the Inter-Governmental Authority on Development (IGAD) must play in helping Somalia recover from the effects of a long period of civil war.

The chapter, which utilizes information from primary and secondary sources, is divided into four broad sections. Section one introduces and discusses the subject, mentioning the objectives and background documents. Section two examines security issues, in particular the DDR and economic recovery, and section three looks at the challenges and opportunities for fostering social cohesion. Section four concludes by considering issues of security, in particular social cohesion and economics from a regional perspective, arguing that, while the onus of pacifying Somalia lies largely in the hands of the Somalis, the region must also contribute. The section mentions a number of issues that the regional security architecture within the framework of IGAD must consider as building blocks towards the long-term process of enhancing security, social, and economic aspects of the Somalia state.

The Somali Peace Process: Eldoret–Nairobi

15 October 2002 marked the beginning of the fourteenth Somali peace process in Eldoret, Kenya. The IGAD-sponsored negotiations quickly resulted in the signing of a Cessation of Hostilities agreement on 27 October 2002. However, Somali warlords have violated the agreement on numerous occasions. The pace of the Eldoret peace process was slowed by disagreements over representation, in particular the number of delegates, which threatened to derail the whole process. Approximately 700 delegates had attended the original process, even though only 400 were required. Some of the delegates also accused the then mediator Hon. Elijah Mwangale of high-handedness. The number of delegates was finally reduced and the venue of the conference moved to Nairobi, with Kenyan Ambassador Kiplagat appointed as the new mediator in January 2003.

The Somali National Reconciliation Conference set up six committees to discuss and make recommendations for fostering national reconciliation and reconstruction in post-conflict Somalia. These committees were: the Federalism and Provisional Charter Committee, the Land and Property Rights Committee, the Disarmament, Demobilization and Reintegration Committee, the Conflict Resolution and Reconciliation Committee, the Economic Recovery, Institution Building and Resource Mobilization Committee and the Regional and International Relations Committee.

In spite of earlier disagreements between the members of the Federalism and Provisional Charter Committee over the form of government that would be adopted, the Federal Charter, which had been elaborated by some of the members of the committee, was finally agreed upon and adopted. The Conflict Reconciliation and Resolution Committee recommended the establishment of a National Reconciliation Commission whose structure would spread to the village level to resolve inter-regional mistrust, suspicion and conflict. The membership of the commission cut across all social groups including women, young people, traditional leaders and administrators. The Committee on Economic Recovery, Institution Building and Resource Mobilization made elaborate recommendations for developing a comprehensive macroeconomic policy, promoting trade and commerce and the rehabilitation of sectors such as public administration, health, education, physical infrastructure, agriculture and industry.

The Land and Property Rights Committee recommended the establishment of an inter-ministerial committee to address the many international and transnational aspects of the issue of land and property rights. It also recommended the establishment of District-level committees to address conflicts relating to land and property rights at the district level. The Committee on Regional and International Relations dealt with mechanisms for promoting the country's regional security, combating terrorism, and participating in regional integration and cooperation including legal cross-border trade. It also covered mechanisms for the implementation and enforcement of both the Nairobi Declaration on small arms and light weapons (SALWs) and the UN arms embargo and Somalia's cooperation with international agencies in the provision of humanitarian and development assistance for reconstruction and peaceful reconciliation.

The Transitional Parliament was inaugurated in August 2004. The 275-member parliament was established on a clan basis, following the 4.5 formula whereby the four major clans were accorded 61 seats each while the alliance of minority clans was accorded 31 seats. The distribution of seats was made at three levels: clan, sub-clan, and sub-sub-clan. The Parliament elected H.E. Abdullahi Yussuf President of the Somalia Transitional Federal Government and he was sworn in on 14 October 2004. The President then appointed Ali Mohammed Ghedi as Prime Minister of the TFG on 6 November 2004 with a mandate to form a cabinet. The delegates also agreed that the six committees should be re-established to move forward the reconciliation and reconstruction process.

Security in Somalia: Disarmament, Demobilization, & Reintegration & the TFG

Post-conflict peace-building is a multi-dimensional process of complex social, economic, military and political recovery in countries emerging out of conflict or civil war. Peace-building involves engaging various stakeholders, including sub- and para-state militias, in order to resolve ongoing disputes between the warring factions. Moreover, peace-building includes a variety of social recovery aspects, which target both civilians and militiamen, to seek reconciliation between victims and aggressors.

Disarmament, demobilization, and reintegration (DDR) is a mechanism of post-conflict peace-building, which is designed to transform heavily militarized societies. As a peace development strategy, DDR seeks to disarm militias engaged in factional civil wars, especially those where there are numerous competing groups controlling segments of the country. Demilitarization programs aim to disarm sub-state military groups, with the aim of developing central authority. Transformation of war-torn societies requires social, economic and military strategies targeting ex-militia groups. Conversion of war economies not only requires an effort to reduce and eliminate active militarism; there is also a need to develop a new economic modality structured for post-conflict recovery, which will not only target disbanded militias, but also address issues of resource scarcity, environmental damage, war-related poverty, and landmine contaminated agricultural land. In order to maintain demilitarization, it is essential that a post-conflict economic recovery model be implemented. An effective DDR program requires that a comprehensive strategy be developed to tackle the sources of conflict in divided societies, including competition for resources and social aspects, such as economic factors, race, ethnicity and tribalism.

Somalia: Small Arms and a Case for DDR
After fifteen years of political anarchy and civil war, the prevalence of small arms and light weapons (SALW) in Somalia has become an enormous problem, which has entrenched a culture of warlordism and militia rule. The newly formed TFG has the opportunity to put an end to the long-standing strife and militarization of Somali society. An effective and well-implemented disarmament program could not only remove weapons from Somali society, but also ensure the security and legitimacy of the new government. DDR is an essential prerequisite for the political, social and economic development of the country. The success of the new government is contingent on the effectiveness of the DDR program.

The new parliament of the transitional government consists in a large part of Somalia's most influential warlords, representing the various factional groups, each of which is a party to the Declaration on the Cessation of Hostilities (2002) as well as the Federal Charter (2004). Participation in the new government should give the parliamentarians an impetus to collectively demobilize the militia factions, which threaten the existence of the TFG. They understand that participation in the political development process is essential, as the country's state of anarchy has shown no evidence that any militia group can attain hegemonic dominance over its rivals. According to the Charter, during the transitional period an effective government-run demilitarization program will consolidate the government's hold on military power.[1] Numerous MPs who hold military fiefdoms and private militias will be asked to disarm and demobilize, in an effort to end competitive conflict between factions and give authority to the new government.

The cessation of hostilities agreement signed at Eldoret in October 2002 stipulates that all parties should abstain from violence as a means of resolving conflict, and that militias should maintain only defensive postures.[2] This agreement has been violated countless times since its inception, but it still forms the basis of the current peace accord. As noted above, six committees were developed through the Eldoret peace initiative in 2002, to aid in the development of post-conflict Somalia.[3] The new Federal Charter (2004) stipulates the re-establishment of the six original committees, the draft documents of which produced at the Somali National Reconciliation Conference in Eldoret will probably inform the new committees under the TFG.

The draft report of the DDR committee in 2002 provided the framework for a future DDR initiative to be promoted in Somalia. The committee requested international assistance through UN observers, and stressed the need for a broad-based Somali government to take a leadership role in disarmament. The National Disarmament and Rehabilitation Commission (NDRC), charged with the task of disarming the factions, would utilize the assistance of military and civilian expertise. The committee also requested the support of the business community in funding the DDR program. The NDRC advocated widespread weapons collection, with targets of demobilizing 100,000 militiamen in the first phase at specified DDR sites, to be completed in a six-month period. While the estimates for the timeframe were highly optimistic, the program design was voluntary in nature, and did not advocate the forcible disbanding of militias.[4]

The DDR report provided for the reintegration and psychological rehabilitation of Somalia's ex-combatants wishing to leave military service. For those wishing to continue in military service, the committee also recommended the construction of a national military. Not only would the creation of a state-run military consolidate government authority, but through the DDR program former militiamen could also be absorbed into the new armed forces, providing them with meaningful employment. The Committee on Conflict Resolution and Reconciliation also noted that, as an essential aspect of developing peaceful conflict resolution mechanisms, a thorough review of, and concerted effort to resolve, the problem of small arms proliferation in Somalia was needed. The committee encouraged all clans, communities and regions to collect arms and assist with the DDR process, and requested that the international community actively prevent the flow of arms across Somalia's borders.[5]

However, if the militias responsible are to be held accountable for crimes committed during conflict, there may be an incentive for certain militias to continue fighting rather than submit to criminal charges. As such, there is a conflict between the DDR initiative and the need to hold the perpetrators of gross human rights violations to account.

Challenges to DDR in Somalia

The DDR process is not only a way of ending the problem of weapons proliferation in the country, but is also a way of ending the fragmentation of Somalia and fostering a sense of national unity. If all parties operate in accordance with the peace process and the DDR initiative, there is an opportunity for the new government to move the country into a period of post-conflict peace and demilitarization. However, in a classic prisoner's dilemma, inter- and intra-clan factions are unwilling to take the first initiative in disarmament, lest opposing factions withdraw from the process. Years of mistrust and suspicion make DDR a challenging task in post-conflict security and reconciliation efforts. In order to legitimize the new government, private militias must relinquish their private fiefdoms. Essential to disarmament is a thorough peace and reconciliation process, designed to overcome the barriers of mistrust, so that an effective DDR process can occur on the ground.

There are a number of key challenges to the DDR initiative in Somalia. First, the number of weapons in circulation is immense. Somali society is armed at numerous levels, from religious authorities to bandits, that retain weapons for either defensive or offensive purposes. Importantly, the precise quantities of military hardware in the country have not been, and perhaps cannot be, determined by means of statistical survey, due to the extraordinarily high level of arms in Somali society and the lack of security in conducting quantitative field studies. The lack of statistical data on the number and design of SALW in Somalia is a challenge to the DDR process. Without adequate information on the nature of the arms problem on the ground, developing an effective DDR implementation strategy will be especially difficult. The types of weapons in Somalia include heavy artillery as well as small arms and light weapons, though the quantities and ratios of weapon types are unknown. There also exists a significant landmine problem across the countryside, of unrecorded scope. General disarmament is a necessity in the collection and destruction of known and identified weapons caches, so that attention can be paid to recovering from the physical damage of war, including landmine clearance and reconstruction of destroyed villages. Substantial international funding is required in order to research, develop, implement, and evaluate a countrywide DDR program.

Second, in order for warlords to maintain their commitment to the peace process, the prisoner's dilemma must be resolved. It is therefore essential that DDR initiatives be implemented in a way that exemplifies transparency and trust. Most importantly, DDR must be implemented universally, with particular attention paid to group politics and the problems related to unequal disarmament. Unless a universal disarmament program is administered with legitimate and non-preferential terms of implementation, the likelihood of a return to violence is high. The suspicion that clan and sub-clan groups will use disarmament as a means to weaken their enemies while secretly maintaining their own private militias, could undermine the participation of competing factions in the DDR program.

Third, according to research conducted by the UN Monitoring Group on Somalia, warlords are not the only actors that benefit from small arms and private militias. There is an emerging business community in Somalia that engages in drug and arms trade, money laundering, smuggling and other illicit activities. The elites of the business community have capacity for military mobilization that often greatly exceeds that of the warlords in parliament. Armed militias are hired to protect economic interests, and the elite businessmen and women have the ability to instigate and put a stop to conflict at will. As such, demilitarization efforts must consider the participation of the business people engaged in both legal and illicit activities. The fact that militias are able to earn higher wages working for private businessmen may frustrate DDR initiatives, if they are designed to target only warlord-controlled militias. Actors such as businesspeople and qaat traders are potential spoilers of the warlord-focused demilitarization attempts.[6]

Finally, because warlord- or business-controlled militiamen are dependent on ongoing violence for their financial maintenance, an effective DDR program must respond to the need to provide alternative employment for the ex-combatants, and will require the government and the business community to develop a solid job-creation strategy and training. Unless there are economically viable alternatives for militiamen who participate in the DDR program, the potential to return to violence and illegal activity remains high. The cost of vocational training and job creation for hundreds of thousands of armed individuals will be substantial, and will require the assistance of both the international community and the regional business community.

Opportunities for the TFG

The creation of the new government is a crucial step in alleviating the country's current state of anarchy, and developing countrywide peace-building programs. In particular, the existence of a government creates the opportunity to establish a state-run, internationally funded demilitarization program. There are numerous reintegration strategies in existence that Somalia can learn from. The case of Somaliland provides a useful example of how former militias could be accommodated in a post-war environment by affording them the opportunity to work in the national military or the police force, and then demobilizing and reintegrating those individuals wishing to leave formal service. As such, the demilitarization strategy adopts a Remobilization, Demobilization, Reintegration, and then Disarmament (RDRD) approach. Through this method Somaliland has had success in disbanding militias, centralizing authority, and building up stability, though at high financial cost to the government.[7]

In Afghanistan, ex-combatants have the option of participating in mine clearance work, which not only provides meaningful employment to former fighters, but also helps communities to accept DDR program participants and re-establish trust between the victims and perpetrators of war. In mine clearance work, ex-combatants are seen as risking their lives for the betterment of the community, and contributing to the fostering of peace and reconciliation efforts. Absorbing former militiamen into a legitimate, national armed force and the creation of mine clearance programs are practical methods of ensuring alternative employment for DDR program participants, while encouraging post-war transition to peace and stability.[8]

Demilitarization models for post-war Somalia must be designed to address the country's complex context, with attention paid to clan and cultural dynamics. The new federal government has the opportunity to develop a responsive program that will establish security in Somalia's troubled cities. Cooperation between factions for the common goal of state security can act in a conversion capacity for Somalia's war-torn economy.

Successful peace-building in Somalia requires that political, military and socio-economic problem-solving initiatives be engaged in at all levels of society. Of primary importance is the universal implementation of a state-run, internationally sponsored DDR initiative, in order to disband Somalia's numerous factions based on clan and sub-clan affiliation, and foster a national military that commands principal authority in the use of force. However, equally important is the development of social institutions that can bridge differences between rival factions and promote conflict resolution mechanisms. Not only do victims of violence and human rights abuse have the right to justice and truth in the post-conflict reconciliation process, but also the system of accountability must be designed in such a way as to prevent militias from acting as spoilers.

Moreover, the illicit use of private militias by businesspeople suggests that demilitarization strategies need to take into account the complex nature of small arms proliferation. It is also essential to the DDR initiative that the reconciliation process addresses the need for the reintegration of former combatants, the majority of whom will have victims in the societies they join.

The primary challenge to security in Somalia remains the prisoner's dilemma among members of parliament, and the success of post-conflict peace-building remains contingent on the commitment of the warlords to the new government, in which they hold office. If those members of parliament with private armies fail to relinquish personal power for the sake of centralized authority, the likely outcome will be the resumption of civil war. The realization of security in Somalia is thus contingent on the capacity to build sufficient trust and transparency in the DDR process, so that respective members of the new parliament will consider simultaneous disarmament.

Economic Recovery in Post-Conflict Somalia
Even before the collapse of the Somali state in 1991, Somalia scored badly on standard economic indicators among developing countries in the world. As people living in one of the world's poorest countries, Somalis have traditionally engaged in pastoral and agricultural activities, as well as trade through its seaports. Somalia has had to struggle with the harsh effects on its livelihood of drought, which threatens survival in this highly rural economy. However, the detrimental effects of war and state collapse on the economy have compounded the problems of drought, environmental disaster and underdevelopment. War has not only caused stagnation in the Somali economy, but according to the draft report of the Committee on Economic Recovery, 'Somalia has retrogressed in all targets of the Millennium Development Goals' over the course of the past fifteen years.[9]

Given that there is no effective central government to regulate cross-border trade or contain illicit activities, the Somali economy has collapsed into a state of warlord-controlled profiteering. Trade in qaat, illicit drugs, and weapons is prevalent. Agricultural and pastoral activities have been disrupted by violent warlord clashes and resource competition, as well as extensive landmine use.

Traditionally an agricultural and pastoralist economy, the war has had a profound effect on Somali livelihoods. Destruction of dams, irrigation systems, and other land and water infrastructure has undermined farming and herding activities, which form the basis of Somali subsistence. Pre-war agricultural production included livestock, crops and fisheries. These products formed the basis of Somalia's exports, and were the fundamental basis of the economy. Over half the population relied on livestock herding as a primary means of income, exporting livestock and livestock by-products. Fruit and banana production also makes up a significant proportion of the Somali economy, and has been a source of resource-based conflict during the war period. Over the course of the past fifteen years of civil strife, agricultural and pastoralist activity has declined, and in some cases crop production has ceased entirely.

Qaat remains a key aspect of the economy. The UN Monitoring Group estimates that militiamen spend a third to a half of their daily income (ranging from US$3 to $5 per day) on the narcotic. Not only does qaat provide revenue for the warlords who run airport landing strips for importers, but also Somali wholesalers and retailers generate income from sales across the country. [10]

Since the collapse of the economy and the descent into political anarchy, a number of key criminal activities have emerged. Smuggling of contraband goods, such as weapons and illicit drugs, is a lucrative industry, as Somalia's ports allow duty-free access for Arab and Asian goods to be brought into Africa. Moreover, the production of forged passports and refugee documentation has emerged as a commonplace black-market activity. Another form of illicit activity is the kidnapping of both Somali and foreign persons for ransom. Several warlords now members of parliament have allegedly engaged in kidnapping activities.

The Somali economy is a complicated scenario. The collapse of the state has resulted in the pervasiveness and entrenchment of criminal activity in daily business dealings. Moreover, the destruction of physical infrastructure and land resources has impeded traditional agro-pastoral activities.

Challenges to Economic Reconstruction

The environmental damage incurred during the war period is significant in scope. War-related destruction of infrastructure and environmental integrity will require a physical reconstruction to take place to restore agricultural and commercial activities. Essential irrigation systems have been destroyed and need to be rebuilt to support a return to normal farming activities. In addition to pastoral and farm land rendered unusable by landmines and other damage, the illegal dumping of hazardous waste materials and the exploitation of natural resources by foreign and local actors has created an environmental crisis in Somalia, which threatens economic recovery.

The Committee on Economic Recovery recommended an environmental assessment for natural resource management, particularly to evaluate fisheries, water resources, land and mineral resources, and wildlife.[11] The study of the current environmental conditions in Somalia is crucial to develop a post-conflict economic reconstruction and development strategy. The challenges to implementing such a research design are threefold. First, the security situation stemming from the prevalence of anarchy and land-mines in Somalia restricts the free movement required to conduct evaluative studies. Second, the expertise required to administer a country-wide environmental assessment must be obtained from either domestic or international personnel. And third, procuring sufficient funding for countrywide environmental programs will require the international community to commit itself to long-term evaluation and reconstruction efforts in Somalia, rather than short-term solutions to war-related economic collapse. This will require the TFG to demonstrate willingness to maintain the ceasefire and to use international funding appropriately.

Also needing international funding support are social, health and poverty alleviation projects. Given the particularly violent history of Somalia, the need for disarmament will present the largest cost to the TFG. In particular, the cost of carrying out a countrywide disarmament initiative, as well as providing vocational training and jobs for thousands of ex-militiamen, will be extraordinary. Absorbing ex-combatants into the new army and police forces is a costly exercise, which will fall on the new government. In the case of Somaliland, where all factions were absorbed into military and police service at the declaration of independence, a substantial portion of government revenue has gone into maintaining the armed forces. As such, international financial support for the TFG and transitional programs such as DDR is crucial to the success of the interim period.

Existing security conditions in Somalia have presented multiple complications for economic reconstruction. Compounded by the problem of drought, famine has become a countrywide crisis, and militia rule has made it exceedingly difficult for international aid agencies to deliver relief to the victims. The need for international emergency assistance is not only hampered by security considerations, it also acts to exacerbate conflict situations. Militia exploitation of international aid delivery may be funneled into warlord activities. This scenario creates a paradox in which aid is needed because of famine and war, but can act to worsen the humanitarian situation. International agencies entering Somalia must be fully aware of the precarious nature of their involvement in the crisis zone (Anderson 1999).

Famine and extreme poverty also act as stagnating factors in the Somali economy, as large segments of the population become vulnerable to disease and death, rendering them unable to contribute actively to the country's economic reconstruction and growth. The existence of an incapacitated and impoverished population is one major hurdle that economic development specialists need to address in post-conflict recovery.

Another challenge to economic recovery in post-conflict Somalia is the lack of financial and monetary institutions. Collapse of the government led to the destruction of the existing institutions and subsequently an absence of state monetary control. In circumstances of political anarchy, the Somali currency has become non-uniform, and the warring factions commonly print counterfeit notes. The production of counterfeit money is a means of financing warlord activities, and is also related to countless money laundering and international criminal activities.[12]

Lack of central monetary authority and a federal fiscal structure has made foreign investment in Somalia exceedingly difficult. Moreover, in place of a legitimate taxation system, militias have seized the opportunity to extort duties from residents living under their fiefdoms. The Transitional Federal Government has the responsibility of unifying and regulating a national currency, as well as developing appropriate taxation structures, in order to develop a national economy that has the capacity to participate in international trade and commerce. By consolidating power through the federal government, and centralizing monetary and fiscal policy development, the TFG can act to resolve currency, revenue and taxation problems. Moreover, legitimizing the country's economic and financial affairs, the TFG can act to reduce the power of militia factions that extort monies from residents in return for security guarantees.

Opportunities in Economic Reconstruction
and Environmental Rehabilitation

The trade and commercial strategy developed by the 2002 Committee on Economic Recovery has adopted a neo-liberal economic approach, focused on encouraging trade in goods in which Somalia has a comparative advantage in production. Specifically, Somalia produces livestock, livestock by-products, bananas, hides and skins, frankincense, and fish. The committee recommended that the economy seek to diversify, particularly in the production of manufactured goods, as well as to encourage foreign investment in the development of the private sector.

In order to promote international trade and commodities diversification, the TFG must invest in the reconstruction of Somalia's infrastructure, as well as actively prohibiting activities that add to environmental damage. In particular, it has the opportunity to enforce the prohibition of illegal foreign exploitation of Somalia's fisheries. Moreover, many corporations have taken advantage of the political anarchy in Somalia to illegally dump hazardous and toxic waste in the country's coastal waters. The creation of a centralized authority, with legitimate legal and political enforcement capacities, could end this foreign exploitation.

Environmental sustainability is an essential aspect of economic recovery in Somalia. Damage done to forests and rangelands needs to be assessed, as poverty and destitution lead many people to plunder natural resources for survival. The felling of fruit-bearing trees for firewood and the unrestricted hunting of wildlife are examples of unsustainable environmental degradation, which undermines poverty alleviation and development in the long run. The recommendation of the Committee on Economic Recovery to carry out an environmental assessment, including evaluation of deforestation, mineral depletion, soil quality, and fish resources presents an opportunity for genuine post-conflict reconstruction. An evaluation of the extent of the damage will inform how the TFG can adequately respond to the resource depletion and physical damage.

The committee recommends action on a number of key points, in addition to establishing peace and security as essential prerequisites for economic growth. First, the decline and cessation of crop production across the country, and in particular in the south and central parts of Somalia, must be countered by means of agricultural technologies, joint ventures, and research initiatives. Moreover, destroyed irrigation systems, flood control channels, and water control structures must be re-developed to encourage the resumption of normal farming activities.

Physical reconstruction activities are costly and require expertise; as a result the committee has requested the support of the international community, in particular the NGO community and the private sector, which have developed a comparative advantage in providing assistance, in the absence of effective government. Moreover, international assistance from donor states is needed in support of the TFG, particularly in developing programs that must be government-run. For example, privatization as a solution to government incapacity to provide services cannot extend to matters of national and regional security, such as disarmament or the policing of illicit weapons trade.

In addition to having the opportunity to increase its international funding, the TFG can also engage the international financial institutions in managing the country's debt profile. Somalia can apply for relief for outstanding international debt through the Heavily Indebted Poor Countries (HIPC) Initiative and similar programs, for which it is eminently eligible, and which will allow its development programs to proceed without concern about payments on past international borrowing. The TFG can also use its political legitimacy to engage international financial institutions in the negotiation of foreign debts. Moreover, it can get involved in multilateral and bilateral international trade negotiations and can decide whether Somalia should to participate in regional economic institutions, such as the Common Market for Eastern and Southern Africa (COMESA).

Developing Social Cohesion in Somalia

Building social cohesion in a society emerging from conflict entails re-establishing shattered social relations, resolving past differences, achieving reconciliation, and building trust. All these are critical in the pursuit of common goals, which in the case of Somalia are peace-building and development.

The dynamics of inclusion and exclusion on a clan basis, rampant corruption and the marginalization of large sections of the population were responsible for the erosion of social cohesion in Somalia. The civil war that continued after the overthrow of President Barre eroded what remained of social cohesion in Somalia, and the division of Somalia into fiefdoms dominated by warlords worsened an already sorry state of affairs.

A number of opportunities for fostering social cohesion have been discussed by various commentators, scholars, and policy-makers, including the existence of a shared social and cultural heritage, the establishment of the new Somali Federal Government, the construction of public institutions, and the presence of civil society. Challenges to such a development have also been highlighted, particularly the Somali peoples' antipathy towards the state, the presence of warlords who have split the state into fiefdoms, the reliance on clans as the basis of the new Somali polity, Somaliland's declaration of political independence, and the weakness of civil society.

Social Cohesion: A Theoretical Background

Social cohesion is a broad concept incorporating many facets including, among others, the absence of latent conflict, whether caused by racial, economic or political reasons, and the presence of strong social bonds, as noted by the existence of trust, reciprocity, associations cross-cutting social divisions and the presence of institutions of conflict management (Berkman and Kawachi 2000). It is the elements that conform to this notion that contribute to the building of communities and the strengthening of social bonds, especially under conditions of civil unrest and hardship. While latent conflict will always be found in any society, the challenge is how to manage it so as to improve social relations and avoid violent conflict. Social cohesion is founded on social capital, 'a glue that holds society together' (Serageldin 1996: 196). Norms, values and social relations are the bonds that hold communities together. In addition, these are the means by which to reach across differences and begin to build trust.

According to Norman Uphoff social capital is 'an accumulation of various types of social, psychological, cognitive, institutional, and related assets that increase the amount (or probability) of mutually beneficial cooperative behaviour'. Uphoff breaks down social capital into structural and cognitive components. Structural capital is associated with networks, relationships, associations or institutional structures made possible via vertical or horizontal linkages between members. Horizontal relationships take place among equals or near equals, while vertical relationships are attributed to hierarchies and/or unequal relationships due to power or resource differences. Cognitive capital includes values, norms, civic responsibility, expected reciprocity, charity, altruism and trust. Ultimately, both domains are intrinsically connected through their shared networks, roles, precedents and procedures, and all come from cognitive processes; while 'structural social capital assets are extrinsic and observable, cognitive social assets are not' (Uphoff 2000: 188).

Horizontal and vertical social capital interact amongst different actors working towards either social cohesion or an escalation of conflict. The greater the extent to which vertical linking and horizontal bridging take place, the more a sense of integration and cohesiveness is established, resulting in inclusiveness in mediation processes and curbing the potential for violent crimes. Conversely, the weaker the reinforcement potential of socialization mechanisms such as values and compliance mechanisms or social control, the weaker the social cohesion. Weak social cohesion also heightens the risk of the crumbling of social institutions, the exclusion of minorities, and disorganization and violent conflict (Genge 2001: 14–15). Social capital can be used in support of social cohesion and can be a constructive element in the building of trust and hope in a conflict-ridden area. But it can just as easily be perverted to hasten social fragmentation and the onset of violent conflict. Most academics who have written on social capital agree that local associations and networks have a positive impact on economic welfare and local development, and are one of the key factors in promoting institutional structures for managing conflict.

Developing Social Cohesion in Post-conflict Somalia
Observers of African nation-states assumed that Somalia was a unique case in the continent as the population shared many social and cultural traits such as language, mode of economic production and religion. Given its cultural base, the state was thought to be viable, however, the country

entered the twenty-first century without a modern state or institutions.

The failure of the Somali state brought with it total institutional collapse. Security structures and public service delivery systems disappeared, along with the legal and normative standards that previously regulated the seriously eroded social interactions. Competing and often contradictory political factions, economic and religious interest groups, and clan elders attempted to fill the vacuum (Mbugua 2004).

The erosion of social capital and social cohesion in Somalia can be traced from the period after independence to the collapse of the state in 1991. The Somalis had high optimism at independence and their nationalism gene-rated incredible fervour and social unity that reflected their hope for democracy and development. The independence euphoria and the unification of former British and Italian Somali lands in 1960 generated a national cohesion that masked the differences between groups with competing agendas. The patriotic fervour induced by the 1964 war with Ethiopia prolonged this spirit (Samatar 2001).

From the time of independence, Somali elite politics was manifested via contradictory political and economic tendencies. One tendency emphasized a Somali-wide identity, nationalism, the protection of the common good and justice in the dispensation of the rule of law. The opposite pre-disposition emphasized sectarianism and clanism, driven by individualistic interests without regard for community well-being. The struggle between these two elite projects marked the state's institutional history from 1960. The first and second republics (1960–4) and (1964–7) embraced a Somali-wide identity. The second republic tried to fight corruption and the abuse of power by bureaucratizing government institutions (Samatar 2001).

The military regime which took control of government in 1969 enjoyed a high degree of legitimacy during its initial years of its tenure; however, with the passage of time, the Siad Barre regime grew increasingly dicta-torial and cast aside citizen's rights. As a result of growing opposition, the regime promoted public employees on the basis of loyalty, with no regard for skills or experience, further damaging the competence of the state apparatus and alienating the majority of the population. Having lost legitimacy, it used its military power to punish entire regions and com-munities deemed disloyal. A highly sectarian and brutal use of the military machine occurred in 1988 when Hargeisa and Burao were destroyed (Samatar 2001).

By the time Siad Barre was overthrown, all national institutions had been ruined. Moreover, the separate opposition movements, which collec-tively destroyed the old regime, were sectarian themselves and had no national reconstruction programme. The prolonged civil war and terror instigated by the warlords reversed integrative national processes. Warlords and faction leaders fragmented the country into 'clan' fiefdoms.

Opportunities for Fostering Social Cohesion in Somalia

The existence of a shared social and cultural heritage in Somalia provides a necessary though insufficient foundation for building state institutions that cater to the collective interest. The ability of cultural resources to bind a society depends on how they are used. The socially unifying appeal of these resources declines when undermined continuously without the society reinvesting in them. The callous exploitation of shared cultural resources not only squanders their richness and resilience, but may turn them into a national liability (Samatar 2001).

The creation of the new Somali government at the conclusion of the Mbagathi peace talks embraced a wide section of Somali society, and provides an opportunity for the evolution of a new Somali nationalism, in place of clanism. The successful completion of the peace talks is an indicator of the Somali people's desire to pursue the common cause of peace and development. Communities and states can steadily generate trust and confidence for common causes. Values shared across communities are the basis of civic bonds and trust in a society, but the state must take the lead in nurturing society-wide civic bonds. Communities, in turn, must scrupulously monitor state actions to ensure that public institutions function in ways that consistently enhance the quality of those shared values. Such partnership between state and community will facilitate the generation of social capital in a relatively short time (Lemos 1998).

As Somalia embarks on the process of state reconstruction in the post-conflict period, it has an opportunity to create new institutions that constrain sectarian entrepreneurs while strengthening shared values and hopes. Such institutions must enhance accountability, rebuild public trust, and advance a common agenda. This will enable the Somali people to develop confidence that they can work together for the common good and establish trust in public institutions. Realizing the need for reconciliation as the basis of social cohesion, the sixth committee on Conflict Resolution and Reconciliation[13] recommended the creation of a National Reconciliation Commission whose membership cuts across all social groups, so as to resolve inter-regional mistrust, suspicion and conflict. Made up of state, regional and local (village) peace committees, the National Reconciliation Commission can work to build social cohesion in Somalia and foster a sense of Somali nationalism.

Efforts to nurture social capital should focus on enabling forms of capital that are socially owned, such as education, health or technology-transfer services. Overall, rehabilitation of social capital can play an important role in the recovery of a war-torn society, but the forms and manifestations of social capital to be restored should be monitored and the reasons for its support regularly and systematically monitored by all involved (World Bank 1998). There is a need to work out a comprehensive educational plan for both the young people and adults that will encourage the values of nationalism. Engaging the media as a tool for dissemination and education of the public on the values of peace can go a long way in fostering the development of nationalism.

The existence of a robust civil society in Somalia, which thrived in the absence of the state, provides another opportunity for the development of social cohesion. However, the problem is that many civil society organizations are weak and partisan, and need to build up trust among civil society and other institutional networks. Civil society initiatives may, however, be thwarted if they are not matched by a strong political will (World Bank 1998). The critical role of civil society in conflict resolution and peace-building was recognized by the Committee on Conflict Resolution and Reconciliation, when it recommended that there is a need to involve traditional clan leaders, religious organizations, women's groups, and civil society in general in playing a part in peace-building and confidence-building.[14]

The success of the Somali people in bringing to an end their conflict presents an opportunity for the collective pursuit of other collective goals. As Staub argues, groups need to form trusting relationships with each other in order to pursue shared goals. Moreover, 'the strengths of existing group identities and previous successes in achieving joint goals affect the extent to which inter group cooperation reduces conflict and results in positive ties' (Staub 1989: 275). By focusing on common goals, there is a greater likelihood of successful outcomes, which will in turn contribute to the nurturing of a positive outlook on the 'other', thereby resulting in greater trust and caring towards each other, which will promote social cohesion and develop nationalism.

Challenges to the Development of Social Cohesion in Somalia

A number of challenges face the regeneration of social cohesion and nationalism as opposed to clanism in Somalia. Traditional analysts of Somali politics have cited two occurrences as evidence of the Somalis' sectarian nature, despite the fact that they share a common language, culture and religion (Lewis 1994). These occurrences are Somalis' recent antipathy towards the state and nationalism and the warlords' success in carving the country into fiefdoms. The state's credibility among the Somalis has been destroyed because it failed to guard the common interest, and the erosion of social solidarity based on inclusive values makes Somali reconstruction an awesome task (Samatar 2001: 5).

The reliance on the clan as the basis of the new polity poses another challenge to the development of social cohesion and nationalism. While it is true that there was no reliable basis for establishing the Somali polity other than the clan, the system of clanism was also responsible for tearing the country apart.

Peace and security, which are critical in the development of social cohesion, are contingent on the capacity to build trust and establish reconciliation between Somalia's warring factions. Building trust and reconciliation in a society that has been at war for over a decade presents a big challenge, because mistrust and suspicion have taken root. Social reconciliation requires institutional development to forestall future conflicts between competing social groups in non-violent ways. Moreover, mechanisms to build reunification and forgiveness between groups that have incurred atrocities at each other's hands will require social, psychological and religio-cultural tools. Building reconciliation in fragmented communities must take steps to bring closure to past grievances and develop instruments for the peaceful resolution of future disagreements.

It is necessary for groups which are caught in a cycle of retaliation and revenge to commit to peace, utilizing traditional and multi-dimensional tools of reconciliation. Moreover, the need for efficient mechanisms that address human rights violations and crimes against humanity is paramount in developing a culture of transparency, trust, and accountability. Establishing such mechanisms in the immediate post-conflict period is a challenge for the Somali Transitional Federal Government. Individual victims of violence and war atrocities must be able to voice their grievances without fear of further aggression. The Committee on Conflict Resolution and Reconciliation recommended that mechanisms of accountability be established, which hold perpetrators of violence to account.

It is important to note that if the militias responsible for committing atrocities during the conflict are to be held accountable for their crimes, they may be more inclined to continue fighting rather than to submit to criminal charges. Given that many militias have been engaged in human rights abuses, it is important to craft accountability mechanisms in such a way as will not alienate militia groups that can act as spoilers of the peace process. At Eldoret, the Committee on Conflict Resolution and Reconciliation concluded that, while truth commissions were necessary in bringing a sense of justice to victims of war and abuse, the emphasis must remain on reconciliation and forgiveness. The draft report declined to recommend holding perpetrators of gross violations responsible for their actions in a legal context.

Post-conflict reconciliation goes beyond the need to punish aggressors for past crimes. Most importantly, resolution of future grievances must be channelled through new conflict resolution methods that do not use violence. The Eldoret Committee on Reconciliation advised the use of traditional and religious leaders in conflict resolution, as well as the participation of women's groups and civil society actors. The challenge lies in developing a broad-based conflict resolution mechanism which draws upon all possible social and political actors. Civil society organizations can complement the state in nation-building and in checking the state's excesses, and can foster social cohesion. However, civil society in Somalia is fragile and divided, which will require the development of a strong civil society network that transcends clan interests, is independent of the state, and is capable of constructively engaging the government apparatus. The TFG should create an enabling environment that will allow for the development of a viable civil society to complement the government's efforts in conflict resolution, peace-building and sustainable development.

Although the incorporation of warlords into the new government as part of the peace deal brought all the stakeholders in the Somali conflict to the negotiating table, the warlords may continue to exercise a negative influence over their fiefdoms and develop parallel centers of power. Warlord power will in turn lead to the development of divided loyalties in Somali citizens.

Because Somalia has had no democratic systems in its political history, developing a culture of democracy in the immediate post-conflict period will present a serious challenge, exacerbated by the fact that the country is coming out of conflict with very visible divisions in its society, particularly along clan lines. Developing a culture of democracy is crucial for venting grievances and fostering positive engagements which will enhance the pursuit of common goals and, ultimately, the development of Somali nationalism.

The existence of the relatively stable region of Somaliland, which considers itself to be politically autonomous, poses another challenge to the development of Somali nationalism. Although the new Federal Charter provides for the existence of semi-autonomous regional units (such as Somaliland), the challenge is how to ensure the peaceful integration of all regions into the federal republic of Somalia and, in addition, how to suppress regional allegiances and emphasize nationalism. The Committee on Conflict Resolution and Reconciliation made a credible recommendation that there is need to facilitate dialogue that will enable people, including those with secessionist sentiments, to share their opinions and views about the new political dispensation and to move towards better understanding.[15]

The total institutional collapse in Somalia provides an opportunity to develop new institutions to promote shared values and hopes; however, developing such institutions will require significant financial and human resources, which the new government lacks. As a result of the civil war and the collapse of the education system and other public institutions, very few if any students have graduated from Somali schools, colleges and universities in the past ten years or so.

Challenges & Opportunities for a Common Security & Defence Arrangement in the Horn of Africa

In the wake of the unprecedented humanitarian calamities and conflict that have afflicted the Horn of Africa since the 1990s, it is more crucial than ever that the common security framework should focus on regional security concerns as one of the central pillars in supporting reconstruction of Somalia and the entire sub-region. Key security issues that should be addressed in the short run include small arms and DDR, terrorism, refugees and internally displaced persons, differences in clan politics and high levels of mistrust.

Political problems once deemed the internal matters of sovereign states, and therefore beyond the concern of neighboring states and the international community, are contested by the reality that domestic conflicts have a propensity to become internationalized. Neighboring states are drawn into a conflict through refugee flows, humanitarian crises and trafficking of arms. This realization partly explains the passing of the first amendments to the Constitutive Act of the African Union to provide a legal analysis of the broadening of Article 4(h) of the Act. The article allows for the right of intervention, to prevent a 'serious threat to legitimate order.'[16] It also explains the revitalization of the Intergovernmental Authority on Drought and Development (IGADD) (with a very narrow mandate around the issues of drought and desertification) as the Intergovernmental Authority on Development (IGAD), to become a fully-fledged regional political, economic, development, trade and security entity, similar to the Southern African Development Community (SADC) and the Economic Community of the West African sates (ECOWAS).

The argument on the regional security framework hinges on the fact that the distinction between domestic and international conflicts has become increasingly blurred. For instance, the absence of a government in Mogadishu continues to impact negatively on the stability of the entire region. The suspected terrorist links in Somalia, the flow of illegal arms to the region, and the impact of refugees, among others, are issues of both regional and international concern. This notion of 'intermesticity' is a sound starting point for a discussion of the role of IGAD in building sound regional security architecture that will support peace and security in Somalia and the Horn of Africa sub-region.

The idea of cooperation between the nations of the Horn to address mutual economic and security concerns prompted the establishment of IGAD in 1986. Since then, the member states have developed structures to address activities ranging from preventing conflicts to encouraging dialogue to resolve disputes. Although relatively new sovereign states, the nations of the Horn have historically not had consistent success in cooperating to resolve mutual security concerns.

Challenges for a Common Security and Defence Arrangement in the Horn
Given the diverse domestic, regional and international interests, a post-conflict peace-building framework needs to be informed by external and internal security concerns. IGAD, like many other African structures and mechanisms for conflict prevention and resolution, is relatively young. Its capacity to deal with Conflict Prevention, Management and Resolution (CPMR) is partly undermined by lack of sufficient human and financial resources.

Limited political will. For IGAD to be a truly supranational body able to deal with conflicts it must be able to marshal the unreserved political will and financial support of its member states and the international community. Numerous unilateral military actions and support of opposition armed groups in neighboring countries by some members have been a frequent sign of the organization's failure to prevent conflict through negotiation and joint action.

Regime security. Since the election of President Abdullahi Yussuf on 10 October 2004, two incidents have continued to worry pundits. First, there was the blast on 17 October 2004 at Wilson airport in Nairobi where it was thought that the President was due to arrive shortly, and secondly, the spirited attack on the President's residence on 17 November 2004 by armed intruders, who engaged Kenyan security forces for almost fifteen minutes. This was followed by a plea by the Kenyan President to have him relocated to another country, as plans were slow for him to move to Mogadishu. Until regime security is guaranteed no further development can take place.

Illegal trade in small arms and drugs. Illegal trade in small arms and light weapons and other clandestine activities continue to thrive in war-torn Somalia. Militia groups have relied mostly on stockpiles of weapons and ammunition captured following the fall of Siad Barre but also purchased on the international market by various warlords and businessmen. Despite the adoption of Security Council Resolution 733 (1992), there have been numerous violations of the arms embargo. The new government faces an uphill task in dismantling arms trafficking cartels to Somalia.

Regional and international instruments must form the basis for dealing with various criminal activities. For example, the UN Programme of Action (2001), the Bamako Declaration on an African position on the illicit proliferation, circulation and trafficking of small arms and light weapons (2000), and the Nairobi Protocol on prevention, control and reduction of SALW in the Great Lakes Region and the Horn of Africa (2004), are good frameworks for addressing small arms in the sub-region.

Clan politics and dismantling clan-based militias. Somalia has a highly segmented clan structure composed of six main clan families, which are further subdivided into sub-clan groups and even further into smaller sub-clan units. Its history and politics are to a large extent embedded in clan structures. Within these clans, militia groups are key players. Clan interest should not be used to undermine the new government, but rather to foster the national interest. The militias hold sway over most of the countryside. The Somali population is scattered over the region and beyond. As a result, family ties have been broken and social cohesion fragmented. The task of restoring old relations and reconstructing new ones will be even more challenging. It must be accompanied by a deliberate policy and facilitation that demands both technical skill and resources.

Weak states and underdeveloped infrastructure, trade and commerce. Somalia is surrounded by weak states with underdeveloped infrastructure and intra-regional trade. As a result, developing domestic trade in hides and skins to penetrate both the regional and international markets requires enormous technical and financial resources.

Refugees and IDPs. Since 1990 Somalia has produced thousand of refugees and internally displaced persons. It is estimated that between 1988 and 1999 up to 2 million Somalis fled the country. In 1992 an estimated 800,000 Somalis were refugees in neighboring countries. By the end of 2001 some 400,000 refugees and asylum seekers were living in about two dozen countries including Kenya, Yemen, Ethiopia, Djibouti, South Africa, Egypt, Libya, Uganda, Eritrea, Zambia, and Tanzania and nearly 8,000 had sought asylum in various countries including the United States. Currently it is estimated that there are over 800,000 to one million Somalis in the diaspora, including 400,000 refugees and asylum seekers.[17] This includes a substantial number of intellectuals and professionals, who should be encouraged to return home and participate in rebuilding Somalia. The regional framework must facilitate their safe return and resettlement. Peace and stability will only be guaranteed if the majority of Somalis are in the country and participating in nation-building.

Unresolved issues. It is unrealistic to presume that suspicions and mistrust among some of the critical players in the Somali peace process have been resolved by the latest developments or that they are going to be resolved soon. The successful implementation of the various agreements hinges on cultivating confidence among the key players.

No Standard Template on CPMR for Reference

Like any society emerging from conflict, Somalia faces many problems that are complex and multi-dimensional. There are no set responses, but strategies must be tailored to suit the unique nature of the country. There is no model for a successful peace and security framework or architecture. In the past, models that appeared to be successful fell apart as circumstances changed. For example, more than a decade ago European conflict prevention and resolution structures were the archetypal peace-building model, until the wars in the former Yugoslavia proved otherwise.

Opportunities for a Common Security and Defence Arrangement

The election of the President and a Prime Minister for the TFG should enhance prospects for common security in the Horn, which will be based fundamentally on a shared perception of the security 'threats' faced by the member states. Although many challenges still exist, the nations of the Horn have the realistic potential to advance a common agenda through a common security defence arrangement and regional integration. Such a development would produce short- and long-term benefits for all nations involved, and advance IGAD's agenda of a region united in its efforts to achieve peace and prosperity.

The promotion of inter-state dialogue as stated in the IGAD charter should enhance political stability and integration in trade, commerce and social relations. A sound regional framework must be linked to people's socio-economic security, with the ultimate goal of reducing human suffering. In this regard, IGAD must be seen as the legitimate channel for dialogue to deal with various disputes rather than the individual manoeuvres employed by some countries to the extent of supporting different militia groups in Somalia and undermining the regional efforts aimed at ending the conflict.

These developments should spur IGAD member states to reopen diplomatic missions with the new government as a way of facilitating a competent diplomatic intervention in disputes. Cooperation should traverse the commercial, cultural and security spheres to promote regional cohesion among IGAD member states. In addition, multilateral and bilateral security structures and defence arrangements can complement the regional framework. Intra-state committees are critical to dealing with cross-border issues, particularly given the kin and kith relations across border areas in the region.

International Support for Regional Economic Communities (RECs)

The relative success of regionalism in Europe and North and South America, despite their varying problems, continues to inspire other regions to strive towards a regional system beyond national frontiers. In the Horn of Africa a number of regional groupings exist including the Common Market for Eastern and Southern Africa (COMESA), the East Africa Community (EAC), and IGAD, although the latter two cover two of the Horn countries with a varying mandate in common security and defence matters. At the international level, this is clearly outlined in the *Agenda for Peace* (1992) (Boutros

Ghali 1995). At a continental level, the 1993 Cairo Declaration of the OAU, introduced the mechanism for Conflict Prevention, Management and Resolution and its operational arm, the Conflict Prevention Management Centre. Somalia must establish its niche within regional groupings such as IGAD and COMESA. Increased integration will promote higher growth, improve resource allocation and quality, facilitate the transfer of technology and improve access to foreign investment. The new leadership must strive to attract foreign investment to the country. There should also be promises of significant long-term development aid. Recognition of the RECs has provided an impetus for resources to flow into regional groupings, which remain a fertile ground for attracting donor funding.

Participation of the Major Warlords in the Recent Initiatives
Although there were some boycotts, the Nairobi peace talks have been credited with bringing the major stakeholders together for the first time. The talks witnessed the major protagonists, specifically the warlords, engaging in serious discussions and establishing personal contacts. They participated in the election of the parliamentarians, the Speaker Ali Shariff Hassan Sheikh and the Prime Minister Ali Mohammed Ghedi. Although their levels of participation vary and some have expressed reservations throughout the process, it is good to note that they are still participating in the process. One of the reasons why the war has persisted in Somalia is that none of the warlords has the capacity to win the war outright.

Unresolved Political Issues in the Horn
There are quite a number of unresolved issues in the Horn, and key among them is the declaration of Somaliland as an independent state. Although it has not been recognized officially by either the regional states or the international community, the issue needs to be addressed, given that the leader of autonomous Somaliland has refused to recognize Mr Abdullahi Yussuf as the new President of Somalia.

Role of the media. The regional and international media should use their power to promote peace and cohesion in Somalia. Destructive elements must be exposed and the international community pressurized to act against those who are bent on undermining the progress towards peace that has been made. More importantly, the media should rally the international community to mobilize resources that will reconstruct the dilapidated social and economic infrastructure in Somalia.

Terrorism. The AU draft Convention on the Prevention of Terrorism, in July 2004, should inform the IGAD member states' endeavours to deal with terrorism in the sub-region. This is critical based on the fact that the region has been described as a 'soft' target for terrorist activities. The framework should be operationalized so that the sub-region is safe from planning and executing terrorist activities. After 11 September, the United States continues to suspect Somalia of harboring some members linked to the Al Qaeda network. It is therefore imperative that regional countries together with the international community support the new government to build up its capacity so that it can guarantee security within and across its borders. The international resolve to fight terrorism should indeed give impetus to the region's policy-makers to improve security, particularly at entry points which have facilitated terrorist activities.

Conclusion

The challenges to Somalia's post-war economic recovery are many. The environmental, institutional and infrastructural destruction resulting from over a decade of civil war will require a substantial reconstruction effort. The damage to land, water and natural resources has drastically undermined Somalia's capacity to resume normal agricultural and pastoral activities. The absence of government has allowed excessive environmental destruction to go unhindered. Furthermore, the absence of monetary and fiscal institutions during the period of political anarchy has created a currency and taxation disaster, which will require an effective central authority to govern Somalia's economic recovery. However, the TFG is uniquely positioned to turn Somalia's economic fortunes around, if it demonstrates commitment to reconstruction to the Somalis themselves and to the international donor community.

Social cohesion is the key intervening variable between social capital and social conflict. Strong social cohesion reduces the risk of social disorganization, fragmentation and exclusion that may lead to aggression and violence (Genge 2001: 23). Considering the fact that Somalia is emerging out of conflict with its public institutions shattered and even the norms and values, which guide social interactions, eroded, it is necessary that the new government take urgent steps to consolidate social cohesion. The complementary role of civil society in conflict resolution, reconciliation and peacebuilding, as necessary ingredients for fostering social cohesion, should also be borne in mind. Social cohesion should be seen as part of the peacebuilding agenda. It is hoped that the development of social cohesion will go a long way in curbing the influence of the warlords and the problem of clanism, and foster a sense of Somali nationalism.

Since the inception of IGAD, regional security dynamics and indeed the tone of the regional security debate have shifted to such an extent that there is a need for a reappraisal of IGAD as a mechanism for conflict resolution, prevention and management and an integrated approach to economic and security cooperation in the sub-region. Thus responses to conflict need to be based in a sub-regional context where local dynamics are assessed and incorporated into peace-building programmes. Genuine security within the region will come only when nations share dependable expectations of peaceful change and act in concert to address common challenges. The path to security in the region will ultimately be through the effects of the information age, loosening state control of data and opinions, through financial and economic interactions with their prerequisite long-term security, and through diplomacy and collaboration in non-military areas, law enforcement and environmental cooperation.

References

Anderson, Mary B. 1999. *Do No Harm: How Aid Can Support Peace – Or War*. Boulder, CO: Lynne Rienner Publishers.

Berkman L.F and I. Kawachi, eds. 2000. *Social Epidemiology*. New York: Oxford University Press.

Boutros Ghali, Boutros. 1995. *An Agenda for Peace*. New York: United Nations.

Bryden, Matt. 2004. 'Somalia and Somaliland: Envisioning a dialogue on the question of Somali unity', *African Security Review* 13 (2): 1–11, (Online) Available at: www.iss.co.za

Genge, C. 2001. 'Learning For Social Cohesion', *Education* 870 (9–13). [Online] Available at: www.unix.oit.umass.educ870/postconflictpapers.

Lemos, M.C. 1998. 'The Politics of Pollution Control in Brazil, State Actors and Social Movements Cleaning Up Cutabao.' *World Development* 26(1): 75–87.

Lewis, I.M. 1994. *Blood and Bone: the Calling of Kinship in Somali Society*. Lawrenceville, NJ: Red Sea Press.

Mbugua, K. 2004. 'Prospects for Peace and State–Building in Somalia in Conflict Trends, an Overview of Conflict in Africa', in 'Conflict in Africa, Conflict Trends', African Centre for the Constructive Resolution of Disputes (ACCORD) (Online) available at: www.accord.org.za

Samatar, A.I. 2001. 'Somalia's Reconstruction: Beyond IGAD and the European Union's Peace Dividend' (Online) Available at: www.somali-civilsociety.org

Serageldin I. 1996. 'Sustainability as Opportunity, and the Problem of Social Capital', *The Brown Journal of World Affairs* 3(2): 187–203.

Staub, E. 1989. *The Roots of Evil. The Origins of Genocide and Other Group Violence*. New York: Cambridge University Press.

Uphoff, N. 2000. 'Understanding Social Capital: Learning from the Analysis and Experience of Participation', in P. Dasgupta and I. Serageldini, eds, *Social Capital: A Multifaceted Perspective*. Washington, DC: World Bank, 215–52.

World Bank. 1998. 'Post-Conflict Unit, Report of the Workshop on Conflict Prevention and Post-Conflict Reconstruction: Perspectives and Prospects.' 20–21 April. (Online) Available at: www-unix.oit.umass.edu

Notes

1 Chapter Fourteen, Article 71, Section 5 of the Charter requires the TFG to embark on a demilitarization program. Schedule I of the Charter states that the TFG will have authority over matters of defence and security.

2 See the Declaration on Cessation of Hostilities and the Structures and Principles of the Somalia National Reconciliation Process, signed at Eldoret, on 27 October 2002.

3 See Somali National Reconciliation Conference committees draft reports: 'Disarmament, Demobilisation, and Reintegration and Conflict Resolution and Reconciliation'. (Online) Available at: www.somali-civilsociety.org

4 Draft Report of the Committee on Disarmament, Demobilization, and Reintegration presented to the Somali National Reconciliation Conference (SNRC) at Eldoret, Kenya (2002).

5 See Draft Report by the Committee on Conflict Resolution and Reconciliation presented to the SNRC.

6 Report of the Monitoring Group on Somalia pursuant to Security Council resolution 1519 (2003) presented to the UN Security Council on 11 August 2004, http:ww.securitycouncilreport.org

7 For a discussion on Somaliland, see Matt Bryden (2004). Information gathered on Somaliland RDRD was gathered from discussions with various special envoys to Somalia.

8 See the Afghan New Beginnings Website at www.undpanbp.org

9 See report of the Committee on Economic Recovery, Institutional Building and Resource Mobilization 'Somalia Economic Recovery, Institutional Building and Resource Mobilization' presented to the Somalia National Reconciliation Conference, March 2003.

10 Report of the Monitoring Group on Somalia pursuant to Security Council resolution 1519 (2003) presented to the UN Security Council on 11 August 2004, http:ww.securitycouncilreport.org

11 See Report of the Committee on Economic Recovery, Institutional Building and Resource Mobilization 'Somalia Economic Recovery, Institutional Building and Resource Mobilization' presented to the Somalia National Reconciliation Conference, March 2003.

12 See ibid.

13 See Committee Six – Conflict Resolution and Reconciliation, Somalia Reconciliation Conference, Phase Two, Eldoret-Nairobi, Kenya, March 2003.

14 Sixth Committee Report, March 2003:69) (Online) Available at: www.somali-civilsociety.org

15 Ibid.

16 The Constitutive Act of the African Union, Article 4. (Online) Available at: www.dfa.za/au.nepad/constitutive.htm

17 'World Refugee Survey', 2002, (Online) Available at:www.refugees.org

10

Peace & War
in Post-Conflict Mozambique

BRAZÃO MAZULA
with EDUARDO SITOE, OBEDE BALOI & GUILHERME MBILANA

In October 1992 Mozambique achieved a negotiated peace. After 18 months of intense negotiations a cease-fire was reached between the Frelimo government and Renamo, ending a war that had meant severe destruction of both human life, and social fabric as well as of economic infrastructure. It is correct to say that a new era began for the Mozambican, not having to flee from the fighting which was almost a part of everyday life. And a new political framework was built by the General Peace agreement itself, the 1990 Constitution and the realization of multi-party elections. Therefore, when on 4 October 2004, 12 years later, Mozambique remembered the Peace Accord, there was indeed a lot to celebrate. Nonetheless, the end of hostilities did not eliminate political conflict. The point is that political conflict has persisted and has the potential to turn violent which has happened in some instances, leading to loss of lives. As indicated in the title, this chapter is on conflict in a post-war setting. The study focuses on the period between 1992 – the year of the Peace Agreement – and 2002, the tenth anniversary celebration.

The study of conflicts in Mozambique raises complex questions that are widely debated in the context of the democratization process in the country. Here we focus our analysis on the conflicts that occurred in the districts of Changara in Tete province (Central region), and Montepuez in the Northern Province of Cabo Delgado. They are taken as examples that uncover the complexities of peace consolidation. *Montepuez* may well represent the highest point of violence in post-war Mozambique. It was well covered by the media and received significant international coverage. *Changara* has been a very low-profile political conflict and has received hardly any media attention. When it was covered, it never reached the front pages. Eventually most people have no knowledge of it. Even for the authors of this study it was only 'discovered' during consultative meetings organized by the Centre for Democracy and Development Studies (CEDE) in Tete Province, which made it clear that this was an important case to consider. By selecting these two different types, we hope to better illustrate the different forms of political conflict in post-war Mozambique.

The new democratizing state born out of the 1990 plural political Constitution is still confronted by multiple difficulties in the exercise of effective and real political pluralism, even though the Constitution established certain liberties and fundamental rights. An example of these is expressed in Article 31 of the Constitution that reads: 'The (political) parties give expression to political pluralism, contribute to the formation and manifestation of the popular will, and are the fundamental instrument for the democratic participation of the citizens in governing the country'.[1]

This study aims to show the existence of conflicts that arise due to the difficulties experienced by political parties when it comes to the issue of political co-habitation, particularly because the political parties in question were until recently involved in military conflict. Conflict research has both academic and practical ambitions. Dealing with life and death issues for many people caught in conflict, research cannot be purely for the sake of research. We agree with Vivienne Jabri (1996: 12) who says, 'the primary aim of conflict research may be explanation, but the field also has a self-consciously practical aim. It is assumed that greater understanding of conflict processes leads to the amelioration of their destructive implications.'

Having this in mind, the study adopted an adapted version of the War-Torn Society Project (WSP) methodology. This is a participatory-action research developed to address the deficit of dialogue in war-torn societies. It strives to fill the gap between research and policy-making. The WSP methodology aims at developing participatory, multi-actor models for collective analysis, consultation, collaboration and coordination that is particularly suitable for the fluid, precarious and highly unstable context of societies emerging from socio-political tensions. Although the WSP methodology is a macro-level tool, the authors have developed experience in Mozambique of a bottom-up approach in their work within the CEDE which is employed here.

Peace and Conflict in Post-War Mozambique: Some Theoretical Considerations

Understanding Conflict and Peace

How can one understand democratization and peace consolidation in developing and conflict-ridden countries, with particular emphasis on sub-Saharan Africa? To begin with, one should note that the literature in this field tends to be pessimistic about the prospects of structural stability and democracy in such countries. Mamadou Diouf (1998: 1) sums it up by saying, 'the key-words today are the (im)possibilities for Africa to achieve a triple demographic, economic and political, if not cultural or civilisational transition.' Seymour Lipset (1994) argues that democracy cannot occur in these countries unless a certain number of socio-economic requisites are met, namely, economic development and political legitimacy. In like manner, G. Almond and S. Verba (1963) argue that the prevalent political culture in these societies does not yet include values and norms that can sustain a democratic form of politics.

Rich bodies of research have accumulated on political transition in Africa. In the case of Mozambique, there has been significant research on the political transformation that brought about peace and multi-party democracy (e.g., Brito et al, 1993; Abrahamsson and Nilsson 1994; Mazula 1996; Macuane 2000; Sitoe, 2003). Such research has helped to clarify the picture of the factors that led to the end of the war and, partially, the political and institutional foundations of the new era. But little attention has been given to the conflicts that have arisen in the post-war setting in Mozambique.

Conflict resolution and peace studies have elaborated extensively on the fact that the termination of war does not lead automatically to sustainable peace (Macamo and Neubert, 2003; Ayers et al. 1999: 10; Nilsson 2001). Johan Galtung's (1969) seminal distinction between negative and positive peace has been particularly crucial in this respect, arguing for the need to go beyond war termination, i.e. the end of direct physical violence, and search for the reduction if not elimination of structural violence (cited by Nilsson 2001: 6; also by Kotzé 2002: 78). Galtung describes conflict in terms of the following necessary components: first, incompatibility of interests; second, negative attitudes in the form of perceptions or stereotypes about others; and third, behaviors of coercion and gestures of hostility and threat (Kotzé 2002: 78–9). This analysis expands the discussion on conflict beyond physical violence to include structural and cultural violence.

This is particularly important as the moral virtues of conflict resolution and peace are often taken for granted. Paul Salem (1997: 12–13) (cited by Kotzé, 2002: 79) warns against culture-specific assumptions. According to him, struggle – and not peace – can be a virtue in certain traditions and contexts. In the same path, Macamo and Neubert (2003) call for a non-normative analytical perspective in dealing with questions of war and peace. They highlight, for instance, that in general the objective of armed conflicts is victory, not peace as such. After victory, positive peace may follow. When victory is no longer a realistic option conflicting parties try at first not to lose the war. Along the same line of thought, Marta Martinelli Quille (n.d.: 7) points out that one important trend in conflict resolution theory is that which takes man as a learning social being as its unit of analysis. Violence in this case is not seen as a result of man's flawed nature but the outcome of learning processes specific to a particular cultural setting and time. 'In other words,' she explains, 'man might be good in nature, but could act violently and engage in violent conflicts with other people, as a result of the social interactions and social memberships he is involved in.'

Laurie Nathan (1998) asserts that, defined as the absence of widespread physical violence, peace is deemed to be an unqualified 'good', in terms of orderly politics and the sanctity of life. Since civil wars lead to extensive suffering and loss of life, it seems obvious that the prevention and termination of warfare are paramount goals. The protagonists in an actual or imminent civil war may have an entirely different outlook, however. Oppressed groups may prize freedom and justice more than peace, and may consequently be prepared to provoke and endure a high level of violence to achieve the rights of citizenship. In so far as popular resistance threatens the *status quo*, peace serves the interests of the regime, the ruling elite and their foreign supporters. The cessation of hostilities is thus less a goal in its own right than an outcome of the antagonists' willingness to reach a settlement, which addresses the substantive causes of violence.

This brings us to further clarifications in our understanding of conflict and peace. As a matter of fact, in much of the academic and policy literature, the term 'conflict' refers to situations of mass physical violence. Thus, conflict is seen as an inherently negative dynamic. This perspective is analytically questionable. Social and political conflict is not only inevitable, but also normal and ubiquitous in all societies which comprise diverse groups. Whether ethnicity, religion, politics or class defines the groups, they have different needs, interests, values and access to power and resources. These differences necessarily generate competition and conflict. Conflict is also a natural social consequence of fundamental change and an expression of a desire for basic change (Nathan 1998).

How we comprehend conflict in general has a critical bearing on our response in specific situations. If we regard the phenomenon as intrinsically destructive, then our efforts will be directed towards suppressing or eliminating it. Such efforts are likely to be counterproductive, raising rather than lowering the level of tension. On the other hand, if we view conflict as normal and inescapable, then the challenge lies in managing it in a constructive fashion; that is, in non-violent ways that enjoy the consent of citizens. States that are stable are not free from conflict, but are rather able to deal with its various manifestations.

It is against this background that Nathan argues that, both ethically and analytically, the primary goal of efforts to prevent and resolve African crises is therefore best formulated as the establishment of peace with justice. What matters greatly is that all sectors of society perceive the political dispensation to be sufficiently just. And she adds

> violence may be a predominant concern (...) but from an analytical perspective it should be viewed as a symptom of intra-state crises. The crises arise from four structural conditions in particular: authoritarian rule; the exclusion of minorities from governance; socio-economic deprivation combined with inequity; and weak states, which lack the institutional capacity to manage political and social conflicts. Sustainable peace and prosperity are possible only if these primary causes of mass violence are addressed satisfactorily. (Nathan 1998: 1)

The risk of violence rises when these conditions are present simultaneously, intertwined and mutually reinforcing, and when they are exacerbated by other structural problems.

> In Africa such problems include the lack of coincidence between nation and state as a result of the colonial imposition of borders; the colonial legacy of ethnic discrimination and favouritism; unstable civil-military relations; land, environmental and demographic pressures; arms' supplies and other forms of foreign support to authoritarian regimes; the debt burden; and the imbalance in economic power and trade relations between the South and the North. (Nathan, 1998)

Another important assumption to avoid is that the challenge of peace is the same everywhere. It is important to highlight that the notion of peace consolidation is constructed in the context of a post-war settlement, following the implementation of some sort of peace agreement. There is a difference in the pursuit of peace between countries whose violent conflicts are in the past and those where the violent conflict is part of recent history. In the latter, building peace faces particular pressure, to avoid the recurrence of conflict or its re-escalation. Here we can say that, while during peace negotiations the focus is on how to terminate violence, in the aftermath of the peace agreement the struggle is to avoid returning to violence. It is telling that during the 1994 breakthrough elections in Mozambique one common fear was 'the Angola path,' where the 1992 elections were queried by allegations of fraud, and soon after the war resumed. 'The comparison with Angola was a spectre haunting Mozambique' (Maia 1996: 169).

Successive Transformations

Since 1994, three genuinely competitive multi-party general elections have been held, all won by the governing party, Frelimo. Despite charges of fraud, the opposition has in general respected the results and expressed its antagonism within the democratic framework of the law. The third round of national elections was held in 2004 and won by Frelimo and its presidential candidate. An important first step towards the decentralization of power, the creation of 33 municipalities followed. Municipal elections were held in 1998 and 2003. And for the first time in the country's history, a party different from the one in central government now governs some municipalities. On the economic front during this period, there have been positive and, at times, very high rates of growth, although from a very low post-war base. 'Especially in view of so much bad news from elsewhere in Africa, it is not without reason that foreign observers delight at classifying Mozambique as an African success story' (Levy et al. 2002: 1).

The transformations have been significant. That is why Mazula (2002a: 25) asserts that 'peace in Mozambique, over these 10 years, is explained, notwithstanding adversities along the path, by the development of a certain capacity for socio-political and cultural cohabitation, in the day-to-day complex of society itself. This development is itself a learning process.'

Building Consensus: Will it Work?

A direct legacy of civil conflict is also the worsening of political and social polarisation and the absence of dialogue. A culture of confrontation prevails and adversaries are excluded on the grounds that any disagreement goes against society as a whole and that dissent is therefore anti-social... (Reuben Zamora, Guatemala as cited in Hampson and Tschirgi 1998: 2).

The structural violence that characterizes war-torn societies and societies with profound inequalities requires not only new institutions and policies but also and above all the establishment and consolidation of consensus on the 'rules of the game'. Mahmood Mamdani (1996: 29; Ayers et al 1999: 11) argues against the notion that

multi-party democracy can lead to democratic outcomes regardless of context, for this can only be when all participants accept the rules of the game. Logically and historically, the creation of a political community must precede multi-party competition. The creation of a political community requires a minimum consensus within that community – of all, not just a majority.

Dirk Kotzé's (2002: 78) summation of some implications of Galtung's (1969) concept of conflict also points out consensus as a requirement:

> Conflict can be prevented or managed if those involved are parties to a figurative agreement about the *rules* in terms of which the competition is managed – an example of such an agreement being the *social contract*. In the absence of such a consensus, conflict becomes prolonged, unresolved and harmful.

In this context – of consensus-building – exercises of national dialogue in post-war situations or in the midst of severe inequalities or injustice in the societal structure have been sought and promoted in several countries. Since the late 1990s the United Nations Development Programme has developed and disseminated National Long-Term Perspective Studies (NLTPS) aimed at assisting in national dialogue exercises for strategizing development in the South. Mozambique has implemented such a process and in late 2003 the final document of its Vision 2025 was adopted by Parliament. As a policy process, the exercise was highly innovative in that it was a civil society-led process, although political leaders were also involved (Norton 2004). The acceptance of the results of the *Agenda 2025* process by the political leadership both government and opposition is well inscribed in the unanimous adoption of the final document in Parliament (*Agenda 2025*, 2003). However, the impact of such an enterprise is still to be seen. Likewise, the commitment by all players to the Vision is something still to be tested. In particular, the question is whether and how the main political actors will foster a political co-habitation as well as decentralized political structures, including the political parties themselves.

Fields of Vulnerability

No one can ignore the fact that the democratization process in Mozambique shows significant progress. This can be seen in the establishment of key institutions in all of Mozambique's democratic foundations. However, one can also argue that democratization is not just a process of implanting formal institutions of liberal democracy; it is rather 'a process of creation and cultural change to facilitate democratic politics, which accommodates diversity, opposition, and which aims at building social consensus around national projects' (Ayers et al. 1999: 21).

A number of recent studies on Mozambique have continued to applaud the country's success in ending the civil war but also point out shortcomings in the peace and democratic consolidation process that should follow the implementation of the peace agreement. A selection of these studies includes some of those discussed below. For example, Brito et al (2003: 5) argue that

> if the pacification of Mozambican society was an undeniable success, the democratisation and political inclusion that should have followed cannot be classified in the same way. The main political forces tolerate, but do not trust, each other. In recent years, distrust has undergone a noteworthy and worrying resurgence, development imbalances continue to worsen, historic fault lines begin once more to show signs of reactivation, and violence could easily erupt.

According to these authors, the factors that generate violent conflict in Mozambique have deep historical roots, and are directly related to the building of the state and the economy of the country since the late nineteenth century. The extremely centralized nature of the Mozambican state, and the greater access by the southern elite to economic resources and power, alongside a marked cleavage between the urban and rural worlds, contribute to a geographical distribution of wealth highly concentrated around the capital. This feeds political dissatisfaction, which is expressed in the electoral geography, and takes on ethnic and regional characteristics.

Elísio Macamo and Dieter Neubert (2003) also analyze the prospects for a stable peace in the country. Basically they argue that the present-day situation is directly related to the kind of peace that was brokered in Rome in the peace agreement of October 1992. The study discusses the post-conflict order that ensued from the Rome peace negotiations. Drawing on an analytical framework that posits a tension between negative and positive peace, it argues that the peace achieved by the Rome negotiations may not be as stable as is generally assumed. The reasons for this are to be found in the negotiating process itself. The paper suggests that peace was bought from the warring parties in exchange for the promise of development aid. While this may have been necessary to bring the conflict to an end it may have been at the expense of a long-lasting peace which might have included, for example, the settlement of human rights issues.

Similarly, Jeremy Weinstein (2002: 150) argues that Mozambique faces a crisis in the making. For Weinstein, the problem lies with the political system.

> Even as it looks back on a successful transition, Mozambique today faces a brewing crisis. Old, deep-rooted divisions linger and threaten to go worse. And the structure of Mozambique's political system is uniquely *ill-suited* to the challenges ahead. It lacks the capacity to govern effectively at either the national or the local level. And what is still more troubling, it possesses none of the levers that it would need to forestall a possible relapse into civil strife after the 2004 presidential and parliamentary elections.

Another study by Levy et al. (2002) analyzes the political situation along five main dimensions: competition, inclusion, consensus, rule of law and governance. The analysis – undertaken in 2002 – concluded that there was less competition then than as recently as two years earlier. Competition between the branches of government, minimal as it was during the period of the first multi-party Parliament (1994–9) had declined, as numerical superiority became all that mattered. The dysfunctional judicial system was no significant check on the executive or any of its officers. Despite superlative constitutional protections and reasonable press laws, the scope for the competition of ideas had contracted. According to the authors, inclusion too was a growing problem. Political tolerance and social trust were low, and appeals to people's ethnic and racial identities as bases for political allegiance were multiplying. Consensus too seemed to have diminished, if only modestly. Certain rules of the game – what is a legitimate form of public protest and what can be discussed in the press – seemed to call forth less agreement than formerly. The rule of law, always a fragile flower in Mozambique, has wilted in the heat of generalized corruption. Accountability of officials to the public is negligible.

The Centre for Population Studies (CEP) of the Eduardo Mondlane University conducted three public opinion surveys between 1997 and 2001 intended to evaluate the level of public support for key democratic values in Mozambique. Two or three conclusions from those surveys are relevant for this overview: although the majority of people support basic democratic principles, they also strongly equate democracy with socio-economic and material well-being, i.e., democracy is only relevant insofar as it brings wealth into people's lives. At the same time, all the surveys indicate that, whereas people are generally satisfied with government performance in the social sphere such as education and health (which is not to say that performance has been stellar – it is just the way people prioritize things in their lives), they are dissatisfied with government functioning in terms of people's access to jobs, food, etc. People are also unhappy with the perceived imbalance in terms of economic development and investment between southern Mozambique and the rest of the country.

All these studies further confirm the picture showing that the current state of affairs opens up windows of vulnerability to social and political conflicts, although not of a civil war magnitude. As mentioned above, Mozambique experienced a successful implementation of a peace agreement, which terminated a long and violent armed conflict. Not only that, war is unlikely to erupt again in the near future. Internally, there are neither sufficient resources to fuel and sustain an armed conflict nor has the war fatigue that helped end the previous war vanished. Internationally, on the one hand, the southern African region would hardly be likely to back a war in Mozambique as happened in the past and, on the other hand, international support for Mozambique seems committed to and satisfied with the current trend of post-war political and economic recovery. It is remarkable that Mozambique is now widely seen as a success story. However, the very fact that war is extremely unlikely in the near future – as a convergence of both internal and external factors, does not say much *per se* about peace. As highlighted above, critical deficits in the country's political culture continue to flourish, which sustain fields of vulnerability, although not of such magnitude as to lead to another civil war.

Multiple Avenues

The discourse of conflicts in terms of an opposition between war and peace has led analysts to give the impression that the termination of war leads to stable peace. But experience shows that the road to positive peace is a complex one. And the absence of war or the low level of probability that the deterioration of the situation might erupt into war does not necessarily mean that the path to peace is secure. Paulo Sérgio Pinheiro calls attention to the multiple avenues following the end of war when he uses the concept of 'no-war and no-peace' to describe the cases of structural violence which are not cases of war. He is particularly concerned with the low levels of peace the world has realized since the end of the Cold War, despite earlier expectations. He points out that

> the pacification of everyday life continues to be an unfulfilled promise almost two decades after the wave of political transitions, even in most societies going though democratic consolidation processes. The effective protection of human rights and the rule of law are far from being effectively established and citizenship is not yet guaranteed for large sectors of the population, which live in dire conditions of poverty and social inequality. (Pinheiro 2000: 3)

We can also note with Pinheiro that countries in transition to democracy, as the *Human Development Report 2000* (UNDP 2000: 59) has indicated, generally face four challenges in promoting human rights. The first challenge is how to integrate minorities and address horizontal inequality between ethnic groups or geographic regions. A second key weakness is the arbitrary exercise of power, especially the abuse of the state monopoly of physical violence by state agencies. When elite groups act as if they are above the law, faith in democratic institutions weakens. The third problem is the neglect of the economic dimension of human rights. Many new democracies fail to address the social and economic rights of the most vulnerable groups. Finally, failing to deal adequately with the legacy of past authoritarianism can lead to the recurrence of violence and the reversal of democratic rule.

The democratic deficits mentioned above suggest that, after the success of ending the war, Mozambique has been less successful in peace 'consolidation'. Some have suggested that Mozambique's success in maintaining peace since 1992 lies not in the country's capacity to resolve the problems that would lead to instability but rather in its ability to postpone them (Brito et al. 2003: 94). While war looks unlikely, the fact that critical issues to overcome structural violence are unlikely to be dealt with adequately may lead the country to a path of 'stagnation' instead of effective consolidation of peace.

New Actors

Concurrent with the debate on the sources and nature of conflict have been extensive discussions on the role and the characteristics of third parties. As Reimann (2000: 4) sums it up:

> in the past, attention has focused primarily on the differences in substance and emphasis between Track I as conflict settlement strategies and Track II as conflict resolution strategies. While Track I was mainly reserved for the official and formal activities of diplomatic and governmental actors, Track II referred largely to more informal and unofficial efforts by other non-governmental parties.

Reimann also sees a movement towards a more integrative approach:

> I would argue that at least since the early 1990s, an appropriate analytical focus on inter-relatedness and interdependence has emerged, and is now occupying the middle ground in this field. By the mid-1990s, it has been possible to see a shift in the literature that stresses an integrative and complementary approach to conflict management. It emphasises further the need to combine conflict settlement strategies, such as mediation and negotiation, with conflict resolution strategies, such as facilitation/consultation. (Reimann 2000: 5–6)

Still following Reimann's arguments, the key point to be raised from these complementary/integrative approaches is that the synthesis of different models and concepts, in the light of complex conflict interests and needs, can bring great value and insight to the analysis. Indeed, some scholars-practitioners have taken the integrative/complementary approaches a step further by introducing the concept of further tracks, which has now been dubbed the 'multi-track approach'. The most recent conceptual development is the creation of an additional single track – Track III. This

Table 10.1 Track I, II and III actors and their strategies

	Track I	Track II	Track III
Actors involved	Political and military leaders as mediators and /or representatives of conflict parties	From private individuals, academics /professionals, 'civil mediation'/'citizens diplomacy' to international and local non-governmental organisations involved in conflict resolution	From local grassroots organizations to local and international development agencies, human rights organizations and humanitarian assistance
Strategies taken	*Outcome-orientated:* From official and coercive measures like sanctions, arbitration, 'power mediation' to non-coercive measures like facilitation, negotiation/ mediation, fact-finding missions and 'good offices'	*Process-orientated:* Non-official and non-coercive measures mainly facilitation/ consultation in form of problem-solving workshops and round tables	*Process- and / or structure-orientated:* Capacity-building, trauma work, grassroots training, development and human rights work

Source: Reimann (2000)

is taken to refer to all process- and structure-orientated initiatives undertaken by actors involved in grassroots training/capacity-building and empowerment, trauma work, human rights and development work, and humanitarian assistance.

De-escalating Tensions in Time of Crisis

In his book *Making Peace*, Adam Curle defines human relationships as peaceful and unpeaceful and as balanced and unbalanced. Conflict is essentially a situation of unpeaceful relationships where incompatibility of interests is dominant. By unbalanced relations Curle means all those relations where one party has the power to impose conditions on the other, and where the advantaged party uses this power to exploit the disadvantaged one. Unbalanced relations are not necessarily unpeaceful, as he points out in the case of parent and child and local/national governments. Nevertheless, Curle notes that exploitative imbalance is a particularly prevalent form of unpeaceful relationship. He views the process of peace-making as one that 'consists in making changes in relationships so that they may be brought to a point where development can occur' (as quoted in Quille 2000: 13).

To help those involved in conflict Curle discusses the importance of training. He defines training as 'to prepare people to play a useful part in resolving conflict, to help those suffering oppression to resist or those threatened by violence and chaos to survive, to protect those in danger of assassination, to care where possible for the traumatised and the other victims of war' (as quoted in Quille 2000: 15).

It has been well noted by critics of the conflict resolution paradigm that 'objective issue-based disagreements do not necessarily disappear as positive relationships develop' (Bloomfield 1995: 152 as quoted in Quille n.d.: 9). However, the importance of these kinds of interventions to de-escalate tensions and conflict cannot be neglected. While counteracting structural violence takes long-term measures, local interventions are crucial to de-escalate tension and restore some 'normality' to the everyday life of the local communities directly affected, as configured in the Track III approach.

The Dynamics of Conflicts & Third-Party Intervention: The Cases of the Districts of Changara & Montepuez

Essentially, the nature of conflict in the district of Changara results from the fact that the Frelimo ex-combatants there (those who fought for the liberation of Mozambique from Portuguese colonial domination) regard Renamo militants (with whom they fought a 16-year-long civil war) as enemies to be destroyed and not as political adversaries. In the country's new political configuration, political adversaries are called to participate in governing the country imbued with the spirit of responsibility and plurality of opinions.

Montepuez, a district located in the Northern Province of Cabo Delgado, became known internationally following the dark events of 9 November 2000, when more than 100 people lost their lives following a political rally organized by Renamo militants. This rally had been organized in protest at the 1999 national electoral results that gave the victory to Frelimo despite Renamo's appeal to the Supreme Court over allegations of fraud and other irregularities. After the 9 November events it became critical to inquire into what happened there in order to situate the nature of conflicts there in the framework of other existing conflicts in the country.

The Changara Case Study: the Issue of Political Co-habitation

The Changara case came to attention after initial contacts between researchers attached to the CEDE and the principal political and civic actors of the province of Tete. These actors included the provincial Governor, the provincial Secretary of the ruling Frelimo party, the provincial political delegate of the main opposition party, Renamo, the provincial commander of the national police, the provincial presiding magistrate of the Judicial Tribunal, the provincial Attorney-General, and national deputies (members of parliament) residing in the province. These contacts were designed to obtain the views of these actors in relation to the role of civil society organizations, such as the CEDE, particularly in terms of how these can participate in the processes of democratization and peace consolidation evolving in Mozambique.

According to the views expressed by several of these political and civic actors, it emerged that in the district of Changara there are situations that pose a threat to the democratization process and political stability in the country as a whole. These situations are characterized by the systematic occurrence of active (political) violence involving militants and sympathizers of the two major political parties in the country, i.e., Frelimo and Renamo. In concrete terms, Frelimo's ex-combatants are said to be the major promoters of the environment of intolerance and difficult political cohabitation in the district. These ex-combatants, it surfaced, were particularly opposed to Renamo's intention of building their district headquarters in Changara from which to develop their political activities. Renamo's intention is clearly established by the national Constitution and embodies a normal practice in a society governed by a democratic political order.

Those interviewed by the researchers (attached to the CEDE) explained that this conflict had remained latent since the end of the civil war in 1992, following the signing of the Rome peace agreement. The conflict, it appears, had gained new and virulent contours following the electoral campaigns preceding the 1999 general elections and their aftermath. To begin with, the campaigns witnessed numerous acts of physical confrontation involving members and sympathizers of both parties.

Based on facts from the civil war era and the contents of interviews with the major political and civic actors in the province of Tete, it is possible to spell out the principal positions taken by Frelimo and Renamo, respectively, in relation to the Changara conflict. Frelimo and government officials, at district and provincial levels in Tete, explain the violent attitude of Frelimo ex-combatants as follows: 'Renamo intended to establish its headquarters in the district of Changara by force, because it lacked effective implantation in the district where during the civil war it never gained any military conquests.' Renamo's lack of popularity in the district of Changara, according to Frelimo circles, results from the fact that 'Changara district is mainly populated by ex-combatants of the war of liberation waged by Frelimo against the Portuguese colonial domination (1964–74). These ex-combatants later fought numerous battles against Renamo guerrilla fighters who made several attempts at establishing themselves in the district during the civil war era.' The Changara case therefore exemplifies a situation of political animosities based on the recently ended political (military) conflict, that meant in large part the partition of the national territory to create zones of control by Renamo guerrillas. Zones of control completely closed the possibility of free movement of people and the co-existence of different political opinions.

Renamo officials read the situation differently. For Renamo, 'Frelimo is deliberately trying to prevent our political activity, using the pretext that the Changara district is exclusively theirs since it is mainly populated by Frelimo's ex-combatants.' According to Renamo officials, the ex-combatants are being urged by Frelimo to 'conduct acts of hostility, to perpetrate physical aggression against Renamo militants and sympathizers including the destruction of Renamo's political headquarters and other party symbols'. Renamo, on its side, was determined to gain political space in the district, regardless of the price involved; it wanted to win the sympathy of the population of Changara district. It became imperative to destroy the myth that Changara was Frelimo's political field where Renamo could never establish itself. Renamo complained that the case they took to the provincial courts did not receive the desired result. At the same time, Renamo concluded that the agents of law and order did not intervene, as they should, when ex-combatants perpetrated acts of violence against Renamo militants and Renamo infrastructures. Thus, according to Renamo officials, the agents of law and order in the province of Tete acted with passivity and partiality towards the ex-combatants. For Renamo, the whole story of the 'Changara case' can be understood as an electoral strategy of Frelimo designed to obstruct indefinitely the political implantation of other political forces in the district, in particular, of course, the main opposition party, Renamo. Here it is interesting to note that the district of Changara borders on Zimbabwe and is situated in the southern part of the province of Tete. Thus, according to Renamo, Frelimo's electoral strategy contained both an element of obstructing the political activities of Renamo and of securing electoral victories in the contests to come.

This inquiry into the conflict situation in the district of Changara, carried out with the main political actors in Tete province, indicates that there are different interpretations as to what is actually fuelling it. At the same time, the search into the nature of the conflict conducted with actors from both sides indicated that Changara is an example of a hot spot that can potentially endanger the consolidation of peace in Mozambique. A prominent figure in one of these political parties – with a seat in the Standing Committee of the National Assembly – confided to CEDE researchers that a major (military) uprising had been imminent. This uprising would have involved Renamo's armed men moving from their former military bases to the district of Changara. It was necessary to intervene decisively to abort the possibility of this uprising, by appealing to the good sense of both sides.

Actions Conducted by CEDE in the Domain of Conflict Mediation and
Management in the District of Changara

First, the CEDE continued with the inquiry into the sources and dynamics of conflict with the main political and civic actors in the province of Tete, including the provincial government, the two main political parties, the agents of law and order, and religious personalities. Secondly, the CEDE sent a team of researchers to the district of Changara to conduct a similar exercise with the local political and administrative authorities as well as approaching the actors directly involved in the violent manifestations referred to above. In the district of Changara the team of researchers interviewed a number of Frelimo militants and sympathizers about the conflict. Interestingly, the team did not come across anyone who identified himself as a Renamo militant or sympathizer. According to a local clergyman, there are people in the district who can be correctly described as Renamo militants and sympathizers, although they do not openly present themselves as such for fear of hostility and the risk of physical aggression. In fact, and according to this clergymen, even the local resident who accompanied the CEDE researchers 'was a Renamo militant'.

The third measure undertaken by the CEDE involved the compilation of all the information gathered in relation to the conflict – stressing its main elements and dynamics – to produce its own reflections about the conflict, which it then distributed among the main political and civic actors in the province. At the same time, the CEDE invited these actors to an open debate in both the city of Tete, the capital city of the province bearing the same name, and in the village of Changara. Finally, the CEDE promoted the organization of a public forum in the city of Tete. This forum brought together government officials, political activists from both Frelimo and Renamo, and civil society activists located in the province of Tete to openly discuss the prevailing situation of conflict in the district of Changara.

These forums were particularly successful because they brought together diverse political and social organizations, as well as ordinary citizens, all of whom voiced their indignation at the events in the district of Changara. This feeling of indignation was also stirred up by the fact that most people simply did not know what was happening in Changara. As a result of these forums, most organizations and individuals began to put pressure on the two protagonists to begin measures of confidence-building and dialogue. Out of these forums was constituted a task force that twice went to the district of Changara to search for a political solution to the problems prevailing there. CEDE researchers were included in this task force.

The first public meeting organized in Changara met with severe resistance as well as some tension since a number of Frelimo ex-combatants openly opposed the CEDE actions. According to the local chief of the ex-combatants, they even intended to prevent (by attacking or burning) the vehicle transporting the CEDE researchers from entering the district. According to this source, the ex-combatants initially thought the CEDE was working in Changara to advance Renamo's political agenda, namely, to establish their headquarters in the district. The second public meeting occurred in an environment of relative openness and moderation. Frelimo's leadership in the district of Changara showed sympathy to the presence of Renamo's militants and sympathizers in the district. This meeting began the process of dialogue between the two protagonists, and all concerned began to acquire the same attitude towards the condemnation of violence and the call for peaceful political co-habitation.

While these events were taking place in the district of Changara contacts at the highest level were also being made in the province as a whole. These contacts involved the leadership of both political parties at the provincial level, the deputies residing in the province, agents of law and order and religious personalities to seek their involvement in the resolution of the conflict. As a result of all these contacts, the provincial (and central) leadership of the ruling party (Frelimo) sent their own personnel to the district of Changara to call on the ex-combatants to cease immediately their blockade of Renamo militants and sympathizers.

Thus, in July 2003, Renamo reinstated its political headquarters that had been destroyed by Frelimo's ex-combatants in the aftermath of the 1999 general elections. At the same time, CEDE convened a workshop on the *culture of peace* that was attended by militants and sympathizers drawn from both Frelimo and Renamo. From then on Renamo militants and sympathizers were able to present themselves openly as such. At the workshop all took part in the different panels and in the plenary discussion and, at the end, a collective photo was taken to document this historic event.

Currently, the CEDE is conducting post-conflict monitoring work, designed essentially to ensure that the confidence gained between the two protagonists, and among the citizenry, is consolidated in order to guarantee the participation of all in the local development of the district of Changara in a real and inclusive manner.

The Montepuez Case Study: When the Local Level Appears as the Resonance of Tensions at the Central Level

The conflict in the district of Montepuez is different in character from that prevailing in the district of Changara discussed above. This is so because one finds hardly any local conflict there. As a matter of fact, recollection of the violent events that occurred in the district of Montepuez in 2000 indicates that the responsibility is shared by the leaders of the two major political parties at the local and central levels, as well as the government officials at district, provincial and central levels. This shared responsibility arises because the deaths did not all occur on the same day, which means that, if the correct political decisions (and actions) had been taken in time, perhaps some lives could have been spared. The case of the conflict in the district of Montepuez is therefore different from the conflict in the district of Changara. In Montepuez, ex-combatants are not involved, and tensions due to ethnicity are also absent.

In 2002 the CEDE conducted a public opinion survey in Montepuez of some 134 respondents representing the entire social spectrum of the district (Mazula 2002b). Some of the results of this survey can be highlighted as follows. First, 80.5 per cent of the respondents believed that the 'November 2000' events sharpened the distrust between political parties, particularly between Frelimo and Renamo. Second, 42.6 per cent believed that political parties were still stirring up agitation. Matters did not become worse because the public (according to 66.4 per cent of the respondents) was tolerant of this behavior of the various political parties. Third, 80.6 per cent believed that unemployment was at the root cause of these events, while 24.6 per cent blamed the lack of political will on the part of the parties, and a similar percentage thought that those events were the explosion of people fed up with their exclusion from the economic changes and development in the country. Fourth, 73.9 per cent thought that the events of November 2000 greatly influenced relations between people: 'nobody trusts anyone else, because they don't know their party affiliation, whether they are from Frelimo or from Renamo' (ibid.: 29). These data show that there was a high level of distrust triggered by an environment of political polarization.

The environment of social and political crisis that prevailed in the country in the aftermath of the 1999 general elections – the results of which were vigorously contested by Renamo/the Electoral Coalition – triggered the events that led to demonstrations held in several parts of the country. In the case of Montepuez, the demonstrations meant the death of over 100 people.

Throughout 2000 Renamo organized a number of political demonstrations in several parts of the country, each manifesting a different character.

For example, while in the city of Maputo, the capital city, MPs and leading Renamo figures took part in the demonstrations in a peaceful and orderly manner, elsewhere it was different. In the city of Beira, the second major city in the country, and in the district of Montepuez, the demonstrations ended in violent clashes between the demonstrators and the national police. In Montepuez more than 100 people died, including demonstrators and police officers. Later, a number of people (from both sides) were charged with causing the disturbances and are now serving prison sentences of up to 20 years.

Soon after the November 2000 events a CEDE research team established contacts in the district of Montepuez with locally influential personalities to assess the situation. These influential figures included the mayor, the local leaders of the two major political parties, Frelimo and Renamo, and civil society activists. These actors deplored the situation of instability prevailing in the district following the November events, specifically the climate of fear that was evolving. Thus, they took up the opportunity provided by the meeting organized by CEDE researchers to recreate spaces for a constructive political dialogue.

Actions Conducted by CEDE in the Domain of Conflict Mediation and Management in the District of Montepuez
The CEDE defined the objectives of its intervention in the district of Montepuez as follows: first, the analysis of the situation using participatory methods (focus groups, etc.); second, the promotion of psychological reconstruction of the political and civil societies; and third, the promotion of debate, based on research findings, as a tool for facilitating internal and external co-existence of the political and civil society actors as well as stimulating proximity between the major political actors, Frelimo and Renamo.

To begin with, a public meeting was organized which was attended by various political and civic actors, including local government officials, district administrators, political party representatives, businessmen, religious personalities, traditional chiefs, and neighborhood authorities. This meeting was the first to bring together Frelimo and Renamo militants and sympathizers after the dark events of November 2000. During the meeting the local actors raised with vigour and without fear their concerns in relation to the November 2000 events. At the beginning of the meeting, however, the representatives of Frelimo and Renamo tended to point the blame for these events at each other. In order to find an acceptable solution, CEDE researchers established contacts with various local political and civic personalities in an attempt to induce them to play an influential role in calling the Frelimo and Renamo leaders to reconciliation.

In a move that constituted a test of the capacity of CEDE researchers to mobilize resources and to gain the confidence of the major political forces in the conflict, CEDE organized a joint meeting, which brought together the Montepuez district administrator, the local mayor, Frelimo's district First Secretary and Renamo's district political delegate, who had requested the meeting. There was an initial lack of consensus regarding the venue for the meeting, which caused delay, but it was later decided that the meeting should take place in a neutral venue. In the end, a venue was found and the meeting took place as planned.

Those present at the meeting, namely, Frelimo and Renamo representatives, plus the district administrator and the mayor, signed a memorandum. The content of this important document indicated a compromise by the local players in favour of reconciliation, dialogue and peace, as well as the need to institutionalize dialogue for the peaceful resolution of differences between them. The memorandum (*Acta de Reunião* 2002) outlined some of the following principles:

(i) from now on, the parties promise to maintain an open, truthful and consensual dialogue;
(ii) from now on, the parties promise to maintain a posture of reconciliation and permanent search of dialogue, with concrete actions that lead to proximity and trust between the parties, without recourse to force;
(iii) from now on, the parties promise to play an important role in the civic education of the population, and not to facilitate, instigate or accommodate acts of violence that may break the state of good co-existence, security and calm;
(iv) in the framework of this memorandum, the parties promise that, in the case of disturbances that might affect this agreement, all parties shall be notified and by consensus they will decide what measures to adopt. This in the spirit of reconciliation, without prejudice to the actions of the relevant institutions, as prescribed by the country's laws.

The content of this memorandum had enormous impact and attracted diverse reactions from the top leadership of the two major political parties, Frelimo and Renamo. Some of these reactions were positive, but others were not. The media and local representatives of the international community received the memorandum very positively. Negative reactions came from those political leaders at the central level who saw the agreement as a breach of party discipline on the part of their Montepuez local party leaders. These local leaders did not consult first with their central chiefs before entering into an agreement with their political opponents – an agreement that brought them all to a common agenda of peace and reconciliation.

Though these negative reactions coming from the central leaders of the political parties were registered, the document remained valid, in particular because it embodied the popular will of the local party leaders and the district and municipal authorities. It also expressed their desire to live in a spirit of reconciliation in order to cultivate together an environment of normalcy and political and social stability in the district of Montepuez. Other public meetings were organized by each of the major political parties which CEDE researchers were invited to attend. These meetings that involved Frelimo and Renamo militants and sympathizers were generally held in an environment of harmony and calm. The population of the district of Montepuez celebrated this normalcy because, as many pointed out, it was the first time since the dark events of November 2000 that people could freely express their political views in public.

The meetings bringing the main local players to the same table were eventually consolidated by the creation of a Municipal/District Forum, assuring a permanent channel for dialogue. Another result of CEDE mediation in the conflicts of the district of Montepuez was the organization of a massive street march bringing together militants and sympathizers from both political parties on 4 October 2003. This is the national day of peace in Mozambique in memory of the day the Peace Agreement was signed on 4 October 1992 between the Government of Frelimo and Renamo in Rome to end the 16-year civil war in the country. The march was the first public event in Montepuez since November 2000 to bring the population together to celebrate a national public holiday without discrimination based on political party affiliation.

Last, but not least, another result of the work of the CEDE to restore normalcy to the district of Montepuez was the peaceful and orderly manner in which the local elections of November 2003 were held in the municipality of Montepuez. From the electoral campaign to the voting itself, and from the counting of the votes to the acceptance of the electoral results, all these phases occurred without major disturbances. This means that the environment of political and social stability has been restored in the district of Montepuez. It also means that the parties will not easily resort to active violence in order to secure their political goals. Today, the political battle is taking place at the level of the local Municipal Assembly that was inaugurated on 9 February 2004.

Conclusion

This study has highlighted some of the complexities of the post-war situation in Mozambique. By focusing on the contexts and dynamics at the local level the study was able to uncover the challenges posed to peaceful co-habitation between local and central actors, particularly within the political parties. Addressing the root causes of conflict is still a major challenge ahead in Mozambique. In the context of immense vulnerabilities, the role of institutions as well of the political leaderships has become particularly critical in fostering a culture of peaceful co-existence. The findings of this study show that compromises on the part of the political elite, such as those expressed in documents like *Agenda 2025*, have only touched the surface of the transformations needed to promote positive peace.

Coherent with the methodology adopted in this study, researchers ventured into action-based research with the intention of approaching and building confidence between political and civil society; this has been achieved, although it has yet to be completed. The research project gave participants in the two communities alternative references for the normalization of the social and political situation in their district. The Montepuez case had national ramifications as shown by the fact that Parliament set up a commission to investigate the incidents of November 2000 in Montepuez. The success or failure of the project of normalization of the political and social situation in this part of the country may have a multiplier effect on other critical cases that may occur in the country.

The impact of CEDE's research programme demonstrated that sociability between the two political forces was possible in both the case of Changara and in Montepuez. The establishment of a Renamo local headquarters in Changara and the common celebration of peace (in October 2002) showed that both parties could demonstrate in public without undermining political and social tranquillity. The compromise agreements on peace and reconciliation signed by the local leaders in Montepuez showed the national and provincial leaderships the interest of the local actors in the normalization of the political and social situation in the district of Montepuez. In the course of this study, and as a result of the initial successes of its action-based research programme, key players in other conflictual sites in the country have expressed interest in undertaking similar exercises. This is the case, for example, of the municipality of Mocímboa da Praia, in the Northern Province of Cabo Delgado.[2] This bodes well for conflict research in Mozambique.

References

Abrahamsson, H. and A. Nilsson. 1994. *Moçambique em Transição: um estudo da história de desenvolvimento durante o período 1974–1992.* Maputo: CEEI (Centro de Estudos Estratégicos e Internacionais) / ISRI (Instituto Superior de Relações Internacionais).

Acta de Reunião. Montepuez, 8 August 2002.

Agenda 2025. Visão e Estratégias da Nação, Final version, Maputo: Comité de Conselheiros, December 2003.

Almond, G. and S. Verba. 1963. *The Civic Culture*, Princeton, NJ: Princeton University Press.

Ayers, Alison et al. 1999. 'IV. Democracy and Identity-Based Conflicts: Problem or Solution?' Draft Working Paper, 1 November. [Online] Available at http://www.ids.ac.uk/ids/govern/pdfs/demcon.pdf

Bloomfield, David. 1995. 'Towards Complementarity in Conflict Management: Resolution and Settlement in Northern Ireland'. *Journal of Peace Research* 32 (2).

Brito, Luís. 1993. 'Estado e Democracia Multipartidária em Moçambique', in Luís de Brito and Bernard Weimer, eds. *Multipartidarismo e Perspectivas Pós-Guerra*, Maputo: UEM (Universidade Eduardo Mondlane)/FES (Friedrich Ebert Stiftung, 15-26.

Brito, Luís, António Francisco; João Pereira and Domingos do Rosário. 2003. *MOZAMBIQUE 2003: An Assessment of the Potential for Conflict.* Maputo: Population Studies Centre, Eduardo Mondlane University.

Curle, Adam. 1995. *Another Way: Positive Response to Contemporary Violence.* Oxford: Jon Carpenter Publishing.

Curle, Adam. 1971. *Making Peace* London: Tavistock Publications.

Diouf, Mamadou. 1998. *Political Liberalisation or Democratic Transition – African Perspectives*, New Path Series, No. 1. Dakar: CODESRIA.

Galtung, Johan. 1969. 'Violence, Peace and Peace Research', in *Journal of Peace Research*, 6 (3), 167–91. London: Sage.

Hampson, Fen Osler and Necla Tschirgi (1998) 'The War-Torn Societies Project and Third Party Neutral Models of Conflict Resolution', A Paper prepared for the War-Torn Societies Project, Second Draft.

Jabri, Vivienne. 1996. *Discourses on Violence: Conflict Analysis Reconsidered.* Manchester: Manchester University Press.

Kotzé, Dirk. 2002. 'Issues in Conflict Resolution.' *African Journal on Conflict Resolution* 2 (2): 77-98.

Levy, Samuel, J. Michael Turner, Thomas Johnson and Michael Eddy. 2002. 'The State of Democracy and Governance in Mozambique.' Commissioned by USAID. Maputo: MSI.

Lipset, S. M. 1994. 'The Social Requisites of Democracy Revisited', *American Sociological Review*, 59: 1–22.

Macamo, Elísio and Dieter Neubert. 2003. 'The Politics of Negative Peace: Mozambique in the aftermath of the Rome Cease-Fire Agreements', *Portuguese Literary and Cultural Studies* 10 (Spring), 23–47.

Macuane, José Jaime. 2000. *Instituições e Democratização no Contexto Africano: Multipartidarismo e Organização Legislativa em Moçambique (1994-1999)*, Doctoral thesis. Rio de Janeiro: IUPERJ.

Maia, Juarez de. 1996. 'Civic Education in the Mozambique Elections', in Brazão Mazula, ed., *Mozambique: Elections, Democracy and Development*, Maputo: Inter-Africa Group, 51–219.

Mamdani, Mahmood. 1996. 'From Conquest to Consent as the Basis of State Formation: Reflections on Rwanda' *New Left Review*, 216, 3–36.

Mazula, Brazão, ed. 1996. *Mozambique: Elections, Democracy and Development*, Maputo: Inter-Africa Group.

Mazula, Brazão, ed. 2002a. *Moçambique: 10 Anos de Paz*. Maputo: CEDE.

Mazula, Brazão. 2002b. 'Paz e Democracia Desafiantes', in Brazão Mazula, ed., *Moçambique: 10 Anos de Paz*, Maputo: CEDE, 25–42.

Nathan, Laurie. 1998. 'Strategies for Peace and Prosperity in Southern Africa'. Paper prepared for the Southern Africa Trade and Investment Summit, *International Herald Tribune*, Cape Town, 1–2 December. [Online] Available at http://ccrweb.ccr.uct.ac.za/staff_papers/laurie_ihl.html#fref1

Nilsson, Anders. 2001. *Paz na Nossa Época: para uma compreensão holística dos conflitos na sociedade mundial*. Göteborg: PADRIGU/ISRI (Instituto Superior de Relações Internacionais).

Norton, Roger D. 2004. 'Long-Term National Visions and Development Strategies and Their Links to Poverty Alleviation: The Case of Mozambique.' Atlanta, GA: Carter Center. April. (Paper prepared in the context of the contribution of *The Global Development Initiative of the Carter Center* to the *Agenda 2025* process in Mozambique).

Pinheiro, Paulo Sérgio. 2000. 'Human Rights Observation in Democratisation Processes: The cases of no-war and no-peace.' Paper presented at Expert Seminar on Human Rights and Peace, Geneva. 8–9 December.

Quille, Marta Martineli (n.d). 'The Nature of Modern Intra-state Conflicts: An appeal for a different level of analysis' [online] COPRI Working Papers. Available at http://www.copri.dk/copri/ipra/AFPREA/martinelli.doc

Quille, Marta Martineli. 2000. *A Response to Recent Critiques of Conflict Resolution: Is Critical Theory the Answer?* COPRI Working Paper No. 23.

Reimann, Cordula. 2000. 'Towards Conflict Transformation: Assessing the State-of-the-Art in Conflict Management – Theoretical Perspectives', in *The Berghof Handbook for Conflict Transformation*. [Online] Available at http://www.berghof-center.org/handbook/reimann.

Salem, Paul. 1997. 'A Critique of Western conflict resolution from a non-Western perspective', in *Conflict Resolution in the Arab World: selected essays*, Beirut: American University in Beirut.

Sitoe, Eduardo. 2003. 'Making Sense of Political Transition in Mozambique', in Malyn Newitt, ed., *Community & the State in Lusophone Africa*, London: King's College, 15–34.

Smith, Dan. 2000. 'Trends and Causes of Armed Conflict', in *Berghof Handbook for Conflict Transformation*. [Online] Available at http://www.berghof-handbook.net/smith/text.htm

United Nations Development Programme (UNDP). 2000. *Human Development Report*. New York: Oxford University Press.

Weinstein, Jeremy. 2002. 'Mozambique: a Fading U.N. Success Story', *Journal of Democracy* 13 (1): 141–56.

Notes

1   Constitution of the Republic of Mozambique, Chapter III, Article 31, No.1, p.14

2   In Moçímboa da Praia a new type of conflict developed between the ruling Frelimo party and its long-term rival, Renamo. It is a conflict that resulted from the historic patterns of alliances and ethnic loyalties that developed, first, during the war of liberation and, later, during the one-party state that prevailed in the country from 1977 to 1992. One interesting finding is that in this district there is a tendency for individuals to join the political party that brings together members of his/her ethnic group. It is therefore ethnic tensions that get politicized and are then expressed in political party competition, particularly since political parties have become the main vehicles for access to power and influence.

11

Post-1990 Constitutional Reforms in Africa
A Preliminary Assessment of the Prospects for Constitutional Governance & Constitutionalism

CHARLES MANGA FOMBAD

After more than three decades of mostly authoritarian, corrupt and incompetent rule that earned Africa notoriety for political instability, civil wars, famine, disease, poverty and other ills, the 1990s began with a slow and painful move towards what many optimistically hoped would usher in a new era of democratic governance and constitutionalism. One of the main features of this process has been constitutional reform. Africa's record on constitutionalism has been an unhappy one. The great enthusiasm that greeted the independence constitutions in the early 1960s had been quickly dissipated by leaders who abrogated, subverted, suspended or brazenly ignored these constitutions.

Constitutional reforms have now become one of the most overt signs of the present democratization process. Since the 1990s most African countries have adopted new or substantially revised constitutions. However, the mere existence of these new or revised constitutions and their effective enforcement may not necessarily be the panacea that will cure the multi-faceted and gargantuan problems that beset the continent, nor even guarantee constitutionalism. After all, the continent's worst dictators have often dissimulated their dictatorship behind written constitutions. The problems have been substantially caused, not by the absence of constitutions but rather by the absence of constitutionalism. After more than a decade of hectic and sometimes frantic constitutional changes, it is now necessary to consider whether these developments are likely to enhance the prospects for constitutionalism in Africa.

In attempting to assess the prospects for constitutionalism under the new constitutional dispensation of the 1990s, this chapter identifies what can now be considered to have emerged as the core elements of modern constitutionalism. It is contended that a well-designed constitution built around these core elements is crucial to the existence of constitutionalism. Although the presence or absence of constitutionalism could arguably best be assessed by a careful examination of how the constitution actually operates in practice, an analysis of the provisions themselves can provide a reasonably satisfactory or even conclusive indication of the prospects of constitutionalism under any given constitution. The assumption underlying this analysis is that, in the absence of constitutional provisions that enhance the possibilities for constitutionalism, there is little chance that the actual implementation of the constitution will itself result in constitutionalism. Although Africa's post-independence history is littered with many false starts, this study shows that the recent developments indicate some promising signs, especially with shining examples like South Africa and Ghana, but there remain some dark spots, with countries such as Cameroon and Mauritania, where the prospects for constitutionalism have instead diminished during the 1990s.

The Concept of Constitutionalism

We shall start by examining the concept of constitutionalism itself. In order to fully appreciate the meaning and significance of constitutionalism, it is necessary first to consider the meaning of the word constitution. Constitutionalism must therefore be distinguished not only from the word constitution but also from other concepts such as democracy.

The Meaning of Constitution

There is no generally accepted definition of the word constitution. It has sometimes been described as a 'power map'(Curry et al. 1997: 3, 8), deriving its whole authority from the governed which regulates the allocation of powers, functions and duties among the various agencies and officers of government and defines their relationship with the citizenry. In its broadest sense, a constitution consists of all the collection of rules, whether written in a formal document or not, that limits both government and governed with respect to what may or may not be done. As power maps containing legal rules, constitutions form the source as well as the basis of governmental rule-making and therefore act as a check against capricious or arbitrary rule-making. From this rather broad description of a constitution, a number of points are worthy of note.

First, a constitution may be contained in a single document, as is the case with most African constitutions, or may not be formally written or contained in a single document, like the British constitution (Andrews 1968: 31–65).[1] Secondly, there is no fixed or standard form or content for a constitution. It may be brief and simple, like Eritrea's 1996 Constitution,[2] or lengthy, detailed and so convoluted as to defy the wisdom of Chief Justice Marshall's celebrated dictum in *McCulloch v. Maryland*,[3] such as the Nigerian Constitution of 1999, which contains 318 Sections and 7 Schedules, with many detailed rules that would normally be found in ordinary legislation. Thirdly, the very essence of a constitution is to prevent both tyranny and anarchy. To achieve this, it must sufficiently empower the government to enable it to be strong enough to operate effectively, whilst imposing reasonable restraints on it that do not make it too weak and create the risk of anarchy (Holmes 1995: 270–71). Finally, it should be noted that a constitutional government means something more than a government operating in accordance with the terms of a constitution. It means a government controlled by rules as opposed to an arbitrary government, a government actually limited by the terms of the constitution and not a government limited only by the desires and capacities of those who exercise power (Wheare 1966: 137). Nevertheless, this may not necessarily exclude an arbitrary government, if the provisions of the constitution do not contain any restrictions or only weak restrictions, as was the case with many pre-1990 African constitutions. The absence of meaningful restrictions therefore made it almost impossible for many countries to practise constitutionalism. This raises the question of what exactly is meant by the concept of constitutionalism.

The Meaning of Modern Constitutionalism and its Core Elements

The distinction between a constitution and constitutionalism, it has been said, is more than a simple exercise in semantics (Curry et al. 1997: 4). Constitutional scholars have had great difficulties defining the concept of constitutionalism. Some have even confused it with the very notion of a constitution (Nwabueze 1973:1; Gloppen 1997: 43).

The concept of constitutionalism certainly defies any easy and simple definition or description. It clearly means something far more than the mere attempt to limit governmental arbitrariness, which is the premise of a constitution, and which attempt may fail, as it has done several times in Africa. Louis Henkin (1998) in his seminal paper on 'Elements of Constitutionalism', provides perhaps the most succinct rationalization of this complex concept in what can be considered as its modern form. The concept can be said to encompass the idea that a government should not only be sufficiently limited in a way that protects its citizens from arbitrary rule but also that such a government should be able to operate efficiently and in a way that it can be effectively compelled to operate within its constitutional limitations. In other words, constitutionalism combines the idea of a government limited in its action and accountable to its citizens for its actions. Two ideas are therefore fundamental to constitutionalism thus defined: first, the existence of certain limitations imposed on the state particularly in its relations with citizens, based on a certain clearly defined set of important values; secondly, the existence of a clearly defined mechanism for ensuring that the limitations on the government are legally enforceable.

In this broad sense, constitutionalism has a certain core, irreducible and possibly minimum content of values with a well defined process and procedural mechanisms to hold government accountable. Henkin (1998), based on his examination of the US Constitution, identifies 9 core elements, or what he refers to as 'essential' elements of constitutionalism. An analysis of other constitutions, especially recent African constitutions, leads to the conclusion that the core elements of constitutionalism can be stated as consisting of:

(i)   the recognition and protection of fundamental rights and freedoms;
(ii) the separation of powers;
(iii) an independent judiciary;
(iv) the control of the constitutionality of laws;
(v)   the control of the amendment of the constitution; and
(vi) institutions that support democracy.

The central principle in constitutionalism is respect for human worth and dignity. It is by no means a static principle and the core elements identified are bound to change as better ways are devised to limit government and protect citizens. It is the institutionalization of these core elements that matters.

Constitutionalism and the Rule of Law

Constitutionalism as defined above is closely linked to the rule of law. This revered doctrine, which has an ancient lineage, was popularized by A.V. Dicey (1968), the most eminent British constitutional scholar of the nineteenth century who viewed it as one of the crucial elements of English constitutionalism. Nevertheless, the expression remains ambiguous and has been defined differently by different writers. Dicey (1968: 187) himself, in his much acclaimed, *Law of the Constitution*, first published in 1885, admitted that the expression though possessing 'real significance', was 'full of vagueness and ambiguity'. According to him, the rule of law, in the context of the British constitution, had 'three meanings' (ibid.: 202) or included 'at least three distinct kindred conceptions' (ibid.: 187–8). First, the principle of legality, which states that nobody may be deprived of his rights and freedoms through the arbitrary exercise of wide discretionary powers by the executive. This could only be done by the ordinary courts of law. Secondly, the principle of equality, according to which nobody is above the law and everybody is subject to the jurisdiction of the ordinary courts. Thirdly, the general principle that in Britain the rights of individuals are effectively protected by the action and decisions of ordinary courts rather than by guarantees contained in a constitution.

Although Dicey's formulation of the doctrine proved to be acutely controversial, and has been regularly criticized, the underlying concepts of this doctrine as formulated by him still constitute the roots of most of the modern conception of the doctrine. In fact, his ideas have now been enlarged and made universally applicable by various jurists and international organizations (Marsh 1961). In Western political and legal tradition, the doctrine is generally conceived in negative terms: the rule of law is contrasted with the rule of men (Tremblay 1997: 32). The notion of the rule of men refers to governmental decisions that are arbitrary, whimsical, tyrannical or despotic, and are exclusively dominated by passions, desire or self-interest. The contemporary interpretations of the doctrine refer to a cluster of ideas, the best known being related to the principle of legality, the prescription of procedural standards in the administration of justice, the separation of powers, the promotion of material justice and individual rights and the maintenance of public order.

Whichever of the many definitions of the rule of law one adopts, one thing seems clear; many of the core elements of constitutionalism listed above are also necessary for the rule of law to exist, but the latter concept is slightly narrower in scope. Respect for the rule of law on its own may not necessarily lead to the existence of constitutionalism. Nevertheless, constitutionalism is safeguarded by the rule of law and without the rule of law there can be no constitutionalism.

Constitutionalism and democracy

Democracy has almost become established in a position of co-legitimacy with constitutionalism. However, just as the existence of a constitution is not a guarantee of constitutionalism, so too the existence of democracy or certain democratic values or institutions within a country does not necessarily indicate that there is constitutionalism. Whilst there is no inherent contradiction between democracy and constitutionalism because some constitutions promote both, there are, however, situations where democracy can be used to subvert constitutionalism. In spite of this, democracy is an essential prerequisite of constitutionalism.

If the underlying idea behind democracy is no more than rule by the popular will, this can well be achieved with or without a constitution. But even where it is based on a constitution, this may not necessarily produce or result in constitutionalism. Many of the notorious absolutisms of the twentieth century have been produced by popular elections. In Africa, examples include the notorious dictatorships of Idi Amin and Jean Bedel Bokassa, and beyond there is Hitler's Germany and the former Soviet Union. Reliance on the popular will alone is capable of and has indeed resulted in a tyranny of the majority or of a minority or more often of one man.

Neither a constitutional nor a democratic government is synonymous with constitutionalism. However, as Ulrich Prewss (1996: 11– 13) points out, modern constitutionalism involves the reconciliation of the democratic rule of men with the constitutional rule of law. A constitutional and democratic government must not only be based on the popular will of the people but should operate within constraints that prevent any arbitrariness for there to be constitutionalism. In the final analysis, the concepts of democracy and constitutionalism can easily be reconciled. For a democracy to be stable and function properly it needs a constitutional framework; for constitutionalism to thrive, it needs a democratic pedigree.

Post-1990 African Constitutions Analyzed in the Light of the Core Elements of Constitutionalism

At independence, most African countries adopted constitutions that had been crafted by the departing colonial powers. The leading types were the British parliamentary or Westminster model, prepared in the Colonial Office in London but slightly modified to suit the circumstances of the different countries that adopted it. Most of the Anglophone African countries that adopted the Westminster model often added elements of the US presidential model to it. The other major Western constitutional model that was adopted was the Gaullist constitutional system based on the French Fifth Republic Constitution of 1958, which was essentially an admixture of the Westminster parliamentary and the US presidential systems. This model has been widely adopted in Francophone Africa and variations of it were adopted in Lusophone Africa. Although, before 1990, there had been quite significant changes to the constitutions that were adopted at independence, and different historical contexts had generated different preoccupations and priorities leading to quite different constitutional structures, the changes that have emerged remain largely within the received Western models.

To ensure a balanced representation of the different constitutional traditions operating in sub-Saharan Africa, the analysis that follows will be based mainly on the constitutions of the following countries, Angola of 25 August 1992, Cameroon of 18 January 1996, Republic of Congo of 15 March 1992, Eritrea of July 1996, Gabon of 26 March 1991, Ghana of 7 January 1993, Mali of 26 March 1991, Mauritania of 12 July 1991, Mozambique of November 1990, Namibia of February 1990, Niger of 18 July 1999, Nigeria of 1999 and South Africa of May 1996.[4] We shall now examine the prospects for constitutionalism using these constitutions as examples in the light of the core elements identified earlier.

Fundamental Human Rights

The protection of fundamental human rights and freedoms has become a standard of constitutionalism recognized and accepted by all countries. The basic foundation to the universal approach to human rights is laid down in the Universal Declaration of Human Rights of 1948. This was subsequently supplemented by the International Covenant on Civil and Political Rights of 1966 and the International Covenant on Economic, Social and Cultural Rights of 1966. At a regional level, the major instrument is the African Charter on Human and Peoples' Rights (ACHPR) of 1981, which has been ratified by all African countries and has, as a main advantage over all the other international instruments, the fact that it incorporates all the so-called three generations of rights.

The full listing of what are usually considered as the three generations of fundamental human rights is not necessary here. Nevertheless, it is important to note that the first-generation rights, usually referred to as civil and political rights correspond with what is often strictly referred to in the West as fundamental rights and freedoms. The second-generation rights correspond with the protection of economic, social and cultural rights and actually require the state to make every reasonable effort to put in place programmes for the full realization of these rights. The third-generation or fraternity rights, which, at the international level, are currently only reflected in the ACHPR, are the newest and most controversial of these rights. These consist of a catalogue of vague rights and duties incumbent on both the state and the citizens.

The exact extent to which these three generations of rights should be included in modern constitutions is debatable. However, whilst inserting civil and political rights in a constitution has become a matter of course, and it is certainly desirable also to include the social, economic and cultural rights, it is doubtful whether the inclusion of solidarity rights will serve any useful purpose. Two main patterns emerge in the incorporation of fundamental rights provisions in the constitutions examined in this study.

The first pattern, that reflects the Gaullist style, is by way of incorporation of international human rights instruments by reference. Although this was the system adopted by many Francophone constitutions, in the post-1990 constitutions examined, only the Cameroonian Constitution has maintained this style. The constitution itself, unlike all the other constitutions studied, contains no Bill of Rights or provisions recognizing and protecting fundamental rights and freedoms. All it does in the preamble is to affirm the peoples' 'attachment to the fundamental freedoms enshrined in the Universal Declaration of Human Rights, the Charter of the United Nations and the African Charter on Human and Peoples' Rights, and all duly ratified international conventions relating thereto' (Fombad 2003a: 12-13), and then proceed to state as 'principles', but in often obscure and circumlocutory language, some of the standard rights and freedoms found in a Bill of Rights. Although Article 65 of this Constitution states that 'the preamble shall be part and parcel of this constitution', this, for reasons that will become obvious later, does not in any way amount to a recognition and protection of fundamental rights and freedoms.

The more common pattern that features in almost all the other constitutions examined is the inclusion of provisions under the heading 'Bill of Rights',[5] or 'Protection of fundamental rights and freedoms',[6] which set out in some detail the specific rights and freedoms recognized and protected. Whilst older constitutions, such as the Constitution of Botswana of 1966, usually cover only the first two generations of rights, most of the recent constitutions, taking the hint from the ACHPR, cover all three generations of rights. The Angolan Constitution goes even further in Article 21(2) and states that the 'fundamental rights provided for in the present law shall not exclude others stemming from the laws and applicable rules of international law'.[7] To underline the importance of human rights protection, some constitutions provide special procedures for their enforcement. Thus, Article 33(1) of the Ghanaian Constitution states that any person who alleges that a provision in the constitution dealing with the fundamental human rights and freedoms has been, or is being or is likely to be, contravened in relation to him, may apply to the High Court for redress.[8] The significance of fundamental rights is underscored in South Africa, by Section 7(1) of the Constitution, which states that the 'Bill of Rights is a cornerstone' of the country's democracy.

Apart from Cameroon, and to a certain extent Mauritania, where the fundamental rights and freedoms are merely listed in Article 10 of the Constitution, the general pattern that is discernible is that most post-1990 African constitutions now clearly recognize and protect fundamental human rights and freedoms and also provide for their judicial enforcement. However, whilst legal enforcement of the first-generation rights is possible, the same cannot be said of the second- and third-generation rights. For example, Section 26 of the Constitution of South Africa recognizes the second-generation right to housing thus: 'everyone has the right to have access to adequate housing', but then qualifies it by stating that 'the state must take reasonable legislative and other measures within its available resources, to achieve the progressive realisation of this right'. Even where these rights are constitutionalized in apparently categorical terms,[9] the only obligation that is incumbent on the state is to take reasonable steps to implement these rights progressively within the limits of the resources available to it. The advantage with having these rights constitutionally entrenched and rendered legally enforceable is that it is possible to bring an action against the state either on the grounds that the measures taken are insufficient or simply that the state has unreasonably omitted to perform

Table 11.1 General freedom in Africa trend for the period 1980–89[a]

	No. of free countries		No. of partly free countries		No. of not free countries	
1980	4	(7.8%)	18	(35.2%)	29	(56.8%)
1981	4	(7.8%)	18	(35.2%)	29	(56.8%)
1982	3	(5.8%)	19	(37.2%)	29	(56.8%)
1983	3	(5.8%)	19	(37.2%)	29	(56.8%)
1984	2	(3.9%)	18	(35.2%)	31	(60.7%)
1985	2	(3.9%)	15	(29.4%)	34	(66.6%)
1986	2	(3.9%)	15	(29.4%)	34	(66.6%)
1987	2	(3.9%)	16	(31.3%)	33	(64.7%)
1988	2	(3.9%)	14	(27.4%)	35	(68.6%)
1989	3	(5.8%)	14	(27.4%)	34	(66.6%)

Note: a) This table is based on an analysis of the information provided by Freedom House in their *Freedom of the World Country Ratings 1972 through 2003*.

Table 11.2 General freedom in Africa trend for the period 1990–99[a]

	No. of free countries		No. of partly free countries		No. of not free countries	
1990	4	(7.6%)	18	(34.6%)	30	(57.6%)
1991	7	(13.4%)	23	(44.2%)	22	(42.3%)
1992	8	(15.3%)	25	(48%)	19	(36.5%)
1993	8	(15%)	17	(32%)	28	(52.8%)
1994	9	(16.9%)	18	(33.9%)	26	(49%)
1995	9	(16.9%)	20	(37.7%)	24	(45.2%)
1996	9	(16.9%)	20	(37.7%)	24	(45.2%)
1997	9	(16.9%)	20	(37.7%)	24	(45.2%)
1998	9	(16.9%)	21	(39.6%)	23	(43.3%)
1999	9	(16.9%)	25	(47.1%)	19	(35.8%)

Note: a) This table, like the previous one, is also based on an analysis of the information provided by Freedom House in their Freedom House in their *Freedom of the World Country Ratings 1972 through 2003*..

this positive obligation within the limited resources available to it. This raises the possibility of an action for unconstitutionality for omission, a notion that will be examined below.

Some indication of the possible effects of the post-1990 constitutional changes on the quality of human rights and freedoms enjoyed by Africans can be gleaned from an analysis of Freedom House's *Freedom in the World Country Ratings 1972 through 2003*.[10] These give some reasonable indication of the extent to which there might be a correlation between the provisions of a constitution and constitutionalism. This has been summarized in two tables that try to compare the evolution of both political rights (PR) and civil liberties (CL) in African countries for two periods of ten years. The first, 1980–89 is just before the onset of the so-called third wave of democratization (Huntington 1991) that hit the continent, and the second period, 1990–99, is when the process could be described as at its peak.

What these tables reveal is that there has been some improvement in the quality of freedom enjoyed by Africans, generally speaking. For the period

1980–89, an average of 2.7 (5.2 per cent) countries were classified as free, 16.6 (32.5 per cent) as partly free and 31.7 (62.1 per cent) were classified as not free. By contrast, for the period 1990–99, the number of free countries had almost trebled to 8.1 (15.2 per cent), whilst the number of partly free countries had increased to 20.7 (39 per cent) and there was a fairly significant drop in the number of countries classified as not free, 23.9 (45 per cent). Perhaps the most interesting finding from the survey itself is that a number of countries for the entire 20 years covered by this survey have the dubious distinction of being classified throughout as not free. The nine countries in this category are Chad, Democratic Republic of Congo, Equatorial Guinea, Libya, Rwanda, Somalia, Cameroon and Mauritania, the last two of which have been deliberately included in this study. By contrast, Botswana is the only country that has been classified as free throughout the 20-year period. Although the explanations for the lack of freedom in any given country are many and complex, the preceding analysis on the constitutionalization of fundamental human rights and freedoms and the discussion that will follow, will show that there is certainly a causal relationship between the absence of constitutionalism and the lack of freedom.

The Separation of Powers

The suspicion and distrust of power in general and the concentration of power drive the separation of powers, as one of the fundamental preoccupations of modern constitutionalism, in particular. As Lord Acton had observed a century and a half ago, 'all power tends to corrupt, and absolute power corrupts absolutely' (Curry et al. 1997: 4). The abuse of the often exorbitant powers that many African leaders arrogated to themselves has been one of the major causes of the continent's woes. One of the main ways in which many governments today try to display their new democratic credentials has been through the introductions of constitutional provisions that apparently provide for a separation of powers. This is not surprising, for the French revolutionaries considered the separation of powers so important that in Article 16 of the Declaration of the Rights of Man and the Citizen of 1789, they stated that any society in which the separation of powers is not observed 'has no constitution'.

The doctrine of separation of powers, in its simplest and probably extreme form, basically requires that the three branches of government, namely the executive, legislature and judiciary, should be kept separate from each other.[11] African constitutional engineers, in incorporating the doctrine, had three main Western models to choose from. The first model is the semi-rigid presidential form that appears in the US Constitution. The second is the Westminster model, which, whilst recognizing the three branches of government, provides for extensive fusion and overlapping, especially between the legislative and executive powers. The third model is the French, which is essentially a mix of the other two and provides for a close collaboration rather than a strict separation of powers, with the only peculiarity being the dominance of the executive and the subordinate position of the judiciary. The prevention of tyranny is the common thread that ties all three models, although the approaches adopted in achieving this common goal are quite different.

All the constitutions examined in this study expressly or implicitly provide for a separation of powers. Most of the constitutions of Francophone African countries have copied the French model. A typical example of this is the Cameroon Constitution that has adopted *holus-bolus* the approach of the French Fifth Republic Constitution. Whilst purporting to introduce a separation of powers, it provides for an all-powerful and 'imperial' President who appears to exist and operate outside the classic division of legislature, executive and judiciary.[12] The Constitution of Niger takes this even further in Article 44, which provides that during his period of tenure, the President is not supposed to be the leader or executive member of any political party or national association. A President who has been elected on a party political platform is suddenly required to distance himself from his political base and become apolitical. The whole idea of separation of powers under the Cameroonian Constitution becomes even more of a farce in the face of a number of provisions that enable the President not only to dominate the legislature but also to completely control the judiciary.[13]

Most modern Anglophone African constitutions, insofar as the separation of powers is concerned, whilst predominantly influenced by the Westminster model, have infused many elements of the US approach. There are, however, very wide variations. Most of them provide for a separation of powers, but with many instances of a fusion of legislative and executive powers. In spite of the apparently dominant position of the executive, the all-encompassing feature is the independence of the judiciary.

The main conclusion that can be drawn here is that most post-1990 constitutions do provide for a separation of powers in the sense of checks and balances that can reduce the risks of despotism and thus enhance the chances of constitutionalism. The provisions dealing with this in the constitutions of Anglophone African countries do allow for a partial and limited intermixing of powers but on the whole are capable of preventing executive excesses. By contrast, the provisions in most Francophone African constitutions are unlikely to be very effective, even though most have tried to improve on the somewhat defective French model, with the exception of Cameroon where the purported separation of powers is purely symbolic. However, the possible effectiveness of any separation of powers provision depends to a large extent on the extent to which the judiciary is independent.

The Independence of the Judiciary

A constitutionally entrenched independent judiciary is absolutely essential not only to ensure the enforcement of the fundamental human rights and freedoms provisions but also to guarantee that the checks and balances provided for through the separation of powers are effective. The extent of independence of the judiciary is usually judged using two barometers; that of personal independence and that of functional independence. The personal or what is sometimes referred to as relational independence of the judiciary is determined by factors such as the nature of judicial appointments and their terms and conditions of service.

In dealing with the judiciary most recent constitutions have adopted either the Westminster or the Gaullist model. To the extent that the executive appoints members of the judiciary under both, it can be said that the executive controls the judiciary. However, both models profess to provide both personal and judicial independence, but in very different ways and with fairly different consequences.

The French model that has been widely copied in most Francophone and Lusophone African countries has been significantly influenced by the obsessive Gallic fear of the threat of legal dictatorship through a 'government of judges', that can be traced back to pre-revolutionary France. Most constitutions in these countries state that the President of the Republic is the guardian of the independence of the judiciary, which clearly suggests that the judiciary is not on a par with the executive but rather below it. This conclusion is reinforced by the powers given to the President to appoint, promote, transfer and dismiss judicial personnel, which effectively compromises their personal independence.[14] The strong political interference in the process of judicial appointments, promotions, transfers and dismissals is often mildly disguised by provisions that require the President to act on the 'advice' of, or receive the 'opinion' of, the Higher Judicial Council or similar bodies, which are bodies whose composition is essentially determined by him. As a result of this, in spite of constitutional provisions that require judges to act solely in accordance with the dictates of their conscience and to be guided only by the law,[15] there is too much scope for political interference and manipulation of the judiciary for there to be any chance of either functional or personal independence. The situation in Lusophone Africa, more specifically Angola and Mozambique, is not very different from what obtains in Francophone Africa.[16]

In contrast, Anglophone African countries have made tremendous strides towards making the judiciary independent of both the executive and the legislature. For example, although the executive makes appointments, as well as taking certain decisions on the transfer, promotion and dismissal of judicial personnel, it is often required to act on the recommendations of a Judicial Service Commission or similar body. Unlike such bodies provided for in the constitutions of Francophone and Lusophone countries, these bodies are usually composed of specified independent legal experts who are more likely than not to act objectively and impartially.[17] It is also unlikely that the executive will disregard their recommendations. The composition of the Judicial Service Commission also provides little scope for political interference.[18] Other measures that have been introduced in the constitutions of Anglophone countries to enhance the prospects of judicial independence include clearly defined judicial tenure,[19] and provisions that judicial salaries, allowances, gratuities, pensions and other benefits are not to be reduced and are to be charged on the consolidated fund.[20] As a result of the latter, judicial payments are permanently authorized and cannot be arbitrarily reduced by the government as a means of putting pressure on the judiciary. This is important, for as Alexander Hamilton explained, 'in the general course of human nature, a power over a man's subsistence amounts to a power over his will' (Hamilton et al. 1996).

Most recent African constitutions therefore recognize and sometimes purport to protect the independence of the judiciary. However, because of the substantial scope for political interference, the prospects for effective judicial independence in Francophone and Lusophone countries are quite limited. In contrast, many Anglophone constitutions, especially those of Ghana and South Africa, contain provisions that can considerably enhance the chances of the judiciary operating relatively independently.[21] A judiciary that operates without pressure, threats or intimidation will clearly enhance the prospects for constitutionalism in the country.

The Control of the Constitutionality of Laws

A constitution is only as good as the mechanism provided within it for ensuring that its provisions are properly implemented and that any violations are promptly sanctioned. An important bulwark of constitutionalism is therefore the existence of an efficient and effective mechanism for controlling and compelling compliance with the letter and spirit of the constitution. In the absence of this, the constitution is not worth the paper on which it is written and is probably virtually non-existent. In addition, most recent African constitutions expressly or implicitly proclaim the supremacy of the constitution over all other laws.[22]

Although most African independence constitutions adopted different methods for controlling the constitutionality of laws, the choice was mainly between the American system of judicial review and the French system of quasi-administrative/quasi-judicial review before a Constitutional Council. Most Anglophone African countries adopted the American system of judicial review. The review was carried out either by the ordinary courts or by specially created constitutional courts. An example of the former is provided for in Article 2 of the Constitution of Ghana. It provides that 'a person who alleges that an enactment or anything contained in or done under the authority of that or any other enactment; or any act or omission of any person is inconsistent with, or is in contravention of a provision of this Constitution, may bring an action in the Supreme Court for a declaration to that effect.'[23] In South Africa, the Constitution provides for a Constitutional Court with two unique features. First, it combines the power of reviewing actual violations with that of reviewing potential violations. The latter, in the form of a pre-promulgation of legislation control, has the advantage that it prevents the adoption and eventual implementation of unconstitutional legislation and in this way ensures a reasonable degree of cohesion, consistency and certainty in the legal system. Secondly, litigants are not only provided with a remedy when the authorities violate or threaten to violate the constitution but they may even take action where the alleged 'violation' consists of a failure to fulfil a constitutional obligation. This may result in a declaration of unconstitutionality for the omission to carry out a constitutional obligation and is to be welcomed on a continent where the executives and legislatures are well noted for regularly ignoring the implementation of constitutional provisions. This unique remedy is probably designed to cajole or force these two branches to fulfil their constitutional obligations and for the first time guarantees that compliance with constitutional obligations is not a matter that lies within the exclusive and absolute discretion of these two branches.

The second pattern of reviewing the constitutionality of laws is that modelled on the French Constitutional Council and, as is to be expected, has been widely adopted in the constitutions of Francophone and, to a certain extent, Lusophone African countries. Whilst most of these countries have in their post-1990 constitutions introduced some changes that have tried to remedy some of the serious defects of this model, Cameroon, in its 1996 constitutional amendment, copied the French model in its pure and undeveloped form with all its defects and weaknesses (Fombad 1998; 2003b). The same observation could also be made about the approach adopted in the Mauritanian Constitution. The Cameroonian Constitution reserves exclusive powers to control the constitutionality of laws to the Constitutional Council, an essentially quasi-administrative rather than a judicial body, composed of persons who are not necessarily judges and are appointed almost exclusively by politicians, who are also the only persons who have the power to seise it. Three main flaws of this form of control need be noted here. First, in limiting the Council's jurisdiction essentially to a pre-promulgation review of legislation, this not only prevents it from playing an active role in interpreting and adapting constitutional texts, which are often complex open-ended legal documents, to the changing realities but also prevents the Council from serving as the keeper of the nation's constitutional conscience. Secondly, whilst in Anglophone countries most laws are enacted by Parliament and these laws are subject to judicial review for conformity to the constitution, in Cameroon, like in most Francophone countries, a majority of 'laws' are made by the executive as part of the so-called residual legislative powers, in the form of decrees, orders, rules and regulations. All of these escape any control for conformity to the constitution. Finally, the most serious flaw with the system is that individual citizens, minorities and other vulnerable groups have no right to challenge the constitutionality of any laws, even those which affect them directly or indirectly. Only the politicians themselves, who make these laws, have unrealistically been given the exclusive right to challenge them.

Whilst Cameroonian and Mauritanian constitutional positions remain today an aberration,[24] some of the changes introduced in the recent constitutions of some Francophone African countries have gone some way towards improving this model, but without substantially eliminating its structural and functional defects.[25] As regards Lusophone countries, the Constitution of Mozambique provides for the establishment of a Constitutional Council with wide powers to review the constitutionality not only of legislative but also of regulatory acts.[26] It also suffers from some of the defects noted above.[27]

The excessive powers with which the executive branch is usually conferred or which it arrogates to itself under African constitutions mean that an efficient mechanism for reviewing the constitutionality of laws needs to be firmly in place to check against any abuses. The effective removal of the review of constitutionality from the ordinary courts of law and placing it before anomalous quasi-administrative bodies whose composition is determined wholly or partly by politicians compromise the chances of ensuring that the constitution is not violated. As the analysis has shown, the Anglophone constitutions that have adopted the American system of judicial review provide a more credible mechanism for reviewing the constitutionality of laws. It is therefore contended that there can be no constitutionalism, in terms of respect for the constitution and the values and principles that underlie it, if there is no secure mechanism, whether in ordinary courts or other specialized courts or bodies, that can independently and impartially enforce the provisions of the constitution and check and control any abuses of its provisions.

The control of constitutional amendments

A constitution is or should be an enduring document. It is a law but, as we saw above, it is unlike any other law, and is usually declared explicitly or implicitly as the supreme law of the land based on the sovereign will of the people. It will lose its value as the supreme law of the land and the will of the people will be subverted if it can be altered easily, casually, carelessly, by subterfuge or by implication through the acts of a few people holding leadership positions. Constitutionalism implies that the constitution should not be suspended, circumvented or disregarded arbitrarily by the political organs of government, and that if it is to be amended, this should be through a clearly laid down procedure that ensures that the will of the people is not defeated in the process. The existence of a constitution that is not overtly vulnerable to governmental manipulations through arbitrary amendments provides a sense of certainty and predictability that enhances the prospects for constitutionalism.

From the perspective of constitutional amendments, written constitutions, such as those examined in this study, are commonly classified as either rigid or flexible, according to the ease with which they can be amended. Whilst flexible constitutions are easily adaptable and adjustable, the opposite is true of rigid constitutions.

The main methods of modern constitutional amendments that have been identified can be classified as follows:

(i)   amendment by the ordinary legislature, but under certain restrictions,
(ii)   amendment by the people through a popular vote in a referendum or plebiscite,
(iii)   amendment by a majority of all units of a federal state, and
(iv)   amendment through a special convention. (Strong 1972: 142)

Although arranged in increasing order of rigidity, indicating the number of legal obstacles that exist to amendments, most constitutions, as we shall shortly see, usually combine two or more of these methods.

The problem of controlling the frequent and arbitrary constitutional changes that were so common prior to the 1990s appears to have been on the minds of many African constitutional reformers. Almost all the constitutions examined in this study, insofar as the restrictions placed on their amendments are concerned, can be put in the semi-rigid category, although the exact extent varies from country to country. A good number require that these amendments are approved in Parliament by a special majority of two-thirds or three-quarters[28] or that, failing such a majority, the proposed amendment be put to a referendum.[29] In some constitutions, amendments must not only get the approval of a special parliamentary majority but must also be submitted to a referendum.[30] Article 290 of the Ghanaian Constitution, in dealing with constitutional amendments, distinguishes between what it refers to as 'entrenched' provisions and 'non-entrenched' provisions. The procedure provided for amending the former is quite cumbrous, stringent and complex as compared with the procedure for amending the latter. In fact, the general rigidity of the process is such that it is unlikely that any alterations can be made to the Ghanaian Constitution lightly, without due notice, elaborate consultations and the full and active participation of the people. By contrast, the Cameroonian Constitution can be amended by an ordinary law with the only special requirement, according to Article 63, being that the proposed amendment should be signed by at least one-third of the members of either House of Parliament and that the amendment itself be approved by Parliament meeting in congress by an absolute majority. Apart from the obvious weakness that it can be altered at the whims and caprices of the government, one common feature that this Cameroonian Constitution shares with some of the others discussed here is that it contains an 'unamendable' provision.[31] Two observations need to be made about the concept of unamendable provisions, and the significance of a controlled procedure for amending a constitution and constitutionalism.

First, nothing is utterly immune from change. The purpose of a controlled amendatory procedure is not to prevent change but rather to prevent the process being abused by dictators to serve their own ends. The concept of unamendable provisions, it is contended, is an illusion. One constituent body cannot make constitutional provisions that prevent a future constituent body from repealing the constitution, even where it introduces an express provision that purports to do this. Arguably a constituent body is omnipotent in all save the power to destroy its own omnipotence.[32] A constitution, or provisions in it, could with time become antiquated and if there is no procedure for amending it, or if this is too cumbersome, this may provoke violent changes through revolutionary means. A better approach, it is submitted, is to strictly regulate and control the manner in which amendments can be made, in order to ensure that this is done with due notice, with deliberation, not lightly and wantonly, and in consultation with the people to ensure that the general will of the people is not subverted by a few selfish individuals.

Secondly, the mere fact that a constitution contains a number of legal obstacles to its amendment that make it harder to alter does not necessarily mean that it will be less frequently altered than one which contains fewer or no special obstacles. The ease or frequency with which a constitution is amended will depend not only on the provisions which prescribe the method for effecting changes, but also the predominant political and social groups within the community and the extent to which they are satisfied with or acquiesce in the organization and distribution of power within the constitution (Wheare 1966: 17). Nevertheless, the existence of a defined process for effecting changes and the nature of this process indicate the extent to which the popular will counts, and to that extent indicate the prospects for constitutionalism in the country.

State Institutions that Support and Sustain Constitutionalism

Implanting and sustaining constitutionalism in Africa's fledgling democratic transitions needs something more than the mere entrenchment of the core elements discussed above. There is need to establish a solid basis on which a new constitutional culture can transform the constitution into a 'living document, building ownership around it, making it available and accessible to all in society and encouraging the people to deploy it in defence of their individual and collective rights' (Ihonvbere 2000: 22). Africa and Africans do not have any history, tradition or culture of constitutionalism to count or build on but have to develop and nurture this almost from scratch, especially because the basic political and social substratum on which the present democracy is built is very weak and tenuous. Constitutional design must therefore include a framework for cultivating the ethos of constitutionalism. There are already many promising signs of this in some of the constitutions examined in this study.

What has rightly been described as probably South Africa's most 'important contribution to the history of constitutionalism' (Klug 1995:1-11) appears in Chapter 9 of its Constitution, under the title, 'state institutions supporting democracy'. This provides for the establishment of a number of institutions with the avowed purpose of strengthening constitutional democracy in the country. The mere listing of these institutions on their own is not novel, for many constitutions do provide for some of them. What is perhaps unique about the South African approach is that there are four legal principles that are spelt out to ensure that these institutions are an effective log to the constitutional wheel and not a political charade of symbolic value only. The four guiding principles provide that:

(i)   These institutions are independent and subject only to the constitution and the law, and they must be impartial and must exercise their powers and perform their functions without fear, favour or prejudice.
(ii)   Other organs of state, through legislative and other measures, must assist and protect these institutions, to ensure the independence, impartiality, dignity and effectiveness of these institutions.
(iii)   No person or organ of state may interfere with the functioning of these institutions.
(iv)   These institutions are accountable to the National Assembly, and must report on their activities and the performance of their functions to the Assembly at least once a year. [33]

Something close to these principles are referred to in some constitutions as 'directive principles of state policy,'[34] but these, unlike the principles in the South African Constitution, are stated in purely hortatory terms. The six institutions provided for under the South African Constitution are:

(i)   the Public Prosecutor (commonly referred to elsewhere as ombudsman)
(ii)   the Human Rights Commission
(iiii) the Commission for the Promotion and Protection of the Rights of Cultural, Religious and Linguistic Minorities
(iv)   the Commission for Gender Equality
(v)   the Auditor-General
(vi)   the Electoral Commission

Many of the other constitutions provide for one or more of these institutions,[35] but what distinguishes the South African institutions is that they have been constitutionally entrenched in such a way that they can operate as independent sites of oversight and supervision as well as enforcement of the constitution. Creating many such independent centres of oversight outside the government should provide additional means to control the enormous powers that governments possess and enhance the chances for constitutionalism taking root.

Conclusion

Although, in form and content, there is no ideal or standard constitutional design or model that is irreproachable and unimpeachable, a constitution that does not guarantee constitutionalism is not worth the paper on which it is written. At the heart of modern constitutionalism is the desire not just to limit government but to actually ensure that governmental power has effectively been limited. Constitutional developments in the last two decades now provide some indication of the core elements that can be used to assess and gauge the prospects for constitutionalism in any country. But why are the prospects for constitutionalism so important?

A number of reasons can be suggested why constitutionalism in the broad sense defined in this study is important, especially to African countries struggling to escape from the trap of political instability, economic decline and social disorder. The presence of constitutionalism as manifested by the existence of its core elements, namely, constitutional provisions that protect fundamental human rights and freedoms, that provide for the separation of powers and an independent judiciary, that control the constitutionality of laws and the process of constitutional amendments and that provide institutions that support constitutional democracy, is a clear and unambiguous sign of a pre-commitment to what must now be considered as certain minimum standards of civilized state behaviour. In this respect, Walton Hamilton is right when he defines constitutionalism as 'the name given to the trust which men repose in the power of words engrossed on parchment to keep a government in order' (as quoted in Kay 1998:16). If a constitution manifestly embodies the values of constitutionalism, it will certainly include what most people hold as dear, and consider as *prima facie* right and good, and will most likely be treated with great respect, if not veneration. Constitutionalizing government provides for predictability because individuals will know in advance how they stand with the government, how far the latter can go in interfering with their life and activities. It also indicates that a government will be responsive and responsible to the people and will act in a just and fair manner. Consistency and predictability are good for long-term planning and reduce the risks of political opportunism and expediency. Many crucial and sensitive matters are placed beyond the whims and caprices of transient or popular leaders and ruling majorities. If one of the greatest injuries of totalitarianism can be described as uncertainty, one of the special virtues of constitutionalism is that it reduces and controls the potentially enormous powers of the state by the imposition of rules.

If the post-1990 constitutional changes were designed to give African countries a fresh start, as most modern constitutions since the American Constitution of 1788 usually try to do, then the general result of this process must be considered as mixed, insofar at the commitment to constitutionalism is concerned. There has been tremendous progress in some cases and dismal failure in others. The South African Constitution clearly stands out as an exemplar of modern constitutionalism and provides a rich source from which many African countries can learn. Amongst the many innovations is the possibility of unconstitutionality for omissions that is a good answer to the perennial problem of non-implementation of constitutional obligations in Africa. The establishment of a Constitutional Court to deal with constitutional matters not only underscores the importance of constitutional matters but also reflects the trend against the desultory efforts of controlling the constitutionality of laws outside the mainstream of the legal system. Another equally liberal and quite progressive constitution is that of Ghana.

There are positive signs of an attempt to move towards constitutionalism in the constitutions of some countries such as Angola, Gabon, Niger, Mali, and Mozambique. The Cameroon Constitution of 1996 is perhaps the best example of a constitutional reform exercise that was carried out to institute the new creeping phenomenon of autocratic multi-partyism. It creates a false heaven in which the lion lies down with the lamb biding his time. As Julius Ihonvbere (2000:21–2) has observed, 'a visionary, committed, enlightened, and democratic brand of leadership is needed to recognize the urgent task of carrying the people, irrespective of ethnic, religious, regional, gender, and other identity forms along in the process of political renewal, democratic reconstruction, and national rebirth'. There is no longer any need to stick to inherited colonial stereotypes which experience has shown are ill-suited to the problems that currently confront the continent.

The emerging trends in constitutionalism in Africa today are taking place in contexts that are radically different from those in the immediate postcolonial situations. Many lessons have been learned the hard way and the errors of the past do not have to be repeated. The mammoth political, economic and social challenges of the future cannot be confronted head-on without an irrevocable commitment to constitutionalism and all that this principle stands for. Once a country has crossed the constitutionalism Rubicon the chances of it backsliding into anarchy or dictatorship are considerably reduced. The absence of constitutionalism in the constitutions of many African countries explains why there is still doubt as to whether the third wave of democratization will do any better than the preceding ones. The good prospect for constitutionalism in certain countries such as Botswana, Ghana and South Africa certainly does not guarantee constitutional rule, good governance or democracy. Nevertheless, its presence makes the task of a dictator or tyrant more difficult and acts as a powerful bulwark of defence that will be quite difficult to overcome.

References

Andrews, W.G., ed. 1968. *Constitutions and Constitutionalism*. Princeton, NJ: Van Nostrand.

Curry, James A., Richard B. Riley, and Richard M. Battistani. 1997. *Constitutional Government: The American Experience*. 3rd edn. St Paul, MN: West Publishing.

Dicey, A.V. 1968. *Introduction to the Study of the Law of the Constitution*. 10th edn. New York: Macmillan.

Fombad, Charles Manga. 1998. 'The New Camaroonian Constitutional Council in a comparative perspective: Progress or retrogression?', *Journal of African Law* 42: 172–86.

Fombad, Charles Manga. 2003a. 'Cameroon: Text of Constitution', in R. Blanpain ed. *International Encyclopaedia of Laws*. The Hague: Kluwer Law Publishers.

Fombad, Charles Manga. 2003b. 'Protecting Constitutional Values in Africa: a Comparison of Botswana and Cameroon.' *CILSA* 36: 83–105.

Fombad, Charles Manga. 2005. 'The Separation of Powers and Constitutionalism in Africa: The Case of Botswana', *Boston College Third World Law Journal*. 25: 301–42.

Gloppen, Siri. 1997. *South Africa: The Battle Over the Constitution*. Aldershot: Ashgate.

Hamilton, Alexander, James Madison and John Jay. 1996. *The Federalist* No. 79. London: Everyman.

Henkin, Louis. 1998. 'Elements of Constitutionalism', *The Review* 60: 1122.

Holmes, Stephen. 1995. *Passions and Constraint: On the theory of liberal democracy*. Chicago: University of Chicago Press.

Huntington, Samuel. 1991. *The Third Wave: Democratization in the late Twentieth Century*. Norman, OK: University of Oklahoma Press.

Ihonvbere, Julius O. 2000. 'Politics of Constitutional Reforms and Democratization in Africa', *International Journal of Comparative Sociology* 60: 45–65.

Kay, Richard S. 1998. 'American Constitutionalism', in Larry Alexander, ed., *Constitutionalism: Philosophical Foundations*, Cambridge: Cambridge University Press.

Klug, Heinz. 1995. 'Constitutional Law', in *Annual Survey of South African Law*. Cape Town: Juta and Co., 1–11.

Marsh, N.S. 1961. 'The Rule of Law as a Supra-national Concept', in A.G. Guest, ed., *Oxford Essays in Jurisprudence*, Oxford: Clarendon Press, 223–64.

Nwabueze, B.O. 1973. *Constitutionalism in the Emerging States*. London: C. Hurst and Company.

Prewss, Ulrich. 1996. 'The political meaning of constitutionalism', in Richard Bellamy, ed., *Constitutionalism, Democracy and Sovereignty: American and European perspectives*. Aldershot: Ashgate, 11–27

Strong, C.F. 1972. *Modern Political Constitutions: An introduction to the comparative study of their history and existing forms*. London: Sedgewick and Jackson.

Tremblay, Luc B. 1997. *The Rule of Law, Justice, and Interpretation*. Montreal: McGill-Queen's University Press.

Wheare, K.C. 1966. *Modern Constitutions*. London: Oxford University Press.

Notes

1 Most of what many consider as the key elements of the British constitution are written but not in a single document. These documents include the Magna Carta of 1215, the Petition of Right of 1628, the Bill of Rights of 1689, the Act of Settlement of 1701, and the Parliament Act of 1911, as amended in 1949.

2 This is one of the shortest on the continent with just 58 articles.

3 'A constitution, to contain an accurate detail of all the subdivisions of which its great powers will admit, and of all the means by which they may be carried into execution would partake of the prolixity of a legal code, and could scarcely be embraced by the human mind. It would probably never be understood by the public. Its nature, therefore, requires, that only its great outlines should be marked, its important objects designated, and the minor ingredients which compose those objects be deduced from the nature of the objects themselves.' 4 Wheat. 316, 407 (1819).

4   Unless otherwise stated, any references to the constitutions of these countries should be taken as references to the constitutions on or after these dates. All the constitutions cited here can be found at http://confinder.richmond.edu/ as well as the official web site of each of these countries.

5   See, for example, Chapter 2, Constitution of South Africa.

6   See, for example, Part II, Constitution of Angola; Title II, Constitution of Rep. of Congo; Chapter 5 Constitution of Ghana; Title I, Constitution of Mali; Part II, Constitution of Mozambique; and Title II, Constitution of Niger.

7   See also Section 39 of the South African Constitution.

8   See similar provisions in Section 46 of the Constitution of Nigeria; Article 5 of the Constitution of Namibia; Article 19 of the Constitution of the Congo Rep; and Article 38 of the Constitution of Eritrea. Section 38 of the Constitution of South Africa, besides the special procedure, allows not only the person affected by any violation to approach the courts but also anyone acting on behalf of another person who cannot act in his own name, anyone acting as a member of, or in the interest of, a group or class of persons, anyone acting in the public interest or an association acting in the interest of its members.

9   See, for example, Article 37 of the Constitution of Congo Rep.

10 See, http://www.freedomhouse.org/ratings/ The Freedom House Survey itself provides a fuller explanation of the methodology used in carrying out the survey and the criteria used in ranking countries as either free, partly free or not free.

11 See, generally, Fombad (2005).

12 See Articles 35 and 44 of the Cameroon Constitution.

13 As regards the extensive powers of lawmaking, see Articles 27 and 28 of the Cameroon Constitution, and as regards the judiciary, see the section on judicial independence below.

14 See, for example, Article 37(3) of the Cameroon Constitution, Article 69 of the Constitution of Gabon, Article 89(1) of the Constitution of Mauritania, and Article 100 of the Constitution of Niger.

15 See, for example, Article 37(2) of the Cameroon Constitution; and Article 90 of the Constitution of Mauritania.

16 See Articles 66 and 130–1 of the Constitution of Angola; and Article 161–72 of the Constitution of Mozambique.

17 See for example, Sections 103–4 of the Botswana Constitution; Articles 153–4 of the Constitution of Ghana; and Article 85 of the Constitution of Namibia.

18 See Section 178 of the Constitution of Namibia.

19 See, for example, Sections 97 and 100, Botswana Constitution and Article 82, Constitution of Namibia.

20 See, for example, Section 122 (5), Constitution of Botswana, Article 127 (4), (5) and (6) of the Constitution of Ghana, and Section 176 (3) of the Constitution of South Africa.

21 See Article 127 of the Constitution of Ghana and Sections 174 and 176 of the Constitution of South Africa.

22 See, for example, Section 1(1) and (3) of the Constitution of Nigeria, Article 1 (1) of the Constitution of Namibia, and Section 1(c) of the Constitution of South Africa.

23 See further, Articles 130–1 of that Constitution, and similar provisions in Articles 79 and 80 of the Constitution of Namibia and Article 49 of the Constitution of Eritrea.

24 See Articles 81–8 of the Constitution of Mauritania.

25 See Article 148 of the Constitution of the Republic of Congo, Article 91 of the Constitution of Mali, Articles 83–6 of the Constitution of Gabon, and Article 110 of the Constitution of Niger.

26 See Article 181 of the Constitution of Mozambique.

27 See Article 183, ibid. and also Articles 43 and 134 of the Constitution of Angola.

28 See, for example, Article 158 of the Angolan Constitution, Article 135 of the Constitution of Niger, and Article 116 of the Constitution of Gabon which, in addition, requires that proposals be put before the Constitutional Council for an opinion, although it is not clear what the purpose of such an opinion is. For example, will an adverse opinion mean that Parliament should not be allowed to discuss the proposal or that it should not be put to a referendum?

29 See Article 116 of the Constitution of Gabon, and Article 135 of the Niger Constitution.

30 See, for example, Section 89 of the Botswana Constitution, Article 178 of the Constitution of the Republic of Congo, and Article 118 of the Constitution of Mali. Under Article 99

of the Constitution of Mauritania, the President may avoid the inconvenience of holding a referendum by ensuring that he obtains three-fifths of the votes of Parliament convened in congress.

31   See Article 64 of the Constitution of Cameroon.
32   By analogy from the analysis of the supremacy of Parliament by Sir Robert Megarry in his judgment in *Manuel v Attorney-General* [1982] 3 AER 833.
33   See Section 181(1), (2), (3) and (4) of the South African Constitution.
34   See, for example, Articles 34–41 of the Constitution of Ghana and Sections 13–24 of the Constitution of Nigeria.
35   See, for example, the Ghanaian Constitution which provides for an Electoral Commission (Article 43–54), a Commission on Human Rights and Administrative Justice (Articles 216–30), a National Commission for Civil Education (Articles 231–9), a National Media Commission (Articles 166–73) and the Auditor General (Articles 187–9). The Namibian Constitution provides for an Ombudsman (Article 142) and an Auditor-General (Article 127), and the Eritrean Constitution provides for an Auditor-General (Article 54 and an Electoral Commission (Article 57), whilst the Angolan Constitution provides for a judicial protectorate (an Ombudsman, in Article 142).

Index